# Women and medicine

TAVISTOCK WOMEN'S STUDIES

# Women and medicine

JOYCE LEESON & JUDITH GRAY

TAVISTOCK PUBLICATIONS

First published in 1978 by
Tavistock Publications Limited
11 New Fetter Lane,
London EC4P 4EE
Printed in Great Britain by
Richard Clay (The Chaucer
Press) Ltd, Bungay, Suffolk

© Joyce Leeson and
Judith Gray 1978

ISBN 0 422 76020 X (hardbound)
ISBN 0 422 76030 7 (paperback)

This book is available in both
hardbound and paperback
editions. The paperback edition
is sold subject to the condition
that it shall not, by way of trade
or otherwise, be lent, re-sold,
hired out, or otherwise
circulated without the
publisher's prior consent in
any form of binding or cover
other than that in which it is
published and without a similar
condition including this
condition being imposed on the
subsequent purchaser.

# Contents

# Acknowledgments

We have received help from so many individuals, sisters, and colleagues, and from women's and other voluntary organizations as well as trade unions, that is is not possible to mention all of them by name, and we can only say thank you to them collectively. However, some people we must name. Jeb Kahn brought the idea of Women and Health groups to Manchester and started the movement going here, bringing together women who have given us much help and encouragement. Nancy MacKeith and Mary Ann Elston have made useful comments. Doris Shelton aided in the research and typed the many drafts of the manuscript. The references were typed by Hazel Moore and Dodie Ritman. David Purdy and Alwyn Smith read the manuscript and made many suggestions, some of which we accepted. The Rathen Road household and Zola and Helen helped us to survive the rigours of writing a book.

We are grateful to all of the above, and we hope they will find the end results worthwhile. The imperfections which remain, in spite of their efforts, must be attributed to us.

# Preface

Why write a book about women and medicine? How do women differ from men patients and why not say 'doctors' rather than 'medicine'?

One of the purposes of this book is to discuss just these points, but by way of introduction we should explain that we are concerned not only with doctors, but with all women health workers, and with the relationship between the sexes within the health care industry. We see the relationship between doctors and their female colleagues and subordinates as an essential background against which the interaction between doctors and their patients takes place.

Doctors in our society are predominantly male: most of them come from middle-class backgrounds and they are members of a respected profession. Their patients differ in being mostly working-class and non-professionals; their women patients differ further in their gender, which adds another dimension to the social distance between them. The distance may be lessened if the patient is middle-class and a professional; and the same may apply for women patients if the doctor is a woman.

The woman doctor who has graduated from a male-dominated medical school is likely to have taken on certain of the attitudes of her male teachers towards both women patients and other women health workers. After taking time off to rear children, she may return to her career feeling insecure about her own professional status and competence, and consequently adopt a defensive and distant attitude. However she lives her life in a woman's body and so can identify and empathize with women patients who have the same physical problems as herself. She also shares social experiences with other women. If she has a family she faces the difficulty of trying to combine her work with caring for her husband, children, and home. She suffers from the lack of child-care facilities and opportunities for part-time training and employment, just as other women workers do, in the health service and elsewhere.

The woman doctor, then, is subject to contradictory pressures, but potentially can be brought closer to other women health workers and women patients, with mutual benefit.

There may be therefore three major barriers between doctors and other health workers, and between doctors and patients and these are class, profession and sex. All of these factors are important and interact but we have chosen here to focus on sex, which we believe has been less fully explored than the other two.

We should stress that this is not a 'women and health' hand-book – there are excellent ones available for those who want them, by the Boston Women's Health Collective (1971) for example, and the book by Nancy MacKeith (1977). We do feel however that our readers should not have to consult medical dictionaries before they can make sense of what we say, and have therefore included in Part II some background information about the health problems we discuss.

# Introduction

## Women health workers today

In most parts of the world the health industry is predominantly staffed by women workers (Navarro 1975; Brown, C. A. 1975). It is a labour-intensive industry, and most of its workers are low paid. This is not to say that doctors are all low paid, but of course most health workers are not doctors; they are nurses, orderlies, porters, domestics, technicians, etc., and a large majority of them women. In Britain, many health service workers are immigrants. At one time the only sure way for the unskilled to gain entrance to Britain was to get a work permit to be a nursing auxiliary – a job to which you were then tied. Many other newcomers to Britain, with little occupational choice, are found in hospitals in unskilled and semi-skilled jobs; nurses and junior hospital doctors too, in many areas, are predominantly from overseas. The labour-intensive low-paid public sector of health, like other public services, is heavily dependent on black and brown workers. Unlike other industries, however, most of these workers are doubly disadvantaged – they are women as well, and this has enabled a relatively comprehensive national health service to be run on a comparatively low budget.

Women in the health industry usually play subservient and supportive roles, as they do elsewhere. Their subservience is a result both of their gender, and of their position in the industry's class hierarchy, with the doctors (mostly male) at the top and the ancillaries (mostly female) at the bottom (Navarro 1976).

Within the health service, and particularly within the hospital, the distribution of power and the existing social relationships can be seen as mirroring the 'natural' position of men and women in the home, as indeed Florence Nightingale thought it should. Decisions are made by the men doctors and the subservient women ward staff exercise authority over the patients on their behalf, as if they were fathers, mothers, and children respectively.

For this reason, the position of women in health care should not be considered an isolated phenomenon; it is intimately related to the position of women in society in general, both materially and ideologically. We will therefore begin by examining the position of women workers in general, before going on to look more closely at the history of women and the healing arts, and the ancestors of today's health workers.

## Women at work

Women health workers are women workers, and many of their experiences and attitudes overlap with those of other women workers. Recently a government minister, trying to justify the continued discrimination against women under social security legislation in Britain, said that there is 'a widespread view that a husband who is capable of work has a duty to society ... to provide the primary support for his family'. But the truth is that, regardless such 'man's duty', in most of the industrialized world the majority of women are also gainfully employed. For example, in England in 1971, 42 per cent of wives were employed; of mothers with dependent children, 40 per cent were employed; of those with children under five years of age the figure was 19 per cent (Department of Employment 1975). In the US in 1974 nearly half the women of working age were at work, and this also applied to married women up to the age of fifty-four. More than half the work force of the Soviet Union are women (Pennell and Showell 1975).

The problems faced by women, on the whole, are those of people who have to do two jobs, one at work and another one at home. Those without home responsibilities may have fewer difficulties. Single women are rare these days, but in academic life in the US they do as well as their unmarried male colleagues. Over the age of fifty, 41 per cent of them are full professors, compared with 44 per cent of single men. The married *men* do better – no doubt due to the back-up services they enjoy, and 76 per cent of them are professors. Married women, by comparison, do much worse, and only 20 per cent of them occupy these senior posts (Blackstone and Fulton 1976). Why? Why should the responsibilities of marriage and often family, seem beneficial to one sex, and not to another? Of course they may just have started out as different types – cleverer men, who marry, and cleverer women, who don't – but a more likely explanation is found in the circumstances that life imposes on married women.

Leaving aside the question of the educational and other options offered to girls as compared with those offered to boys, the social, psychological, and practical pressures on career women have to be experienced to be believed. Some of them are discussed later as they apply particularly to women doctors, but it should be remarked here that, as well as subtle social mores, more obvious legal discrimination was, and in some respects still is, a reality. In Britain, women civil servants and teachers used to lose their jobs when they married; mortgage and hire purchase facilities were often denied to women, and for married women could only be obtained with the husband's permission. Marriage laws assumed that the woman's contribution to family assets through housework and child care counted for nought.

Recent legislation has modified some of these disadvantages, but the inferior position of married women is still a bedrock of the Welfare State (Wilson 1977). The Beveridge Report carried the notion of the male as the real breadwinner over into post-war legislation, and created a sub-class of national insurance contributors, consisting of married women who were by definition dependent on their husbands, and could not therefore be required to pay full contributions or receive full benefits. It is true that a flat-rate contribution would weigh heavily on married women, as it already weighs on single women and those who opt to pay full contributions, because of women's low pay (CIS 1976). But the only solution to that problem is to eliminate discrimination against women workers, and to ensure that they occupy the same proportion of well-paid jobs as men – a target that still seems a long way away in Britain in spite of recent legislation.

Other repercussions of the myth that women are and should be dependent include the notorious social security 'cohabitation rule', whereby virtually any man in a household is likely to be held responsible for supporting any otherwise unattached woman and her children. A working woman paying full contributions cannot claim additional sick benefit for her husband and children unless it can be shown that her husband is unable to work. For a man to choose to stay at home and look after young children whilst the wife works must be a threat to social order that the Welfare State cannot condone! Likewise many pension schemes automatically cover widows of male contributors, who, being women, must no doubt be dependent, but exclude widowers of female contributors (who have paid the same amounts) – unless the man can be *proved* to be dependent (Land 1975).

Even in countries with advanced social services for child care, such as the USSR, these are often based on the assumption that they help *women* with *their* children, that is they enshrine the notion that problems of child care are women's business. The German Democratic Republic legislates that fathers and mothers have equal responsibility for their children (Fogarty, Rapoport, and Rapoport 1971) but only in Sweden, it seems, has this principle been incorporated into a social security law. There, *either parent* may claim sick leave to care for a sick child.

So as we noted earlier, when we talk of women workers we are usually talking of people with at least two jobs, one of them to do with maintenance of dependent people (not only children – the sick and the old usually depend on women too)[1] and which therefore *has* to come first. There is very little choice involved in deciding not to go to work when a five-year-old child is at home with earache, and would be alone if you went out.

Women amongst the top earners, like doctors or dentists, may be able to pay for an alternative care-taker, whilst those lucky enough to have available kin (usually women, too!) who can be called on to help may solve some problems this way, although in both cases this may not be possible immediately, or for an indefinite period. So the same women on whom the health service and other sectors of the economy depend, are also indispensable to many other individuals. In an emergency these single dependants invariably take priority over the job, with the result that women are often considered 'unreliable workers' by administrators. When studying the problems of women health workers we have to recognize that as long as society places on women alone the obligation to care for family members, these difficulties will persist.

The attack on these problems will have to be launched on many fronts, and we welcome the demands of some of the health service unions for hospital-based creches and holiday care facilities for children of all health staff; we also warmly support the call of the Women's Trade Union Congress for a TUC campaign for better child-care provision. Such social services are a part of the changes we consider necessary for women to play a full part in all aspects of life, but they are not sufficient in themselves. Also necessary is the demand made at the 1976 Women's Liberation Conference for the responsibility for housework, and the care of dependents at home to be shared by all household members, male and female. This could not be enforced by law,[2] and is unlikely to be achieved for all in our lifetime, but individual households are striving towards it, benefiting the women who live in them, and leading the way forward for others to follow.

# PART I
# Women providers of health care

# ONE

# How did we get here?

## Historical perspective

From the beginning of humankind's existence ill health has been part of common experience, and as language evolved, people must have talked of earlier episodes and compared them with their own or others' present illnesses. Sooner or later associations would have been made leading to speculations about possible causes of disease and factors promoting cure. Anyone who lived long might have gained enough experience to advise younger members of the group how to avoid or treat ill health. When hunting, and later herding, large animals began to take the menfolk 'away from home', it was the women elders who were available and who knew most about disease and about helpful remedies. Women who had borne children themselves were also most likely to be midwives to others.[1] Thus treating the sick and assisting at deliveries, which, in spite of opposing claims,[2] may well have been the first forms of specialization in human activities, and hence the oldest professions, were probably originally women's work. They combined both of the functions which would now be distinguished as 'doctoring' and 'nursing'.

Although historical records all date from male-dominated times after what Engels calls the historic defeat of the female sex (Leacock 1972), women have always been recorded among the healers. Mead (1938) has documented them – in ancient Egypt, Sumeria, Greece, and Rome, recorded on tablets, depicted on reliefs, and appearing in legends. As is often the case in history, those mentioned were women at the courts of rulers, and little is recorded about ordinary folk. However, until recently, and in many places even to this day, the 'wise women' ministered to humble folk, using herbal remedies from antiquity, and helped their daughters to give birth (Ehrenreich and English 1974a).

Historically, the notion that only men can make suitable doctors is a relatively recent idea, and in very few places has general medical care ever been provided by men. As we shall see, those countries in the modern world which have the greatest success in making modern medicine accessible to the whole population, in town and country, in field, office, and factory, are those where women are, once more, heavily involved as providers of medical care.

The currently accepted wisdom of western Europe and North America that a doctor's duties are more suitably performed by men than by women is so patent an aberration, local in time and place, that one might think it is not worth pursuing further. However, the problems of women patients or women health workers today are not solved by a *broad* historical perspective, however intellectually comforting it might appear, so we do need to examine recent history in more detail, as well as the present situation and current trends, in order to find our way through our difficulties.

### Attempts to drive women out of medicine

The relative or total exclusion of women from the ranks of the healers seems to have been an integral part of the process of professionalization. We shall look at this process more closely later, but for the moment we may define it as the conversion of a general human skill which any person with experience may try, into an exclusive craft to be practised only by a closed group of initiates.

At first women were not totally excluded, and even the development of universities which later became totally sexist, did not drive them out. The famous medieval medical school at Salerno in the eleventh century accepted men and women among both teachers and students, including the well-known woman medical teacher, Trotula.

Attempts to establish a closed shop, and to exclude women, seemed to have begun in earnest in Britain in 1421 (Poynter 1961) when a petition from the universities (that is, from Oxford and Cambridge) was received and approved by Parliament, recognizing the dangers of allowing 'ignorant and unskilled persons' to practise medicine and surgery. The Privy Council was given authority to restrict practice to 'adequately trained and competent physicians'. (The strong belief that such training as existed led to competence was based more on faith than evidence – as we shall discuss in connection with midwifery.) This law would have largely excluded women, who were not admitted to training, but it was a dead letter, for there were in fact extremely few 'educated physicians'.

The situation remained as it was until Henry VIII set about extending centralized state power in various spheres, and arranged for the enacting of the Medical Act of 1512. The preamble to this indicated the shape of things to come:

'Physic (& surgery) is daily ... exercised by a great multitude of ignorant persons ... that common artificers, as smiths, weavers and *women* boldly and customably take upon them great cures ... in which they partly use sorcery and witchcraft ... to the ... grievous hurt ... of many ... people.' (Our italics)

Practice was to be restricted to those licensed by bishops. The licence depended on both competence and moral suitability, including religious reliability which became of increasing importance later. However, a degree was not absolutely necessary, nor was being a member of a guild – the doctors were not yet powerful enough to have such clauses inserted.[3] Later in Henry's reign the so-called 'Quacks Charter' restored the right to practise (by implication without a fee) to 'honest persons ... men ... (and) women, whom God hath endowed with the knowledge of ... herbs'.

This was all London business. Meanwhile, for most people, who lived in the country, life went on much as before. McConaghey (1961) has described some features of medical care in one corner of England, the south west. There, from time to time, the Bishop of Exeter duly granted licences. In 1568 he granted two permitting the practice of surgery – one of these to a woman. McConaghey also found that churchwardens kept records of parish payments for treating the sick or injured poor. Many of these payments were made to women, though few seem to have been professional doctors, as indeed was the case for the men. Nevertheless women seemed to have functioned regularly as surgeons, physicians, midwives, and home nurses during the seventeenth and the beginning of the eighteenth centuries.

Mention should be made here of the witch-hunts which were so common in Europe from the fourteenth century onwards. The first execution for witchcraft in Britain was in 1479, and before the laws were repealed in 1735, about 30,000 people died. The majority of those deemed to be witches were women, and many of these were believed to be knowledgeable about herbs and magical means of promoting or destroying health and intervening in childbirth. It has been argued (Ehrenreich and English 1974a) that the persecution of witches was primarily a campaign against women and particularly against women healers, and although we may consider it an over-simplification, there is plenty of evidence to support this view.

*Malleus Maleficarum*, the guide book to witch-hunting, was clearly concerned with the sexuality of women and their intervention in what was termed 'the venereal art'. Witches were accused of

- inclining the minds of men to inordinate passion
- obstructing their generative force
- removing the members accommodated to that act
- changing men into beasts
- destroying the generative force in women[4]
- procuring abortion.

Witchcraft was thought to come from carnal lust, 'which in women is insatiable', and induction into a coven was reputed to involve sex with the devil.

The document's attitude to women healers was similar to that expressed by the Royal College of Physicians, although the penalty advocated by the Church was rather stronger: 'If a woman dare to cure without having studied, she is a witch and must die.' If 'study' in this context meant university study, this, as we have already noted, automatically condemned all women healers (and most men).

It seems likely that witches *were* familiar with some potent herbs (Forbes 1966). The 'flying ointment' which was rubbed on, and which caused witches to fly away to orgies and other delights, is now believed to have contained many psychotropic substances of plant origin – such as hyoscyamus from henbane, atropine from deadly nightshade, and aconite from monkshood, likely to result in quite spectacular 'trips'.

Midwives were a particular group who were subject to many charges of witchcraft, perhaps because they were all women, and were involved in 'venereal' matters. They also had access to what were believed to be prize witchcraft materials – newborn babes, placentae, and umbilical cords. Magical rites of a 'holy' nature, were not unknown, and no doubt other, less holy, devices were used. A Scottish midwife in 1591 was accused of using a magic stone and powder for relieving pain in labour, and was executed as a witch for the offence.

The Church was very concerned about midwives for another, though not unconnected, reason. No child should be allowed to die unchristened and yet sometimes, even often, babies died during or immediately after birth with no-one there except the midwife. It was essential, therefore, that the midwife could be relied upon not only *not* to offer the baby to the devil, but also to christen it in an emergency, and in fact she was required in ecclesiastical law to do so. From the middle of the sixteenth century – soon after medical practitioners were required to be licensed by bishops – midwives were likewise required to appear before a bishop. There, they had to swear an oath and give evidence of good character and midwifery experience, before paying a fee to be licensed 'to exercise the office of a midwife'.

Thus women practitioners were forced out of medicine or into subservient positions, at least officially, as the sway of central power extended from the capital to the rest of Britain, and the men doctors struggled to acquire a legal monopoly of medical practice. However, in the middle of the nineteenth century, a handful of women eventually began launching counter-attacks.

In the middle of the nineteenth century, colonial America had markedly different attitudes towards medicine in general and the role of women in medicine in particular. But the differences were declining at about this time and an important transatlantic link was created by the pioneer Elizabeth Blackwell whose story is given in Bell's *Storming the Citadel* (1953).

Elizabeth Blackwell was born in Bristol in 1821, and went to America with her family while still a child. One of a group of sisters who were determined to pursue careers, she decided to go to university to study medicine, and after having her applications refused many times she approached the University of Geneva, New York State. The Faculty felt unable to take the responsibility of deciding whether to accept her, so they passed the application on to the medical students, who

'Resolved : that one of the radical principles of a Republican Government is the universal education of both sexes; that to every branch of scientific education the door should be open equally to all; that the application of Elizabeth Blackwell to become a member of our class meets with our entire approbation ...'  (Bell 1953)

(Sad to say the rest of our story contains few such enlightened attitudes from men students!)

Elizabeth Blackwell graduated MD in 1849, with honours in all subjects, and left for London and Bart's Hospital. Here she was given the run of the hospital, except of course for the ward for Women's Diseases. (The Professor of Gynaecology could not approve of a lady studying his subject.) On returning to New York she faced many obstacles in entering practice, until she gained the support of the Society of Friends who backed her in opening a women's dispensary in an immigrant tenement area. From this base, she launched the New York Infirmary for

Women and Children. Similar efforts were being made in Boston and Philadelphia.

The following year, 1858, Elizabeth returned to England to give some lectures on 'Medicine as a profession for ladies'. These had several results: she was included in the Medical Register, which was established that year;[5] a committee was set up to further medical education for women and a spark was struck in another Elizabeth – Elizabeth Garrett, who decided at that point to follow her in becoming a doctor (Manton 1965). The saga of the second Elizabeth's struggles, and those of her successors, can also be found in *Storming the Citadel*. In brief, her successes nearly led to her downfall – her examination honours were kept secret, but when she was the only one to answer questions correctly in class, the men students insisted that she should go! She attempted to be admitted to degree examinations at London, St Andrews, and Edinburgh, but was refused. However, she had completed the necessary conditions to become a Licentiate of the Society of Apothecaries, and after her father threatened litigation, lawyers advised the Society that they had no option but to license her.[6] She thus joined Elizabeth Blackwell on the Medical Register – where they remained the only women for twelve years while the battle raged. Following her example, Sophia Jex Blake, Elizabeth Thorn, Edith Pechey, and two others later became the first five women undergraduates at university in Britain, when they were accepted by the Edinburgh Medical School in 1869. However, they were subject to such harassment, chicanery, and intimidation by the Medical Faculty, that *The London Times* was moved to write 'it is the strongest argument against the admission of the young ladies to the Edinburgh Medical Classes, that they would attend the lectures of gentlemen talking in this strain'.

Then the reserves were called in – the male medical students. No such noble sentiments as moved the students of Geneva, New York, were displayed. The managers of the Infirmary were petitioned to refuse the women admission to the wards, and a riot was staged outside a hall where the women were sitting examinations. Classes had been released early to take part, so it was clear that the men students did not expect to get into trouble for such activities. At this point Edinburgh University, which had accepted the women's fees all along, found that they were unable to graduate them after all. There was only one possibility left – to start a women's school, and this was founded in London in 1874, with the help of friendly members of staff of existing London schools. But the problem of clinical work, and of a recognized qualifying examination remained.

In 1876 supporters in Parliament passed a bill enabling all universities in the UK and Ireland to graduate women. The students who had done clinical work at Edinburgh went post-haste to Ireland and persuaded the Irish College of Physicians and Queens to admit women, and six more joined the Medical Register. During this time the Royal Free Hospital was prevailed upon to provide clinical tuition for students from the Women's School. Two years later the University of London adopted a new charter allowing the admission of women to all degrees.

Women, or perhaps it would be more appropriate to say ladies, had arrived in medicine (in spite of Queen Victoria's opposition – she threatened to withdraw her patronage from a medical conference if women were admitted). They entered all spheres, including the mission field – the Queen did approve of women doctors for India. But 1914, and even 1939 revealed that some doctors were still more equal than others. During the First World War, the War Office refused the services of groups of women doctors offered by the National Union of Women Suffrage Societies, and they and the Women's Social and Political Union sent units to France and Serbia independently. Later, the women were reluctantly incorporated into the Army Medical Services, but there were no commissions, nor badges, for them.

During the inter-war years, women doctors were not accepted in all fields, despite their increasing numbers. And when the Royal Army Medical Corps finally accepted them well into the Second World War, the women were given a 'contract of service', not a commission, with 'the relative rank of officers', a uniform and, this time, badges. Not until 1950 were women commissioned in the RAMC. But during the War, the Goodenough Report of 1944 made far-reaching recommendations, in an attempt to drag medical education into the modern world. Among these was that single-sex medical schools, which were still the norm in London, should now accept students of both sexes. In the years that followed, women gradually increased their proportions in medical school, although these were held down to a maximum of one third in many places. The recent outlawing of discrimination in education on grounds of sex has forced the last strongholds to abandon this policy of restriction, and despite the strong objections from some quarters, trends suggest that there may be equal numbers of women and men students in British medical schools in the future.

## The struggle in North America

For the first 150 years of the American colony, practical necessity and sentiments against foreign elites and 'professionalism' meant that many tried their hand at healing – including women. In the eighteenth century apprenticeship to existing doctors became more common, and in the process the number of women doctors decreased. However, at the beginning of the nineteenth century in New Jersey, medical practice was reported to be still mainly in the hands of women (Shryock 1967). The numbers of 'regular', or orthodox, trained doctors increased from then on, and by 1830 nearly all the States of the Union had introduced regulatory licensing laws. These required new entrants to medical practice to pass examinations set by medical schools or State Boards.

What is interesting is that this early development in the process of professionalization did not progress any further. Shryock offers various explanations for this. He notes that egalitarian sentiments were even stronger in 1850 than they had been in 1750 and that the commercial regular (or orthodox) medical schools had very low standards; 'ill-informed legislatures still thought one sort of medical practice as promising as another', so that irregular or sectarian schools were allowed to establish themselves – for example the homeopathic, the eclectic, and the botanics – whilst regular doctors who protested were 'accused of seeking a monopoly'. This does not seem to be entirely due to legislatures being ill-informed, for Shryock himself concedes that 'the superiority of orthodox medicine still lay to some extent in the general education of its leaders, rather than any therapeutic advantage. Indeed the mild practice of homeopaths was probably safer than that followed by regulars – though equally ineffective.'

While some of the sectarian schools admitted women, the regular ones did not until Geneva admitted Elizabeth Blackwell. It was easier for her to go on to establish a Women's Hospital and Medical School at Philadelphia in 1857 and to gain recogni-

27

tion for the graduates, than it was even later in London, because of the less stringent licensing laws, which allowed graduates of new and struggling schools to be registered. The medical societies continued to ostracize women doctors, regular or irregular. In the last quarter of the century registration of doctors became general, and entry onto the registers could be obtained by graduation from many schools, regular and irregular, good, bad, or indifferent.

But American society was changing, with increasing urbanization and the growth of an affluent elite. Doctors were anxious to improve their social position, and the American Medical Association was growing in power. Regular medical science seemed to be developing in a way likely to provide the basis for improved practice. Eventually, the Carnegie Foundation financed a report on medical education by Abraham Flexner (1910), which sounded the death knell of many irregular schools – and many regular ones too. In 1905 there were 154 medical colleges; by 1914 there were seventy-five. The intended rise in standards may have been achieved, but the purge certainly succeeded in reducing the number of doctors. In 1910 there were 154 doctors per 100,000 population, but by 1930 this had fallen to 121 per 100,000.[7] Other effects resulted too – whether intended or not. Between 1910 and 1940 the proportion of women regular doctors fell. In that period only about 5 per cent of students were women, many schools remaining exclusively male, some until the 1960s. Blacks, Jews, and Catholics were also largely excluded from some schools. Shryock (1967) notes further that the reforms of 1910–20 may have gone too far; it had been easier for poor boys to secure professional training prior to that era.

The professionalization of American medicine was now accomplished – it had become a WASP (White, Anglo-Saxon, Protestant) and *male* profession. In our own day too, the current shortage of doctors, and moves to train sub-doctors and to seek medical aid in the form of medical graduates from the third world can be seen as direct results of these American Medical Association (AMA) policies – as can many well-known and widely criticized characteristics of American medicine today.

28

## What do we mean by the medical 'profession'?

The term 'profession' keeps appearing in this discussion, and before going further it would be as well to discuss it here. This widely-used term eludes a simple definition; many when asked to define it reply something to the effect that it is 'like medicine' – which is not much help to us. In the English-speaking world, medicine's rank on the scale of learned professions is certainly historically junior to the Church and the Law, but nowadays it is seen as the prototypic 'profession'. Freidson (1970) has discussed definitions and characteristics at length, and more thoughtfully than most, and he suggests that whilst a profession is basically an occupation, in other words a job done by people to earn their living, it is one of a set of special sorts of occupation. Its special nature is that it has been granted the right to autonomy – to determine *what* its work is, *who* can do it, and *how* it should be done. In medicine, this right has been granted by the ruling elite, who based their patronage on a recognition of learned content – the scientific body of knowledge on which medicine is based, and on its believed ability to produce desired results for the public good. There is also an assumption of underlying vocation, or service to humanity.

Freidson argues that worthwhile results are essential prerequisites for a service profession like medicine to establish itself, or rather, to obtain a legal monopoly. Indeed the United States gives some credence to this view, since medical registration, the statutory enforcement of the medical monopoly, was not achieved until after the great developments in basic medical science, and the emergence of modern bacteriology, therapeutics, and surgery which took place at the end of the last century and the beginning of this. However, in Britain the Apothecaries Act of 1815 and the Medical Registration Act of 1858 were passed long before the profession had proved itself in any demonstrable way (although of course, at the time, current medical practices were believed to be beneficial). An organized pressure group, with influential friends well placed among the elite, was able to attain a monopoly position in spite of the limitations of medical science.

What other occupations should be called 'professions'? In the light of our definition, the title itself clearly carries some desired connotations, and many groups aspire to it. Nurses are one such group, as are social workers, and the occupations controlled in Britain by the Council for the Professions Supplementary to Medicine, such as dieticians, occupational therapists, orthoptists, physiotherapists, and radiographers. These occupations are sometimes referred to as semi-professions.

Because of their sexist content, recent writings on professions and semi-professions compel us to pay more than a passing attention to the topic. In a book edited by Etzioni (1969), American sociologists make assessments of the nature of professions, which are not only distorted by parochialism, but also assume that professionals are all men. It follows that 'woman's work', like nursing, cannot by definition be professional. Etzioni puts it succinctly; he believes that the principles and values of professions (and of organizations) are incompatible with female employment. Physicians must be detached from the patient, not get involved with him, or seek unique solutions to his problems. The professional sphere is science, so the doctor cannot be concerned with details of the patient's life – even when these are relevant to the person's illness and its treatment! The argument, which tries to show that nursing cannot be a profession, suggests that the nurse can only meet the 'non-scientific' needs of the patient – like caring for him, relating to him, and helping him solve the problems sickness has brought to his life-functions – needs which these experts believe have no place in modern medicine. No wonder so many Americans are looking for alternatives to the services of such a profession!

It seems, then, that because the nurse cares, she is not a professional. Instead of being task-oriented, she is humanitarian and wants to relate to the whole person, a notion harmful to professionalism. The final condemnation is that she lacks competitiveness, and so cannot develop a professional ideology (Simpson and Simpson 1969).

These arguments are the result of the following underlying assumptions. 'Culture' defines woman's primary responsibility as being to the family, so by definition work comes second. Further, 'society' is less willing to grant professional autonomy to women. The semi-professions – nursing, primary-school teaching, social work, occupational therapy, and others – are seen to have a rapid staff turnover, because 'that is what women do', so no *esprit de corps*, essential to a profession, develops. (Many other jobs, such as resident hospital doctors, have a higher turnover, but that is neither here nor there: the men are moving on for promotion, a reasonable (and professional) thing to do.)

It must be noted that these writers are not the first or the most damning to have taken this standpoint, although they may be the first to seek to legitimate their point of view. As George Bernard Shaw (1931) reminded us, all professions are a conspiracy against the laymen, and he did have medicine particularly in mind. More recently Illich (1975) has argued that the medical profession is a threat to health.

Even if these very different analyses of the medical profession are only partly right, they add up to a strong criticism. The aim of many reformers of medical education is to create a humanitarian doctor, both scientifically well-trained *and* sensitive and responsive to human needs, but the above arguments suggest that the aim may be in conflict with professional trends, certainly in the US and perhaps even in Britain. Other societies may be more likely to achieve success; 'serve the people' is not only a slogan, but a basic precept of the health services of the Chinese Peoples Republic (Sidel and Sidel 1973). But then they *have* 'deprofessionalized' in many respects. Health care has been democratized, so that all health workers (not just doctors) are involved in decision-making, and the people's needs for basic preventive and curative medicine take precedence over the technological developments which may be more interesting for doctors. A large number of people are involved in health care, from those with limited training, to the best among them who are selected for advanced training. Women are a significant force in all this; they comprise the majority of the bare-foot doctors, between 30 and 40 per cent of physicians, and half of all medical students (Sidel 1975).

Doctors might argue that the Chinese approach may provide immediate advantages, and for a backward country, but that medical advances and high standards of modern medical care would be sacrificed by it. However, it seems that in China too advances continue. For example, they are pioneers in the reattachment of severed limbs, and the development of low dose oral contraceptives. In spite of the marvels of modern medicine, we would argue that professionalism, meaning the sort of technological elitism which Etzioni and others imply, has conspicuously failed to deliver appropriate health care not only to the poor countries but also to the large numbers of people in the developed world.

Modern health problems in industrial society are predominantly those of identifying and alleviating the effects of incurable chronic diseases, and modern medicine often fails to do this. According to the above analysis it is inherently incapable of doing so – or at least when the qualities exhibited by women health workers are excluded. While rejecting the sex stereotyping which assumes that women alone can perform 'caring' tasks, we suggest that with better utilization of the skills and interest of a wide range of health workers, including nurses, ancillaries, occupational therapists, and others, who are mostly women in our society, and of the women doctors, we might make a better attempt at tackling these problems. We believe that women health workers are more likely to see the need for transforming the relationship between doctor and nurse, between nurse and ancillary, and between health worker and patient. Such a transformation seems to us an essential part of the profound changes necessary for the solution of the health problems of today.

# TWO

# Women doctors today

## Women doctors in Britain

When Dr Elizabeth Garrett decided to marry, many of her supporters assumed it was surrender, abandoning the vantage point won. They were quite wrong. She had chosen a man, Shelton Anderson, who must have been a remarkable husband by the standards of the time; he moved into her house–consulting rooms after their brief honeymoon while she resumed her career as before. She bore three children, likewise with very little interruption to her routine, except that she gave up some of her extra-professional activities.

Without detracting from her considerable achievements it should be noted that she started off with only 'a cook and a parlourmaid', as her biographer, Manton (1965) puts it, with a nanny and a wet nurse added when her daughter Louisa was born. She had no need to fear criticism for this delegation of maternal duties. A most devoted mother, she did only what every woman of her station did. The difference was the use to which she put the time thus freed. It may seem ironical that the hard struggle to force open the door for women to enter or re-enter medicine should have begun to be successful at the same time as practical difficulties and new ideological pressures began to create a new set of obstructions.

The fact that far fewer women now are only able to earn their living by working in other people's houses doing housework and looking after children, is obviously a great victory for the women's cause, and one that must be applauded whatever the subsequent difficulties for a few. Smaller houses, smaller families, joint responsibility shared by men and women, modern aids to heating, cleaning, and cooking, and social facilities like creches, should more than balance the loss of domestic servants' services for would-be professional women, in a society concerned to make the best use of the talents of all its citizens. Unfortunately, we do not live in such a society, and the lack of facilities is justified by reference to the works of Freud, and the Freudians, particularly Bowlby (1951). One particularly forceful argument is that of maternal deprivation.

Although there is virtually no historical or anthropological evidence that there has ever been a society which bound a child exclusively to its mother for more than a brief period of physiological dependence, lasting at most a year or two, one current myth is that a child needs the undivided attention of one adult female for years, and that the one must be the mother. This myth has blighted the lives of many modern women, made them feel guilty if they did not adjust their lives accordingly, and has been used as an excuse by local and national governments for not paying attention to the provision of facilities for the social care and education of young children. Its curious survival in the face of many damning exposures, for example Rutter's *Maternal Deprivation – Reassessed* (1972), can only be explained by its great convenience for some powerful forces in the home, and in society in general.

The earlier age at which many people marry today has affected women medical students and doctors too. Although they are, on average, several years older at marriage than their non-medical sisters, most of them are wives by their mid-twenties, and mothers not long afterwards. Women doctors who have qualified since the last war have found themselves in a situation where they cannot win: three equally unsatisfactory courses are open to them. They can be exceptions and remain single or childless and bear the social cost and stigma entailed; or they can reproduce and pursue their careers, and be condemned as inadequate wives and mothers, or they can give up their work to minister to their husbands and children and be condemned for having wasted the nation's investment in them and for having kept a prospective male doctor out of medical school by selfishly occupying his place. Each of these solutions clearly carries a cost not expected by the bright young woman who shone so well in medical school. Until recently this has been seen as an individual dilemma, and the business only of the woman concerned – except when it came to pontificating, or more seriously restricting entry to medical school to a certain quota of women (Elston 1977).

## Medical woman-power

Medical man-power, as it is usually called, has been a big issue in past decades. Following the recommendations of the Willink Committee in Britain (1957) – the AMA had got there first with the Flexner report (1910) – that intake to medical school should be reduced, the demand for doctors has raced ahead of the output of medical schools and the availability of local practising doctors. An important and much discussed factor in this was medical emigration but in the early sixties, when well-qualified women were pounding on the doors of the medical schools (although still nowhere near in proportion to their numbers in the age group) another issue became fashionable – the 'wastage of women doctors'. Surveys began and multiplied, mostly of the 'where-are-they-now?' variety, tracing graduates of particular periods from particular schools.[1] Two studies, those of the Medical Practitioners Union (MPU) (Elliott and Jefferys 1966) and the Medical Women's Federation (Laurie, Newhouse, and Elliott 1966) were wider, and attempted to cover all women doctors.

Their findings were interesting, remarkably consistent, but not surprising. For example, the MPU enquiry, conducted in 1962–3, elicited information from more than 8,000 women doctors. Of these, 47 per cent were working full-time, 32 per cent part-time, and 19 per cent were not working at all; over the age of forty-five, 90 per cent were working. Those who were not at work were mostly married women with children under five, although some with older children or with no children were not working either. Only one fifth of women with young children, and one third of women with older children were working full-time. For some people, this latter finding demonstrated the futility of educating women doctors. However, some interesting features emerged. The percentage working varied from 71 per cent in Scotland to 86 per cent in Birmingham; the majority of the non-employed women wanted work, particularly part-time work, but found none available in their locality. Many of them had the particular problem of having not completed their post-graduate training, and could see no way of doing so. This seriously limited their chances of a rewarding professional career. For two-thirds of those who were not working, the reasons included the lack of a suitable job, and later studies confirmed this finding.

An interesting study by Stanley and Last (1968) considered a national sample of men and women doctors in their late twenties. Among those who were single there was little sex difference in their working status, post-graduate training, or career aspirations. Married doctors were different; married *men* had most often firmly decided on a career, and more of these than of single men had opted for general practice. A large proportion of married women had not firmly decided on their careers, and those who had decided, were more likely than single women to prefer general practice and public health. The authors noted in an aside that sixty women were not currently employed – a number comparable with the sixty-three (sex unspecified) who had already emigrated or who definitely intended to do so.[2]

The MPU publication emphasized that note should be taken of the practical difficulties women in our society faced, which prevented their making the contribution they were able and and wished to make to medicine. These difficulties included domestic problems, particularly of child-care, and the lack of part-time employment. It was argued that there was an unmet need for further training or retraining facilities to encourage women, who have had to withdraw for a time, to re-enter the profession.

It was some time before any national effort was made to take action along these lines – in fact not until staff shortages in some specialities led to an increasing need to use these female medical reserves. The urgency and enthusiasm with which opportunities have been developed in different areas vary considerably, and as the number of qualified women increases, the need becomes more urgent. So does the recognition of the fact that some of the proposed solutions create their own problems, perpetuating the second-class citizenship of women doctors in what is supposed to be an era of equal opportunity.

## Where are the women doctors?

Overall, the proportion of all doctors who are employed in hospitals has increased steadily since the beginning of the NHS. Today hospital doctors form a majority of the profession, although in peak career posts there are still two senior doctors (principals) in general practice for every senior doctor (consultant) in hospital. We have seen that past surveys showed women were more likely to be employed, or to want employment, *outside* the hospitals. We can guess the reasons – the junior hospital doctors have only recently realized that their conditions of service and pay for hours worked are not only intolerable but in fact do not have to be tolerated, and can be improved by united action (it has proved easier to improve pay than to win more reasonable working hours). Married men in Stanley and Last's survey, like married women, had faced the problem and the majority of them had voted with their feet, selecting a career in general practice. But it is not going to be easy to enter general practice in future, as traineeship, with a prescribed three years' training including two years in hospital jobs, becomes a general requirement for all new entrants. We can only hope that as hospital working conditions improve, it will no longer seem too difficult for men and women with family responsibilities.

But meanwhile, in spite of everything, many women are already hospital doctors. What are they doing?

In 1974, in England and Wales, there were 29,018 hospital medical staff, and 4,590 of these were women.[3] At pre-registration house officer level – the first year after qualification – they were more than one third of the total; at the next level, post-

37

registration house officer, nearly one half. Passing up through the hierarchy, at registrar and senior registrar level they were one fifth, and at the most senior, consultant level less than one tenth. To a small extent these differences may be accounted for by the number of women doctors in different age groups, since the proportion of women entering medicine has increased somewhat in recent years, but other explanations have to be sought for most of the difference. Some are obvious: biologically, child-bearing women may have found heavily demanding junior hospital posts a strain during pregnancy and lactation. Social pressures, the expectations of society in general and husbands in particular of the amount of commitment that wives and mothers are supposed to give to family life have, up to now, been almost totally incompatible with these residential posts. And without this training, they are unable to acquire the higher qualifications necessary to gain access to senior posts. Older women, returning after rearing children to take up promising careers, have often found the obstacles to obtaining hospital consultant appointments insuperable. Of those who do obtain hospital work, a disproportionate number are found in the sub-consultant 'medical assistant' grade – in 1974 more than one third of these were women.

Such restricted career openings are even less defensible now than formerly, with all the evidence we have of the superior performance of women students in many medical schools and the air thick with talk about equal opportunities.

Paradoxically, it is the senior posts in the hospital service (if only that level can be reached) that are, in fact, often part-time – to allow for private practice – or are based on several hospitals, so that in effect the consultants are part-time at each. Further, as Arie (1976) has pointed out, 'we are all part-timers now', that is, no-one is prepared to be on duty twenty-four hours a day, every day of the week.

Some of the other fall-back, or 'drop out', positions which women were expected to accept gracefully are unlikely to be able to absorb as many women in the future. For example, family planning clinics may well decline now the general practitioners are playing a bigger part in this field, and clinical medical officers in community medicine have been recommended for phasing out, with general practitioner paediatricians to take over their responsibilities (Court Report 1976).

## Calling up the reserves

The Department of Health, not surprisingly, has tried to respond by acknowledging the *status quo*, and making some small gestures 'to help women doctors overcome their problems' – as it is always put. They have not tried to reduce the problems society imposes on women, but defining them as personal ones, to throw a slim lifeline to some of the women concerned. Two schemes, the 'Retainer Scheme' and the 'Retraining Scheme' have been set up, although the impact of these seems very limited, and unlikely to improve during current financial difficulties.

### The Retainer Scheme

This is a rather complicated arrangement introduced in 1972 whereby a non-working doctor is paid a sum of money, at present £75 per annum, in return for an undertaking to 'keep in touch with medicine' – in particular, to remain on the medical register, pay a medical defence subscription, to take a journal, to attend some educational sessions, and to work for a minimum of twelve sessions per year. Not a very attractive proposition, when defence union subscriptions are £40 per annum and the British Medical Journal likewise costs £40 per annum.

It is open to those under fifty-five years of age, and in 1977 more than 200 women, of an estimated 2,000 non-working eligible doctors, were in the scheme (Royal College of Physicians of London 1977).

### The Retraining Scheme

Introduced by the DHSS in 1969, this called for the creation of supernumerary part-time training posts and clinical assistant posts for doctors – expected, of course, to be women – unable to take full-time jobs. Between 1973 and 1976, 113 senior registrars and 153 registrar posts were created. Sharing posts which prove difficult to fill was also recommended – but this has rarely been done. A survey by the Medical Women's Federation found less than half the regions had set funds aside for these posts. Even where funds had been set aside, posts had been refused for financial reasons, and where they had already been allocated, the delays in processing applications were enormous, often a year or more.

In general, it is hard to say whether the scheme could be useful and workable, for it has hardly been tried. An exception is the Oxford region, where in 1967, thirty-three, and in 1975, 122 women were in training. Rue (1975) estimates that for £4,000,000 per annum a similar result could be achieved throughout the country.[4]

Other studies on the operation of these schemes show how inadequate they are in relation to the number of posts required, and how little they in fact do to help the retrained women find an appropriate job in an accessible place. In response to an advertisement asking how married women doctors were faring, twenty-two out of sixty-one women doctors reported that they could not find part-time posts after completing their part-time training (Henryk-Gutt and Silverstone 1976).

*Shortage specialties*
Another approach to the problem has been to focus on the 'shortage specialties'. It has been noted that whereas there is a scramble for jobs in acute medicine, surgery, and obstetrics, this is not so in some other specialties, known as 'shortage specialties'. A possible, and some think, attractive way to solve two problems at once, would be to encourage women to accept posts in the 'shortage specialties'. These include geriatrics, anaesthetics, radiology, pathology, mental handicap, and rheumatology – a mixture of specialties, some without patient contact and others involved with less-valued patients – the old and the handicapped. They are almost all characterized by other features too – few and minor merit awards,[5] lack of opportunity for private practice, and their small influence in medical education.[6]

The 'shortage specialties' have been contrasted with 'prestigious specialties' such as neurology or cardiothoracic surgery. 'A women desirous of entering such important spheres of medicine will find that she is competing with men who give 100 per cent of their effort to their work: she cannot expect to succeed if she tries to combine her specialist training with bringing up a family herself.' She should therefore select a 'less demanding specialty', requiring 'less than maximum commitment' (*British Medical Journal* 1976). Subsequent correspondence has asked why it is less demanding to be responsible for eighty beds, rather than eight, or to be involved in ward, clinic, and community rather than ward, clinic, and operating theatre, but no satisfactory answer has yet been given.

Now we are opposed to private practice and merit awards, and believe that the care of groups like the old and the handicapped should be prominent in medical education, that work with them can be interesting and rewarding, and that doctors should concentrate where need is great, as it is in these groups. We further believe that many women would enjoy such work. But the 'women for unpopular specialties' campaign does not solve these two problems; on the contrary, it legitimates and reinforces the two attitudes which form the roots of the problems, namely that women are second-class doctors, and that the incurables are second-class patients.[7] And in our view, career guidance for women students which aims at persuading them to restrict their ambitions, and to specialize only in those areas where there is little competition is not acceptable.

However, it is possible that there are specialties to which women are particularly suited. The pioneers thought so – these were childbirth and the diseases of women, in other words obstetrics and gynaecology. (As we document elsewhere, from the start obstetricians and gynaecologists were prominent among those striving to keep women out of medicine – and even now they, together with the surgeons, seem most reluctant to make the necessary arrangements to allow part-time training.) But other than these, no case can be made about specialties being suitable for women which is not based on the most dubious judgements, about women and about patients, and about the value to the community of different spheres of medicine.

In addition, real experience belies the supposed big opportunities for women in the shortage specialties. Between 1969 and 1974 the number of women consultants in England and Wales increased by 256, raising the proportion of woman consultants from 7.1 per cent to 8.3 per cent. But there was a slight *fall* in the proportion of women geriatricians from 8.3 to 8.1 per cent, and in the other fields the increases were not dramatic. Fifty-two new women anaesthetists increased the proportion of women from 14.6 per cent to 15.7 per cent, while 28 more pathologists lifted the figure from 9.2 to 9.9 per cent. In the shortage specialties, the number of women consultants increased overall from 412 to 549, representing 11.5 per cent and 12.6 per cent of posts respectively. During the same period women consultants in the other, 'non-shortage', specialties increased from 263 to 342, that is from 4·4 to 5·5 per cent. Even if many women were to opt for shortage specialties through force of circumstance, it seems unlikely that this would result in a rapid increase in the number of women occupying the higher posts in medicine. There is no simple solution to the dilemmas that women doctors find themselves in along this particular road.

We ought to emphasize, however, that wastage of medical personnel is not just a matter of loss of services of women doctors. Bewley and Bewley (1975) have pointed out that losses occur for many reasons. Migration, and early death and disability which are all more common in men doctors also cause loss of trained staff, so wastage is not a 'one-sex' phenomenon.

## The situation in the USA

As the proportion of women in medical school intakes have risen slowly but steadily over recent years, the question of value for money or 'how good an investment?' has inevitably come to the fore in the United States as it has done in Britain. One would expect that American women doctors would be very highly motivated, since the great effort required there to enter and to survive in medical school would surely eliminate all but the most determined (Campbell, M. A. 1973). Presumably, like male students, they too are deeply in debt by the time they qualify and have to struggle to pay the debt off. So it is no surprise to find that more than 90 per cent of women doctors were medically active – in spite of more than half of them being married to doctors, a group whose wives rarely work (Powers, Parmelle, and Wiesenfelder 1969). What sort of work were they doing?

Well, it might be argued that they were not doing enough, for they only put in an average of 2,000 hours of professional activity a year, compared with a 2,831 average reported by male physicians. This works out at between forty and fifty hours a week for women and between fifty and sixty hours a week for men. Comments on this state of affairs can vary from dismay that women work so little, to disgust, or disbelief, that men work so much. But 75 per cent of male doctors were self-employed as compared with 48 per cent of female doctors, so

42

that it is possible we are comparing reasonable working hours in public service with excessive hours in private practice. Incidentally, women's incomes on average, are disproportionately less than those of the men – $28,000 as compared with $48,000. Seven and a half per cent of all specialists are women and the specialties in which women are most commonly found bear a remarkable resemblance to the British 'shortage specialties'.

## Women doctors elsewhere

The 'doctors and nurses' games of childhood indicate an early awareness on the part of children of our society's sex stereotyping – or of the natural roles of men and women in the healing arts, as some would say. Cross-cultural comparisons rather undermine the second hypothesis, as they so often do, when we find that our 'natural state of affairs' would seem a bizarre exotic native custom to anthropologists from other parts of the world. Visitors from quite near neighbours in fact, would find our situation remarkable, for in general, as you go East, women doctors are more common. In the US they form 8 per cent of doctors, in England 22 per cent, in Finland 24 per cent, in Poland 46 per cent, and in the USSR 74 per cent. Other health professionals likewise vary; for example, dentistry has long been predominantly a women's profession in Finland, with 70 per cent at present, much like the Soviet 77 per cent and Polish 81 per cent, but unlike the Swedish 27 per cent. In the US 1 per cent of dentists are women (Pennell and Showell 1975).

Why these variations? This question was discussed at length in Washington in 1975, at the International Conference on Women in Health. The legal position of women, and their statutory right to education, may seem the same – although as noted elsewhere it is only within the last few years that the open practice of discrimination against women applicants to medical school became illegal in Britain. In the socialist countries women are found in a much wider range of occupations, including science-based jobs, but not in such large numbers as in medicine. There are many child-care facilities and the idea of professional training and work for women is the accepted norm. In these circumstances medicine is frequently chosen by women from among the wide range of possibilities and career opportunities open to them, and is less frequently chosen by men.

Interestingly, in both Poland (Sokołowska 1975) and the USSR (Piradova 1975) the presence of a substantial number of women in medicine predates the socialist revolution. The post-revolution majority position was therefore achieved on the basis of a well-established tradition of women doctors and other health workers. It is not at all unusual, in the USSR, for nurses to further their studies and become doctors. In so doing they are given every encouragement, including exemptions from some parts of the course. Women are found in all specialties, and as a majority in almost all, the only exceptions being surgery (except cardiovascular surgery) and anaesthetics.

In the socialist countries, women are still under-represented in policy-making positions, such as Ministers and Directors, but are prominent and often predominant in most other senior positions (Fogarty, Rapoport, and Rapoport 1971). Sokołowska comments that in Poland at least, the necessary redefinition of sex roles within marriage and the family which would allow women equal time to pursue career promotion has yet to take place on a wide scale, and we fear this applies to other socialist countries too. She sees signs of change in Poland, and since women doctors there are experienced at decision-making in a professional setting, she predicts that they will be playing their part as managerial decision-makers in the near future, particularly if medical management training programmes are developed. Obviously men will have to take equal shares of parental and domestic responsibilities if women are to put such training to good use.

Whether the predominance of women in the health services of the socialist countries is, as some say, a new sort of sex stereotyping or is related to the relatively low rank of doctors on earnings tables, as Field (1975) suggests, we cannot say. What we can say is that it is immensely encouraging to those of us elsewhere who want women to play a full part in medicine to see the beginnings they have made. And we wait impatiently with Sokołowska for the next steps.

### Women in medical school

To be a doctor, you need to go to medical school; those who select students and fashion the environment in which they will learn clearly influence who shall be our doctors, and what sort of doctors they will be. We shall therefore turn now to the medical schools to see how women fare before they qualify.

Despite basic similarities, Britain and North America differ to some degree in their selection of students to medical school. On both sides of the Atlantic far more men apply than women, and more men get in. Women 'select themselves' (or social pressure does it for them) so that relatively few, and only relatively well-qualified women enter the race. In many instances they are subject to quotas – not as one might suppose, attempts to raise the proportion of under-represented groups to an acceptable level, but to keep them down. Many schools in Britain operated in this way until the increase in male applications in the late 1960s made it no longer necessary: women could be selected on their merits and still not constitute more than one third. A survey of medical school rejects in 1966–7 found that the academic qualifications of the rejected women were, on average, markedly better than those of the rejected men (Johnson 1971). The Committee of Vice Chancellors and Principals advised against quotas for women just before it became illegal in Britain to use sex as a selective factor – but the secrecy in which most selection takes place makes it hard to check whether this legislation is everywhere respected. In some schools the proportion of women is rising steadily, and parity seems in sight. In others this is far from the case.

Negative quotas operated in Canada until 1967. In the US the number of women students was derisory at about 5 per cent for many years until it started climbing and reached the heady level of 22 per cent in the 1974 intake. These women students often had cause to complain of their minority status and of the sexist behaviour of teachers and fellow students, similar to that inflicted on the pioneers of the last century (Campbell, M. A. 1973).

Critics of students' performance whilst in medical school and after leaving seem to prefer to blame inadequacies on mistakes made in selection. This seems somehow more attractive than examining the content of medical education and the actual circumstances in which young graduates find themselves. Naturally, the 'woman doctor problem' has been subjected to this approach too, and Ulyatt and Ulyatt (1971, 1973) have been prominent supporters of the 'pre-acceptance test' answer. They found that non-working women doctors described more obstacles preventing women following careers than did working women doctors. They presumed that these were imagined difficulties, and attributed the differences in performance to deeply-rooted 'personality-factors'. The authors then turned their attention to women medical students and gave students at two schools questionnaires. The answers seemed to cluster at two extremes and were considered by the authors to be predictive of future working careers. Particular issues concerning the desire to be close to the family and fear of damaging children by any absence were thought to best predict who would be likely to work in the future. It implied that one should ask the applicants about their feelings before accepting them – and admit only future workers.

The extraordinary set of assumptions behind this approach, and its profoundly sexist implications, demand further attention. But clearly, as we have contended earlier and will argue further later, it fits in well with the assertion that children need an ever-present mother – an assertion which serves the interests of some powerful sections of society, but which has never been validated.

The success rates of women medical students are high – they do better than men in examinations according to most reports. In the US they drop out for 'non-academic' reasons more commonly than do their male colleagues (often to support a medical student husband, or to bear his child). There was little sex difference in drop-out rates in the UK in 1963–4 (Jefferys, Gauvain, and Guleson 1965). Only four out of 2,755 women students left for marriage or child-bearing in that year in Britain.

Personality tests, second only in the affections of many educators to intelligence (IQ) tests, have been administered to many a medical student, and in some instances comparisons have been made between men and women. These have recorded men as tending towards extroversion and women towards neuroticism – in other words the women tend to be more anxious. However, the test results also show women to be more patient-centred, as opposed to technology-centred, more aware of psycho-social factors, keener to take on clinical responsibility, and less dependent on their teachers (Walton 1968).

In this light, the documented under-achievement of qualified women seems even more tragic. Society moulds women into more caring creatures in general, allows only the most talented among them to get into medical school, and then wastes the able, well-motivated output of women doctors.

## Women students and minority status problems

American writers have argued that one of the problems women students face is their status as a minority group in medical school, and the lack of any successful women doctors on whom to model themselves. A special interest therefore arises in the fate of graduates from the London Royal Free Hospital School of Medicine, formerly a women's school, where neither of these problems existed. The 1966 follow-up study of their graduates (Flynn and Gardner 1969; Gardner 1976, personal communication) was not, however, very encouraging. Of women who graduated between seventeen and twenty-one years earlier, 35 per cent were working in hospitals, but only 12 per cent were consultants. Among married women, 27 per cent were in hospital work and only 7 per cent consultants. A younger age group, who had graduated between twelve and fourteen years before, had fared even worse. Only 9 per cent of all women were consultants, and 6 per cent of married women. Of course, some of this last group of women may yet be promoted, and the numbers may be underestimates of final status. This explanation is unlikely to account for the poor success of the older group, and it is disappointing to find that these women whose experience as students should have given them a good start (if morale in medical school is influential), had not achieved higher status. That two thirds of those who were working in hospitals were in sub-consultant posts raises many questions about the policies of appointing committees. When we realize that more than half of the *single* women were in this category too, the question of sex discrimination begins to look important.

It seems then that although women students have won the battle to enter medical school, with all the effort that entails, and have thrived within it, they have been unable to overcome the obstacles which stand between them and a 'normal' medical career, even when they have been part of a female majority within a school with many women teachers. The obstacles include marriage, motherhood, social pressures, the appalling lack of child-care facilities in our society, and most likely sex discrimination as well. Explanations involving personal attitudes or individual failings are no doubt relevant in some instances, but are on the whole totally inadequate, defeatist, sexist, and offer no practical solution at all. Profound social change, and in particular changes in the position of women in our society are prerequisites for the total solution of the problem. Some of these changes could and should be implemented now, and the demand for them already forms part of the policy of some of the health service unions. For example, the Medical Practitioners Union (part of the Association of Scientific, Technical and Managerial Staffs, ASTMS), calls for hospitals to establish creches and school-holiday centres for the children of all staff. It also advocates the extension of part-time post-graduate training facilities for doctors in all specialties to all areas, together with refresher courses and flexible working arrangements in career posts for all those who have completed training.

In campaigning for such policies, we can alert women to the trap they are in, and involve them in working for realizable aims which can lighten their present burdens. In the longer term, even partial successes will speed the day when at last men and women parents, and men and women doctors, have equal responsibilities and equal opportunities, without disadvantages to themselves, their children, or their patients, and to the greater benefit of society as a whole.

# THREE

# Other women health workers

As we have noted, women predominate in the labour force of many health services. We began with women doctors, and have so far made only passing mention of other women health workers. Perhaps this represents a bias on our part, as doctors. If so, we apologize and point out in part justification that medicine is dominated by the doctors, in whom most power resides, and the position of women doctors has been seen as central to the struggle for sex equality for many years. They are growing in numbers, and thus their problems are multiplying – and moreover the subject is well documented.

But now we want to see what we can learn about other women workers in health. Who are they? There are some other 'professionals' of whom the largest group are probably the dentists. Then there are the ones who, as we saw earlier, have been termed the 'semi-professionals'. Of these, nurses and midwives form the largest category, with far few physiotherapists, occupational therapists, radiographers, dieticians and orthoptists, and of course social workers, if we define health service workers in the broadest sense. There are also the many other hospital and social service workers not dignified by the title of 'professional', although many state enrolled nurses (SENs) and nursing auxiliaries do work that is often done by state registered nurses. Outside the hospital, the home-helps probably do more 'caring' from the patients' point of view, than all the 'caring professions' put together. In hospitals too, the orderlies and the domestics are often important people in the lives of in-patients, providing advice and support as well as practical help. We will now look briefly at most of these groups, focusing in rather more detail on the nurses.

### Women dentists

According to Goode (1969), dentists have achieved professional status only relatively recently. Adequate scientific foundations were laid down, increased income and prestige were achieved, and a new profession was established, remarkably, in an area which overlapped with the work of some doctors. In this, dentistry differed from anaesthesiology for example, which is now a medical specialty in Britain, while in the US it is practised by nurses under medical supervision. How can we account for this difference? Is one of the reasons the fact that dentistry is largely a male profession?

It is noteworthy that the predominance of male dentists is not universal. As we mentioned earlier, in the Soviet Union and East Europe approximately 80 per cent of dentists are women, and 70 per cent are women in Finland too. In Sweden, the figure is 27 per cent. The proportion of women dentists is rising in England and Wales where it is currently one quarter of those entering the dental profession, and even in the US (where now only 1 per cent of dentists are women) 11 per cent of the dental schools intake in the year 1974–5 were women.

A recent survey of women dentists in England and Wales found many similarities with earlier surveys of women doctors (Seward 1976). Seventy per cent were married, and more than half the married women were married to a dentist or a doctor. Half the women had children under sixteen, and a quarter had children under five. Nevertheless only 15 per cent were not working, one fifth of these because of old age or ill health. Forty-one per cent were working full-time and 44 per cent part-time. More than half the working dentists were in general dental practice, in many cases in partnership with their husbands, and the attitude and behaviour of the husband was often crucial in determining whether it was possible for the woman to follow her career.

Less than 2 per cent of those of working age did not want to work in dentistry, but many, particularly among those not currently working, felt a need for retraining, or for being brought up to date with recent developments in practice. Some needed to be able to make flexible and limited commitments to work, at least for a time. Fortunately, it is easier to do this in dentistry, where an appointment system can regulate work load, than in some other spheres of health work. Nevertheless hospital and community practice could probably attract back more women dentists if courses were organized and attempts made to fit in with the women's other commitments. The parallels with medical women are very close, but the difficulties surrounding the doctors' long post-graduate hospital training do not apply, so the solution should be easier. It remains to be seen if the problems facing dental women will be tackled with the necessary energy; perhaps the prospects are brighter for dentists, where there is as yet no talk of over-recruitment to the profession.

### Professions supplementary to medicine

In 1960 a Council was established to supervise five boards, each of which maintains a register of those recognized as professionally qualified in dietetics, occupational therapy, orthoptics, physiotherapy, and radiography (Martin 1969). These boards maintain standards of training and conduct, and have disciplinary powers. Working in the hospital service in any of these fields requires registration (although this is not necessary for private work outside!). The establishment of the Council represented a step towards independence, but in daily practice the activities of these workers are under medical control to a greater or lesser extent – they are medical hand*maidens*. For of course, the practitioners are predominantly female, and predominantly young, too.

The students training in these areas come from relatively privileged backgrounds compared with those of nurses, though not of doctors. Those who are married tend to have husbands in professional or white-collar occupations.

The pay is poor and the career structure limited. In short, like nursing in the past, the professions seem structured to have a constant turnover of young women, ever replaceable by the next generation, who will likewise work only for a few years before retiring 'home'. In spite of a desperate shortage of woman-power in each of these fields, retaining or retraining never seem to have been seriously considered as means of making better use of trained people. Part-time work is quite common among the married practitioners, but this appears to have developed without planning, and not to be part of NHS policy.[1]

There still seems to be a long way to go before women in the 'professions supplementary to medicine' are able to make the contribution that they could and should make to health care, and to receive appropriate recognition and rewards.

### The midwives

Healers of both sexes in the distant past, we have seen, can be viewed as common ancestors of both medicine and nursing. However, traditionally all midwives were women and as division of labour developed, some women became professional midwives. The men-midwives, as their name implies, were intruders into a women's world. In Britain, they came largely from the ranks of the apothecaries, although some had other qualifications – for example, one of the Chamberlen family[2] was a fellow of the Royal College of Physicians, and MD of Padua, Oxford, and Cambridge.

A nineteenth-century doctor writing on English midwives (Aveling 1872) was well aware that midwives' proposals for the regulation of midwifery might have been based on self-interest. He commented on a comprehensive scheme propounded in 1687 by a remarkable London midwife, Mrs Cellier, for the training and licensing of women practitioners: 'The scheme, though not wholly devoid of merit, was mainly a monopoly and mostly for her own benefit.' This may well have been an accurate assessment – but one which applied equally to alternative schemes proposed by the Chamberlens and to many subsequent proposals which actually received medical blessing, including that of the apothecaries in 1815. Each of these represented an attempted take-over of midwifery – but this does not seem to have occurred to the medical author. Medical writers, then as now, commonly assumed the unassailable correctness of current medical practice, in spite of a paucity of objective evidence. Some historians have made the same assumption, misled by the observation that in general death rates have been falling ever since they have been widely recorded. Since over the same period, hospitals and dispensaries were established, medical education developed, and considerable advance was made in the understanding of the function of the human body in health and disease, they concluded that these lives had been saved by current medical practice.

McKeown and Brown (1955) have questioned this notion of cause and effect and challenged the idea that medical developments in times past have contributed materially to the general health of the population.[3] In particular, the authors evaluated several medical developments in midwifery in the eighteenth century. One was the establishment of lying-in hospitals (the first was in London, in 1749) of which the men-midwives were keen advocates. These were certainly much more likely to have increased maternal and infant mortality than to have reduced it, as the spread of puerperal sepsis took its dreadful toll.[4] Another contemporary development was the somewhat wider use of obstetric forceps, although fortunately they were still used relatively rarely. The forceps began as a monopoly of one family, the Chamberlens, who introduced them, and later became the monopoly of one sex – the men-midwives. Forceps were associated with very high maternal and infant mortality rates, even if occasionally they saved lives.

A more positive development was improved hygiene at delivery which was equally applicable by practitioners of either sex. At the time theoretical study gave no help as the nature of infection and its transmission was not understood, but common sense and experience provided plenty of reasons for advocating and practising cleanliness when caring for women in labour.[5]

Thus, the expectation that better or rather, more, training led to greater competence did not seem to be confirmed, and in the case of the midwives and the medically trained men who sought to usurp and control them, was not borne out in practice. The midwives were often accused of being meddlesome – but it may be that some who meddled were simply getting above their station and emulating the men with their instruments. Virtually until this century, women in labour could only hope that harm would not be done to them, and the midwives, in general, were probably less harmful than the men.

However, the profession of midwifery did come to be regulated finally in 1902. The whole story of the battles preceding the 1902 Midwives Act is a long and complicated one, recently documented by Donnison (1977). Like the nurses' saga which we discuss later, it was interlinked with campaigns for women's rights, and with rearguard action on the part of doctors seeking to defend their self-interests. The British Medical Association (BMA) and the General Medical Council changed position from time to time, as metropolitan doctors and poor provincial general practitioners exerted respective pressures. And Mrs Bedford Fenwick, a leading figure in the campaign for the registration of nurses also had a part to play, oscillating from side to side. In the end, Parliament partly disregarded the main medical pressures (for otherwise there could have been no workable act at all), and established, by statute, the profession of midwifery. It was, however, hedged round with restrictions as no other profession has been, before or since, with rigid regulations and strict control exercised by the Central Midwives Board. The doctors' objective, that of controlling midwifery as a profitable specialty, was promoted by strict regulations requiring a medical practitioner to be called in the event of any abnormality. But up until 1975, midwifery managed to remain a women's profession.[6]

Midwifery, however, has declined as a domestic art and a personal service as more and more deliveries take place in impersonal hospital surroundings, and its claim to be concerned with a physiological, not a pathological, process seems to be under attack, as we shall discuss later. Opposition by vocal women, in alliance with some midwives and doctors, may now be turning the tide against the fashion of intervention to induce labour, and the battle goes on to recover the great benefits of the midwife as the skilled but sisterly helper in the natural process of birth.[7]

In the late nineteenth century, increasing attempts were made by medical men in the US to control and eliminate 'dirty ignorant midwives'. These calls resulted in the closure of midwifery training schools. Nevertheless even as late as 1910, half of all births were attended by the 'granny women', inevitably largely untrained. These were mostly births to the poor, particularly to urban immigrant women and rural black women. Until then, the general practitioners had realized there was little to be gained from competing in this area – perhaps to the advantage of these generally disadvantaged groups, for the record of the doctors was sometimes inferior to those of the 'granny women' (Antler and Fox 1977).

When from 1915 to 1936, the proportion of deliveries conducted by midwives fell from 40 per cent to less than 15 per cent, the maternal mortality rate remained high, at twice the level of that of many European countries where midwives were universal. Each year, 15,000 American women died in childbirth, and proportionately more died in high-class all-doctor areas like Boston than in towns like Newark, New York, and Cleveland, where midwives still conducted half the deliveries (Levy 1923).

The persistently high rates seemed to be associated with increasing obstetric intervention. Caesarean sections (at twice the price of non-operative delivery) increased, and up to half of the women were delivered by 'routine forceps extractions' (perhaps the reader will see parallels with today when the section on childbirth is reached). Patients were blamed for the interventions, since they were said to demand quick painless labour. Antler and Fox report that women's hospitals (staffed by women doctors only) had few operative deliveries and lower maternal mortality rates. Municipal hospitals also had lower death rates, compared with voluntary and private hospitals, in spite of catering mostly for wives of manual workers who would be expected to be in poorer health. Here the mortality rates were probably related to the low rates of operative delivery, since there were no financial incentives to deliver by forceps or caesarean section.

The New York Academy of Medicine (1933) conducted an enquiry into maternal mortality and placed the blame for the high death rates on doctors. They recommended the re-introduction of the midwife with provision for her thorough training, but their proposals went unheeded; the midwife is still a rarity in America. Their recommendations were ignored because doctors were competing keenly with each other for custom. Medical midwifery was an introduction into a family which the young doctor dearly needed and was prepared to see as a 'loss leader' since it often led to a continuing relationship. Thus, in the US, the general practitioners were more successful than in England, and the midwife was eliminated, leaving only a maternity nurse as an aid to the doctor. Later the doctors themselves began to receive more basic obstetric training, and a regular medical review of maternity practice was introduced. Maternal death rates began to fall in the late thirties, but remain relatively high even now, compared with many other industrialized countries.

However, small-town, unprofitable practice does still not attract doctors, and sub-doctors of various sorts are now providing general medical care in some such areas. Midwives too have had to be re-invented to practise there. Recently, sophisticated urban women have been demanding midwives, to avoid giving birth on the obstetric hospital conveyor belt. They have rejected the definition of childbirth as a pathological process, requiring hospital admission, and medical or surgical control, and they are asserting the right to deliver at home with skilled womanly help but the minimum of interference – as we shall discuss later.

**Nurses**

*The history of nursing*
It is only relatively recently, in the last few centuries, that a division of labour has occurred in the healing arts. Medicine was monopolized by men and nursing, which included the rest of the healing functions, was left to women to perform. The history of the development of nursing as a distinct occupation, and the attempts made to elevate it to the status of a profession, began in earnest in Britain in about the middle of the last century. Ever since then, its history has been interwoven with the struggle for women's rights, for many of the leading figures professed feminism.[8]

Until recently, almost all the sick were cared for, that is nursed, at home by those around them. The exceptions were those who were injured or became ill when far from home, who were among strangers and were alone. Apart from times of war or famine, these exceptions were few, and religious foundations here and there offered accommodation to the wanderers, and care for those who fell ill.

Economic and social developments in the eighteenth and nineteenth centuries created a greater demand for institutional care, and caused hospitals to be established in many towns of Britain and Europe. Some were run by religious orders and others sponsored by local burgesses. Their inmates included the chronic sick and dying, the crippled, the old, and the mad, from among the urban poor and particularly from the newcomers to the towns. The Industrial Revolution had led to the passing of the Poor Laws, and the creation of workhouses for the able-bodied poor, where the sick were also often taken.

Although today nursing is a vital part of the British health service, it is still true that most people who are sick are at home and receive most of their 'nursing care' from family, friends, or neighbours about them, as they have always done. The very rich, of course, may have resident nurses to care for long-term invalids – as they did for all significant illnesses in the last century. Those who have the choice, that is can afford to pay for home nursing and doctoring, have only taken to using institutional care during this century, as surgery and other complicated treatments developed. This led to the building of 'private wings' and nursing homes. But more recently, since the creation of the NHS brought improved standards in hospitals, the affluent have taken to using them as well.

Until the late eighteenth century doctors were rarely concerned with hospitals to any great extent. Then however, post-revolutionary France began to take the lead in European medicine, based on extensive clinical and pathological studies. Doctors were appointed, full-time to the *Hôtel Dieu* which they found full to overflowing with the sick poor of Paris. Under these circumstances, the nature of the medical problem was re-defined; the concern became less 'the sick person', and more 'the disease'. Medical students came in to be taught on this 'clinical material', to practise clinical examination and diagnosis, and in due course, post-mortem examination. The prospering bourgeoisie were asked to give charitable support for hospitals for the sick poor, explicitly on the grounds that the doctors could gain more knowledge and experience in them, and thus be better able to treat their affluent patients (Foucault 1973).

Of course, patients still had to be nursed, and the nurse spent much more time with the sick person than did the doctor or the medical student who 'walked the wards'. But the nurse too had been redefined – as a medical auxiliary, working under the doctor, taking orders from and passing on information to him, rather than primarily caring for the sick person and meeting his needs as she saw them.

French medicine became a world leader in defining syndromes and identifying diseases, and the pattern described above soon developed in the big cities in the rest of Europe.

Until the twentieth century, the sick in institutional care were drawn almost exclusively from those groups whose home circumstances were totally unsuitable for any sort of home nursing – the poor and the destitute. In Britain they were housed, respectively, in the voluntary hospitals and the workhouse. The hospital nurses were usually respectable, married, or widowed working-class women – they had learned from the experiences of their own families' illnesses, from watching other nurses, and from the instruction of the doctors. In a word, they were rather superior domestic servants, perhaps close in social class to the patients they nursed. These latter, as they recovered, were required to give a hand with the daily chores. In the workhouse, able-bodied paupers had to care for their sick co-residents; there were very few paid nurses until later in the century.

These early nineteenth century working-class nurses were reviled by the reformers, Florence Nightingale at their head, and this attitude has persisted. No doubt there were good and bad among their numbers (as among nurses today); their educational level was low and their training minimal – although as we noted for doctors, it is not self-evident that training in the current theories of disease and its treatment was a certain advantage. What is sure is that they were badly paid, even by the standard of women's wages at the time, and their conditions of work and accommodation when resident were appalling. Of course, we are talking of ordinary nurses. Sisters were usually of somewhat superior origins – the housekeeper class – whilst matrons were ladies, not necessarily with much nursing experience.

*The demand for training and nurse registration*

It was against this backcloth that the demand for training for nurses arose. As Abel-Smith documents in his *History of the Nursing Profession* (1960),[9] demographic changes led to a surplus of single women; those of the working-class could find some occupation in industry, in mills and sweat shops, and in domestic service, but only the despised and shrinking role of governess was open to gentlewomen. Good works and visiting the sick poor made suitable voluntary activities for married ladies. Nursing, if only it were respectable, could become an outlet for their spinster sisters. The role was feminine, and as we shall see (p. 62), was considered an extension of the 'natural function' of woman, as a help-mate to the men doctors. A small beginning had already been made in several hospitals, but Florence Nightingale's return from the well-publicized and successful expedition to the Crimea, marked the beginning of major changes, the start of nursing as we know it today in Britain.

The result of the reforms was to provide more, better-class, better-trained nurses; greater discipline and cleanliness in the hospitals; more skilled observation and treatment in the wards; and the opening-up of a career for women, allowing them to share a social life with other young women which, restrictive as it was, may have been less so than within the parental home. In other words, a step forward was made both for hospital care, and for female emancipation. But not a very big one, perhaps. For patients, greater efficiency may have been bought at the cost of losing personal and continuing care from mature homely women.

An interesting ambivalence was displayed by the doctors, then and later, to the new-style nurses. Although the ladies protested that they were trained the better to carry out doctors' orders, they became an independent, female, and thus a potentially threatening hierarchy within the hospitals. The matrons were often well-connected, and could go direct to the patrons in the voluntary hospital system – if necessary, Miss Nightingale would even get the ear of Cabinet Ministers!

The lady nurses who filled the top positions, and wielded influence, were little concerned with money. It was status they cared about; and the achievement of professional status, with a monopoly of the title 'Nurse' for those who were properly trained, became a central concern. Mrs Bedford Fenwick,[10] one of the best known top nurses, led the British Nurses' Association from 1887, with the prime objective of restricting entry into nursing training to the daughters of the higher social classes, and establishing a register which would enable the public, meaning the rich, who desired a home nurse, to be able to select the genuine article.[11] Nightingale saw the folly of this scheme, which would clearly mean fewer nurses to meet the expanding demand. She also objected to the proposal that suitability for entry to the register should be decided by examination. 'Dictionaries can answer questions,' she said, 'but nurses require personal qualities which cannot be judged by examinations.' As vested interests of various sorts declared themselves, the 'thirty years war' began and was fought against a background of rampant snobbery, militant feminism, and personal rivalries.[12]

However, Parliament did not find time for a registration bill until after the 1914–18 war, when things had changed irrevocably in many respects. After 1914 the heavy demand for nurses in military hospitals at home and abroad led to the depletion of civilian hospitals, especially of mental hospitals where most of the staff were men. To meet needs, and in response to patriotic appeals, many more women came forward for training. Another, and from our point of view, particularly significant, development was the vast number of VADs (Voluntary Aid Detachments) who were recruited by the Red Cross and Order of St John, and given very variable amounts of training. By the end of the war there were 120,000 of them, many of middle-class origin, as compared with about 18,000 working, fully-trained nurses. Obviously, the definition of 'nurse' was going to be an issue in the post-war world. By 1919, when the vote had been won for some women, and nursing trade unionism was growing, Parliament accepted registration. The new Minister of Health, however, ignored the nursing organizations and drafted his own bill. It was envisaged that existing practical nurses would be registered if they had 'adequate knowledge and experience of nursing the sick' (following the precendent of the 'bona-fide midwives' in 1902), but that henceforth three years training and success in the state examination would be the only way to become a registered nurse.[13] The register had more than one section; the general part was for women only, while the supplements included male nurses, mental nurses, children's nurses, and fever nurses.[14] Men had no means of entering the general section – nor were they eligible for membership of the Royal College of Nursing. The complex and rather exclusive structure, advocated by several leading nurses for many years, had finally been achieved.

However, the expected millennium was not at hand. There was still a desperate shortage of nurses in the expanding hospitals, and the less attractive hospitals continued to have to rely on untrained staff. In 1931 nearly 140,000 women and 15,000 men were entered on census returns as nurses, about three times as many as those on the registers. In reality, the available supply of girls with the right educational background was strictly limited, and the extremely poor conditions probationer nurses had to suffer often discouraged them from continuing – between one third and one half of entrants did not complete their training.[15]

Poor pay, which must have contributed to this wastage did not concern our lady leaders – or rather it did, but in a negative way. They feared that high pay would attract the 'wrong sort of girl'. Luckily for the future of nursing, there were others, in the trade unions, with more insight. Meanwhile a parliamentary committee recognized the need for nursing personnel other than state registered nurses, who would be trained, but with lower educational requirements. From this the state enrolled nurse (SEN) was eventually created, born of necessity in 1943, in spite of the Fenwick group's continued opposition,[16] but it had taken another world war for action to be taken. In the event the SENs, like SRNs, were trained in large numbers, but many did not remain in active work for long.

In the post-World War II era, the National Health Service made it possible to provide more uniform salaries and conditions than ever before, and a 'Whitley Council' machinery was set up, to replace the 1941 salaries committee, as a framework for negotiations for all staff in the hospital service.[17] One issue which remained was 'waste' of time on 'non-productive' domestic work – which Nightingale had felt was character-building – and gradually auxiliaries and other less highly-trained personnel were increased to relieve students of these 'chores'.

## Nursing in the USA

Many parallels can be drawn between the history of nursing in the USA and Britain, but the hospitals in the States were a later creation, specifically to care for the sick. They did not grow out of facilities for the destitute (Ashley 1976), and while some charity patients were accepted, most patients had to pay. Doctors were involved from the start, many with a business interest. This resulted in the long opposition to public hospitals, which were considered unfair competition. The main profitable product for sale was nursing care, on and off the premises.[18]

It seems that doctors expressed little concern to have well-trained nurses staff their hospitals. They shared the ideology that nurses are born, not made, and need intuition and character, meaning obedience, rather than professional expertise. Moreover, using trainees to staff the hospitals kept costs down and profits up. Standards of nursing were not laid down anywhere by legal regulations until 1947 when New York was the first State to implement control.

Today too nursing in the United States and in Britain have much in common (Cannings and Lazonick 1975), but their few differences are mostly associated with the greater commercialism of the American health care industry. Nearly half of the nursing workforce, about 1,300,000 women, are nursing aids with little or no training; of the remainder, nearly 500,000 are 'registered nurses' (now all to be graduates) and half that number are 'practical nurses'. The vast majority of all of these grades are women. There are no clear distinctions among the roles of the different grades of nurses, in spite of their different skills, but there is a tendency for basic bedside nursing to be allocated to the least trained staff, while the most trained staff are either nursing administrators or are undertaking technical and/or medical tasks – these latter are not paid doctors' rates, of course.

*Sexual stereotypes in medicine and nursing*
The sex hierarchy in distribution of power and in earnings in health services in western Europe and the USA mirrors the relative position of men and women in society as a whole. It has also been suggested that it is a reflection of male–female relationships in the family, too (Ashley 1976). The model put forward runs like this:

The doctor-nurse-patient relationship in and out of hospital is largely based on that which usually obtains at ward level. That relationship mirrors the stereotype of the bourgeois family

62

where father dominates and performs the role of decision-taker and protector whilst mother's role is passive, consisting of servicing activities and carrying out the wishes of father. The child's role is subordinate, her rights are limited, she is serviced by mother, her needs are interpreted by mother to father, and her daily performance related to father by mother.

Imagine the ward scene. The consultant goes on a ward round, having been busy elsewhere; his nurse accompanies him, showing him what she has been doing while he has been away. They arrive at the bedside of the patient. They discuss the patient at the foot of the bed. The consultant says to the nurse: 'How is Mrs Jones today?' Nurse says: 'She's opened her bowels and her appetite is better.' Both question and response *could* have been directly put to and answered by the patient but the nurse acts as mediator. The situation is similar in gynaecological outpatients department (Richman and Goldthorp 1977) where, after the consultant leaves the examination suite, the nurse interprets to the patient what she is to do and what the consultant thought. The distance between doctor and patient is thus maintained, and the former's brief and infrequent appearances only serve to increase his importance. The nurse can use the threat of 'doctor's disapproval' if the patient does not comply with certain conditions; promises of his approval can also be held up as rewards.

The analogy can be taken further:

The ward is rather like the home. The home has to be kept clean and tidy. Housework can be a soul-destroying task; it is endless. The housewife keeps herself going with a vision of the house when it is all clean, when the kids are bathed and ready for bed, when the washing-up is done and put away and everything is tidy. The ward sister similarly may have as an ideal the vision of the ward tidy with patients combed and clean, sitting up ready for the consultant's ward round (Coser 1963).

In Nichol's play *The National Health*, there is an underlying theme that the image which helps the nurse keep cheerful in the face of the decrepit hospital ward, the inadequate operating theatre, and the death of patients, is the dream of a Dr Kildare-like hospital. The fantasy hospital adopts the name of her own hospital with herself (glamorized) working in it. All the patients get better. The medicine and nursing which is practised is all acute medicine, drama, glamour, and glitter. In the end a glamorized and smooth version of her favourite doctor proposes to her, and the nurse–wife becomes the real wife.

In the relatively closed community of a hospital beset by many stresses and strains, it would not be surprising if some potential conflicts between doctors and nurses were resolved by sexual means (fantasy or real),[19] which of course sometimes occurs. But the pseudo-family model has political implications too. The statement that 'a family should stick together, bury its differences for the sake of the children' can be extended to the ward where sacrifice for the sake of the patients is also expected. A nurse's responsibility to the patient is appealed to when she is about to go off duty and her replacement has not turned up. In a situation of no overtime, if she stays it will be to do unpaid work. Most consultants would expect it of 'their nurses', especially their ward sister.

That this father-mother-child-like relationship should reduce militancy follows logically. The concept of a sister going on strike is as alien to most consultants as that of a mother going on strike in the home.

Clearly this picture is over-simplified and reality is much more complex.[20] The recent doctors' disputes have of necessity altered their attitude to militancy in other health workers. Nurses too can no longer see doctors as the benign authority figures, totally divorced from materialistic questions such as pay. Things will never be quite the same again (Gordon and Iliffe 1977).

*Nursing structure reorganized*

Two major changes in the structure of the nursing services in Britain have taken place in recent years. The first followed the recommendations of the Salmon Committee (1966) for an elongated hierarchy to give a more rational career structure for nurse managers – or to increase the bureaucratic control of nursing, according to how you look at it. In the well-tried government manner, some experimental areas were set up, to test out the proposed new structure but just as these areas were getting under way, and some major problems were beginning to appear, the decision was taken to implement the scheme everywhere. As nursing staggered through this exercise, 're-organization', this time of the whole administration of the National Health Service, overtook it, and some of the new Salmon grades disappeared or changed names again. Some objections to the changes may have been merely inherent conservative cries against the idea of change itself, others came from doctors who thought that nurse managers were interfering with their control over 'their' nurses. But more sound objections do exist. A rigid, extended hierarchy is conducive neither to professional attitudes nor to good morale. The relatively low position in the structure of the most senior practising nurse devalues nursing as such, and upgrades management at the expense of bedside nursing. Senior clinical nurses, such as ward or theatre sisters may now be less accountable to doctors, but they have less autonomy in other respects, and are more accountable to senior nurse managers. Ironically, more and more of these managers are men, who have been appointed to a disproportionate number of the top positions.

So at a time when their desire to be recognized as 'professionals' is growing and their claim can be justified by some nurses' extended university education as well as well the growing body of nursing research, the current is running very much the other way, in at least two respects. These are the relinquishing of the caring role, and the increasing bureaucraticization introduced by the new structure. One wonders if these two developments, both products of managerialism, are accidental. Certainly there are many who do not wish to see nursing become comparable in status, or remuneration, to 'the professions'. After all, nurses are still mostly women.

*Nurses in trade unions*
Recently in Britain trade union membership in the hospitals has grown rapidly. Today the National Union of Public Employees (NUPE), the Confederation of Health Service Employees (COHSE), and the National Association of Local Government Officers (NALGO) represent more nursing staff than does the Royal College of Nursing (RCN).

Trade unionism grew first among nurses in mental hospitals, many of whom were men, who were formerly excluded from the RCN. In the last three decades there have been considerable increases in the numbers of SENs, auxiliaries, and ancillaries (the last two are not eligible for RCN membership), and more and more of these groups, most of whom are women, have become trade unionists. A variety of factors, some related to general social trends and others specific to the health service, have contributed to this development. There has been a general growth of white-collar trade unionism, particularly in the public sector where earnings are relatively poor. Within the health service, management policies have forced workers to feel the need for organization (Manson 1977). Nearly three quarters of NHS costs are wages, and faced with cries for economy, management has looked towards rationalization, cutting the workforce and increasing productivity. It embarked on work studies, and introduced bonus schemes, and because of these, wages in a particular hospital no longer depended entirely on nationally agreed Whitley Council rates; they were influenced by local negotiations. Even administrators realized that the RCN could not credibly claim to represent most nursing staff, and that they would have to work with shop stewards.[21]

Structural changes in the hospitals following the Salmon Report also had repercussions. The ward sister is no longer responsible for all the staff on her ward; the ancillaries are now centrally controlled by administrators. The general situation can be seen as analogous to the takeover of an old family firm by a big monopoly, which leaves the workers feeling the need for organizations to defend their interests.

The hospital workers strike in 1973 was only possible because trade unions were already strong in some areas, and it led to further recruitment. The main issue was pay, particularly for lower-paid workers, and the next year nurses joined other hospital staff in the streets to demand a decent wage. This dispute attracted a lot of support from other trade unionists, and dockers, miners, textile and building workers, and employees in other parts of the public sector joined in with demonstrations and days of action.

The decision to take strike action is always a serious one for the workers concerned. When your work is 'people work' and helpless patients may suffer as a result, the decision is even more difficult. During the strike it was agreed that emergency services had to be maintained – an emergency being defined by the workers concerned (Carpenter 1977). Even so, some dedicated health workers found it hard to accept that strike action on their part could be justified. Whilst sympathizing with their feelings, we go along with the unions in arguing that under-financing health services, including under-paying staff, damages the health services insidiously but much more seriously than industrial action has ever done. The strike was for a better health service, as well as for decent wages for health workers.[22] The struggle for these objectives is a continuing one, and is of concern to all of us, as well as to the women who work in or are patients in hospitals.

*The future of nursing*
As we have seen 'professionalization' is often taken to involve delegating the 'dirty work' to others, to do under supervision, so that the proponents of 'the rational use of man-power' may find allies in those aspiring to higher status. However the trend in Britain as in the USA for the increasing delegation of basic nursing care to less-trained personnel may lead to unexpected pitfalls. As we have seen, professions are supposed to have unique skills, and dedication to service. Nightingale believed, and many nurses since her, that undertaking the personal care of the sick, doing for the patient what is normally done independently by adults for themselves and doing it in a way which does not infantilize or destroy the dignity of the patient is at the heart of the unique skill and service of nursing. Delegation of such functions in the interest of professionalization may be a mistake that nurses will come to rue; it is certainly well under way already. In 1974 in Britain, of 322,000 nursing staff only 98,000 were SRNs, and 50,000 students, less than half the total nursing personnel.

At the same time many nurses are performing sophisticated roles in high technology medicine, often taking over tasks previously done by doctors. Such developments are warmly welcomed by American feminists, who thus find themselves in the strange company of some medical economists, with their narrowly-based cost-benefit analyses. These latter would favour nurses in preference to doctors every time, since a nurse costs less to train, and is paid a lower salary – female cheap labour, in fact.

However, some nursing schools in Britain feel that this development is leading nursing too much towards 'sub-doctoring', and away from being the wholly different and separate sphere of activity it is in its own right. They maintain that nursing should be making plans for the care of patients and carrying them out independently of, although in collaboration with, doctors, as separate but equal professionals. The medicalization of nursing may mean nurses being good at using high-powered technology, but poor at basic nursing care. A nurse's role, as they see it, is to humanize, civilize, and rationalize the present unthinking adherence to tasks and routines in hospitals and outside. And the only area in which they would consider it suitable for nurses to take over from doctors would be in long-term care of patients suffering from non-acute illnesses (see, for example, Jones 1977, on the nursing process).

Others have argued that nurses should take on more tasks because they are better able to relate to patients not only because of their sex, but also because they are more often of working-class origin, and thus socially closer to most patients than the average doctor.[23] Whilst this is so, the problem might equally be solved by broadening the intake into medical school in terms of both sex and class. Hart (1974) has proposed something of an amalgam of these strategies; he advocates reserving a number of places, perhaps 20 per cent, in medical schools each year for mature people who have already worked in the health service for at least three years (this we have seen is already common in the USSR, and has been proposed in Sweden).

We cannot help wondering if such a scheme in our society might not reinforce rather than break down the medical hierarchy; those who remain as nurses, etc. being by definition those who failed to 'get on' and become doctors. We wonder too about the practicality of it for most women in their twenties and thirties. The proposal would run somewhat counter to other trends which encourage 'team work' between the nurse, social worker, and doctor, each contributing their own distinct skills to help patients solve their problems.

In many parts of the world financial problems loom large and the insufficient and badly distributed numbers of trained medical workers, both doctors and nurses, are unable to provide services for the whole population. The countries of the Third World have vast rural areas without any modern medical service within reach.[24] Although doctors are being trained in increasing numbers, they are expensive and unwilling to live 'in the bush'. Traditionally, trained nurses are not supposed to work independently in clinical practice; so even if they were numerous enough (which they usually are not) and available to work in rural areas (again, not usually the case) they could not automatically meet the need. Some countries are creating a new type

68

of basic medical worker, the most famous being the Chinese 'bare-foot doctor', who has several periods of training, each lasting a few months, and from the end of the first is available to give basic preventive and curative care, combining modern and traditional ideas, to her fellow peasants, whilst continuing to work in the fields herself most of the time. She in no way replaces more highly trained full-time health workers, with whom she frequently consults and exchanges experiences. She may later undergo further training and then go on to take full-time responsibilities herself (Sidel and Sidel 1973).

Other variations include full-time sub-doctors, medical assistants, and rural medical aids, such as are found in parts of Africa, although alongside them in Zambia, for example, experienced nurses also do the same sort of work. Studies in Tanzania suggest that the well-trained village medical aid can be as good as a doctor at diagnosing and treating common conditions (Essex 1976), and can quickly learn which problems to pass on up the medical hierarchy (King 1966). Such experiments, however, are not always successful (Ronaghy and Solter 1974).

Surprisingly, as we have seen, some parts of the United States cannot provide a good enough living to attract any doctors (few American doctors, in any case, want to be general practitioners), and it has been found necessary therefore to explore the possibility of some type of sub-doctor, called a Medex (Smith 1973) in the States. Initially they were physicians' assistants drawn from the ranks of ex-army medical orderlies, and they were predominantly men. After conscription ended the supply dried up and was replaced to some extent by women called nurse practitioners. Australia and Canada are also developing 'nurse practitioners' (Roemer 1975). Even within the ranks of nursing itself there seem to be divisions of opinion about whether such developments are desirable.

Several American nurses who contributed to the International Women and Health Conference held in the USA in 1975 saw the only possibility for them to gain a real say in the allocation of resources and the decisions about priorities being in the extension of the nurse's role to that of 'nurse practitioner'. The nurse would then have greater independence of action and minimum supervision, and be able to extend her nursing and administrative skills as well as develop her creative abilities (Roemer 1975).[25]

A similar model has been put into practice in Sweden, where senior nurses do such things as midwifery, abortion counselling, running family planning clinics, and maintaining treatment regimes with chronic patients, all independently of doctors. There is also a career ladder, enabling a nursing aid eventually to become a fully registered nurse. It is envisaged that in future she may then be able to train to become a physician (Johnsson 1975).

Many of the speakers at the conference saw that nurses could only reach their full potential if they formed an alliance with, and received support from, women patients. It was noted that whereas the Chinese 'bare-foot doctor' was accountable primarily to the people she served, rather than to a medical hierarchy, most women health workers in America and elsewhere remain, at least to some extent, under medical control. Nevertheless, it was argued that women health workers everywhere could seek to extend their own spheres of influence, and could protect the rights of women patients by giving them information about doctors or hospitals, and that the two groups could join to press for health reforms (Brown, C. 1975).

In general, the American Women's Liberation rationale for extending the scope of nurses is that a woman is more likely to be sympathetic to women patients. But we may wonder whether this is automatically the case. If doctors (largely male) feel increasingly threatened by patients who demand to know more about their illnesses and treatment, are not nurses and other women health workers going to feel equally (if not more) threatened? In Britain, for example, some patients complain of general practitioners' receptionists (all women) who appear as 'dragons at the gate'. This is not just because they seem to prevent the patient from gaining access to the doctor, but also because they are felt to be authoritarian. Such behaviour must derive from the position the receptionist finds herself in, with doctors on the one side not wanting to be disturbed and angry if the call is 'trivial', and with the patient on the other, making demands of the receptionist to which she is not trained to respond. And yet she must say something, so her replies are often brusque and defensive. She sees herself as do other women health workers, as part of the medical organization, and behaves accordingly.

While there is nothing automatic, then, about one woman's identification with another woman's problems, we would, however, agree that a sense of identification with women's problems can be fostered more easily in women, who share so many common experiences.[26]

The argument of the doctor–nurse relationship can thus be shifted to one of the health care worker–user relationship. And it is only when seen in this context that we can really progress with the question 'what should the nurse do?' We will return to this at a later stage.

*Trade unions and workers' roles*

It could be argued, as we pointed out earlier, that nurses replacing doctors is just a matter of dilution, using cheap labour to carry out broken-down jobs of more highly paid craftsmen.[27] In the context of 'cash limits' and other devious ways of cutting the National Health Service, we could be heading for medical unemployment (the BMA is already nervous about this). In the same way, the use of volunteers on the wards, though desirable in all sorts of ways, cannot be countenanced if it means that there are no jobs for nurses finishing their training, or orderlies and domestics are being cut back by 'natural wastage'. The truth is that the British National Health Service has been run on cheap labour all along, and still has many areas – in terms of geographical regions and medical specialties – that are grossly under-financed and under-staffed. For example, many wards spend most of the night and part of the day without seeing a trained nurse, many junior doctors are working excessive overtime and in some parts of the country general practitioners have lists that are far too big. In other words, objectively, we need many more skilled staff in the health service, and we need the money to pay them adequately. If we had adequate finance, and the prospect of expansion to provide an equally good service everywhere, it is unlikely that there would be objections to the imaginative development of the skills of nurses, or other workers or volunteers. But when the livelihood of members is at stake, it is difficult to avoid being defensive and even progressive doctors who are increasingly joining trade unions are likely to be hostile to threats of encroachments.

We can see no easy solutions to these conflicts in a society which is plagued by economic stagnation, status ridden and hierarchical. Feminists can begin to make inroads, however, by raising the consciousness of women and their organizational power, with an eye to the future.

## Nursing auxiliaries

Are they nurses, or aren't they? Unable to answer the question, we are tacking them on at the end of the nurses. They and the nursing assistants (and their American cousins, the nursing aids) form a numerically and functionally important part of the nursing labour force. They are almost equal in numbers (in Britain) to the registered nurses – there are about 94,000 of them – and 95 per cent are women.

The DHSS recommends that they should have some in-service training in basic nursing procedures, but in practice, their training seems to range from very little to nothing. They are not supposed to administer drugs, give injections, or change drips, but they can undertake most other tasks which fall to the nursing staff. In many parts of the hospital, and in particular in long-stay areas, they *are* the nursing staff, the only ones apart from one sister or one staff nurse. The implication seems to be that you don't really need to study anatomy and physiology, hygiene, medicine and surgery, and behavioural sciences – you can pick up all you need to know to do nursing by being around on the ward. This is not our view, nor the view of many leading nurses in Britain. (But perhaps it is inevitable if trained nurses prefer to become sub-doctors.)

However we may view it, the reality is that the nursing auxiliary daily finds herself having to take off-the-cuff decisions, which, at best, do not get her into trouble. If she uses her initiative and encourages her immobile patient to try to move, or her anorexic patient to eat, it is always possible that for medical reasons, of which she knows and has been told nothing, she is doing the wrong thing, and that the patient may fall, choke, or go into a coma, and she will get the blame. Much safer to leave them alone in bed, and have a sit-down in the linen room instead. A lay volunteer, coming in equally uninformed, may make the same mistakes of course, but has relatively little to lose; in any case, she has no uniform, is not part of the organization, and no-one expects her to take charge of the ward during lunchtime. The nursing auxiliaries are usually tough and experienced working-class women; otherwise they would not survive. But that is not a good enough reason for giving them low level jobs carrying heavy responsibility – with little training, poor pay, and no prospect for advancement. Once more we find that the health services are exploiting a major group of their women workers.

### Other health service staff

We have discussed many of the workers in the health services, but the majority remain still to be tackled. It is less easy to get statistics about them than about the professionals and 'semi-professionals' already covered and there is also very little written about them.

*In the hospital*

The largest group of such staff are the *ancillaries*, of whom there are more than 250,000. Two thirds of them are women, including most of the domestic staff, laundry workers, and catering workers. Some of them are part-time workers, many of them immigrants, and almost all of them earn wages which are low in the national earnings table. As was discovered during the ancillaries' strike, their official functions are essential to the operation of the hospital service. Anyone who has been admitted to hospital can see that in addition to cleaning wards, and preparing and serving foods, they are essential in many other ways to the well-being of the patients. In-patients know that domestics and orderlies are second only to the other patients as sources of information and reassurance. Who else can, or rather does, tell you what to expect and when, and generally what the formal and informal rules are and how to get round them if necessary?[28] This rich source of care is not usually appreciated by most hospital authorities; they may not even know it is provided in their establishment. Exceptions may be found in therapeutic communities (Martin 1968) where frequent discussions between doctors, nurses, and patients, and sometimes including other ward staff, are emphasized with general benefit all round, we are sure. It is quite ironic that while lip-service is paid to the desirability of talking to patients and responding to their expressed fears and needs, all the professionals seem to find themselves too busy actually to stop and listen. However, the one group who do spend time around the patient, as they go about their other work, and do listen, have no professional guidance at all in handling the problems that come up.

Our point is that these low-paid, non-professional members of staff often are 'part of the team' in the patients' eyes, whatever the professionals may think. In institutions that are more democratic than most hospital wards, they might be recognized and valued as such, and given more job satisfaction, more responsibility, and more patient-oriented in-service training – not to mention more pay. For the woman patient from an ethnic minority group, for example, a woman domestic worker from the same group who can converse, reassure, pass on queries, and report problems, could make all the difference in the world, especially if the domestic worker felt herself to be part of the team. We wonder how often such feelings are fostered – and whether the present structure and organization of the health service makes it likely that they can be.

*Clerical and administrative workers* are another large group, there are 50,000 of them, of whom three quarters are women. (We are prepared to guess that most of the men are to be found in the higher grades.) They are often the people first encountered, by post or in person, by those who go to hospital either as an out-patient or in-patient. Others work as ward clerks and hence encounter patients and enquiring relatives on the ward. Are they counted as part of anybody's team? Or are they often scapegoats, like the general practitioners' receptionists, expected to protect the doctors and pacify the patients at the same time. Have they the power to organize out-patients appointments in a rational way, to devise efficient methods of giving warning of imminent admission, to improve records systems, and are they encouraged to use that power, even if they have it?

We suspect that the answer to those questions is usually 'no' and that this is another band of women, whose talents are under-used, and who could contribute very considerably to improvements in the health service – given the chance.

*Outside the hospital*
We have now moved into the realm of 'community care', that supposedly desirable thing, better (and cheaper) than hospital care, which is being given to all the chronically sick and disabled, the mentally ill, and the handicapped. There must be an enormous army of people, mainly women, working to provide

it. There are mothers, daughters, daughters-in-law, sisters, aunts, cousins, friends, and neighbours who provide help twenty-four hours a day, if it is required, for most of those needy groups, free, or in a few cases, for an 'attendance allowance' of a few pounds a week – it is no wonder it is cheap. But there are of course some paid workers in the community too. There are about 10,000 *home nurses* (compared with 100,000 registered nurses in hospitals). The majority are women who give home care to patients, including more than 1,000,000 old age pensioners, annually, which is about 15 per cent of the retired population. There are about 6,000 *health visitors*, all but a handful of them women, who each year visit among others, 600,000 old people (8 per cent of the retired group). Eleven hundred *chiropodists* care for the feet of around 1,400,00 old people.

Last but not least, we come to the mainstay of care in the community, the *home helps*. Seventy-five thousand of them, all women, we believe, working on average about half-time, each year care for more than 400,000 old people in their own homes, cleaning, shopping, cooking, lighting fires, chatting, washing, keeping them going in fact, and in many instances giving help far beyond the call of duty. They must count their rewards in terms of the satisfaction of helping others, for their other rewards are pitiable. It is true that their services are sometimes valued by others besides the recipients of their help – we know of at least one instance. Dr J. L. Burn, late Medical Officer of Health for Salford, used to meet regularly to talk to and to listen to the home helps. He arranged for speakers to introduce discussions on medical and social matters too – a tradition that others continue there today. We find it hard to imagine a more useful example of keeping in touch with the grass roots, and providing in-service training.

## Social workers

From 1971, social workers became autonomously organized in local authority social service departments, thereby taking a step away from medical hierarchies, into hierarchies of their own. Although the majority of social workers are women, many of the senior posts in the new structure are held by men. Several thousand social workers still work in hospital or clinic settings, but most work outside and are responsible for their own clients.

The responsibility can be heavy; from time to time a disaster occurs, like the death of a child at the hand of its parents. Much of the blame is likely to fall on the social worker involved, who is often made a scapegoat in a way that rarely happens to members of old established professions like medicine.

Many problems beset social work; the workforce has grown rapidly and consists in some areas of a rather incompatible amalgam of untrained, partly trained, and fully trained people with very varying approaches to social work.[29] Society's expectations are often unrealistic, and there is a desperate shortage not only of the general supportive facilities essential for good community care, but also of hospital beds, when they are needed for members of such groups as the elderly.

The newly introduced generic approach, which requires all social workers to undertake work of all types, with the old and the young, the well, the physically handicapped, and the mentally ill, has further increased their burden (and from what we hear from some clients, such as families of the mentally handicapped, has resulted in a serious deterioration in the service they are able to offer).

In a word, the relatively young profession of social work has had to contend, like the health service, with various imposed organizational changes, and is now experiencing severe financial difficulties. Here there is really only one professional group involved, the social workers, of whom the majority are women; but power still seems to rest predominantly with men. It may be enlightening for feminists and students of health care to pay careful attention to what is happening in social work.

### Who controls the British National Health Service?

We will tackle this specific question because it is a centrally administered health service, with organizational charts and so on, which make it seem reasonable to expect that an answer can be found more easily than, for example, for health care in America with its conspicuous lack of a co-ordinated national service. However, the interesting question of how the British health service is controlled may need to be deferred until we can determine whether the health service is controlled at all. In terms of controlling future developments in the service, two apparent modes of planning have been identified: 'incrementalism', that is, same as last year, but a bit more (or in the present day, a bit less) all round; and 'decibel-planning', that is adding on a bit more (or not taking off so much) for those who make most noise.

It is clear that the Department of Health and its predecessor, the Ministry of Health, have been hard put to have any effect at all on the direction in which the health services have been developing. Throughout a period of years in which increasing emphasis has been placed on 'community care' apparently meaning 'care outside the hospital', the proportion of the NHS budget going on hospital services has increased.[30] Probably reorganization of the health services in 1974, and certainly the 1976 proposals of the Resource Allocation Working Party (RAWP), have been seen as means of centrally controlling the juggernaut, and heading it in the right direction. It remains to be seen whether these objectives are achieved to any extent. In as much as these recommendations, particularly those of the RAWP, challenge traditional seats of power in the NHS, the chances are slim, we believe.

### Where is the power wielded?

The effectiveness of the British Medical Association as a pressure group has been well documented by Eckstein (1966), for example, and by Forsyth (1966). It is not unknown, however, for the Royal Colleges to be able to exert even more central influence, and by virtue of the close interlocking of the Royal Colleges, the London Teaching Hospitals, and the General Medical Council, to influence education and research in profound ways too.

We first referred to those bodies in the context of women's struggles to enter medicine in the last century. They have of course changed since then. The BMA admits women members and co-operates closely with the Medical Women's Federation. But, it happens that women occupy only eight seats out of 253 on its major committees. This record is marginally better than that of the Royal Colleges (and Faculties) whose Councils or Boards have eight women members out of 261, and rather worse than the General Medical Council where there are four women out of forty-six members (Bewley and Bewley 1975).

The Royal Colleges on the whole have not been very helpful

in implementing DHSS recommendations on part-time training, although the physicians have produced a useful booklet (RCP 1977). As already mentioned the gynaecologists have just agreed – but as yet they have no part-time training posts, whilst the surgeons are still dragging their feet (there are no women on their Council – less than 2 per cent of consultant surgeons are women, and no doubt some of them would like to keep it that way).

Of course, we do not believe that a token woman here and there will make much difference. Indeed the few women who have 'made it' under the present system are not always aware of how much their own good luck or exceptional talent has helped them to work the system, or how much the scales are weighted against many other women, as can be seen from the correspondence columns of the journals from time to time. What we are trying to do here is weigh up the size of the problem facing those of us, women and men, who want to transform medicine by greatly increasing the contribution women can make. The fact that almost all the decision-makers are men, who have done quite well from the present state of affairs, indicates that our task is not going to be easy. Probably quite a few of the men have specifically and personally bene-fited by the pressures preventing women from playing a full part: competition on the way to the top was reduced and in some instances, medically qualified women sacrificed their own prospects to forward their husbands' careers and relieve them of domestic and child-rearing duties. Even those of whom this can-not be said (and some of whom it can) who are sympathetic to the problems of the woman doctor, can have little first-hand experience of the dilemmas to be faced. They, like many of the women doctors themselves, still see the question in personal terms, of doing *her* a favour, helping with *her* problems. The notion that we are talking of society's problem, created by nothing except economic and social factors, and soluble only by major social change, seems hard to grasp.

The need will have to be strongly-felt – as it may be when the present supply of foreign doctors gradually disappears, to make many influential men welcome women doctors as colleagues. And the big risk will remain that women will be welcomed only in as much as they *do* replace the foreign doctors – i.e. fill sub-consultant positions. The prospect of large numbers of women consultants may well be seen as another matter altogether.

Of course, as we have noted, women already constitute the great majority of health service workers, and democratization within the service should enable many more women to play a part in decision-making. Nurse-managers may indeed be more influential than formerly, now they are members of management teams; not all of these nurses are women, though – fewer than their proportion in the profession would justify. Some of the trade union militants in the struggles of the ancillary workers are women too, and it seems that the influence of women power in the NHS as elsewhere will be forwarded by the unionization of women workers, and their active participation in union work after they join (this would – indeed will – transform the unions, as well as the NHS!).

The running of the health service is locally under the control of the Regional Health Authorities (RHAs) and Area Health Authorities (AHAs), appointed by the Secretary of State for Health to represent professional and local interests. Twenty-five per cent of RHA members are women – we have not been able to obtain information about the AHAs.

The National Health Service establishment bodies, then, are predominantly male, and the organs of the dominant profession, medicine, are likewise nearly all men. Hopes for a slightly greater influence from women seems to lie mostly with those semi-democratic bodies the Community Health Councils, together with the trade union organizations of health service workers and with women themselves, and we will discuss developments in this direction in Part III. Before that, we are going to look at the circumstances that commonly lead to women coming into contact with health services.

# PART II
Women users of health services

# FOUR

# Women patients and women's conditions

We have seen that women are the main providers of health care, although they have little influence in policy-making. We turn now to the users of health services, the majority of whom are also women, and who have even less control over the service.

### Women and general practitioner services

How is it that the majority of patients are women? This question can be answered at several levels, some based on fact, others on speculation.

The most obvious point is that most people are female. From middle age onwards in Britain, women form the majority of each age group, this majority growing greater in each succeeding decade, until among the over seventy-fives, there are two women to every man. So there are more women, and more old women. Other things being equal (which, of course, they aren't), one would expect more ill health in women purely as a result of the age structure of the population. However, we also know from surveys that even when age differences have been allowed for there is more disabling physical illness per 1,000 population among females than among males (Harris 1971), even though male death rates are higher.

One of the reasons for the greater number of women patients is that women are subject to 'medicalization', that is, to being classed as patients, during natural physiological processes such as pregnancy and childbirth. In addition, the organs connected with reproduction in women seem more complex and more liable to cause trouble than those of the male. Menstruation, contraception, and the menopause, in particular, sometimes lead to medical consultation, but sex differences in consultation rates are not eliminated by excluding consultations related to conditions of reproductive organs, although the differences become considerably less.[1] Nathanson (1975) has suggested that when we see sex differences in consultation rates, we are looking at differences in 'illness behaviour' rather than illness itself. The argument is that it is more acceptable for a woman to admit weakness or distress, and to seek aid for it from a doctor, than for a man to do the same. There may well be some truth in this, particularly when the symptoms are psychological. Further, women often have to take sick children or old people to a doctor and therefore know the ropes, or can mention problems of their own in passing; those who are at home can go during the day without loss of pay, which is not the case for most men.

We do not believe, however, that this tendency for women to act sick more than men is a universal phenomenon; on the contrary, there is much evidence that many women cannot afford to be really sick, in other words to take to their beds and abandon all their usual roles (see Koos 1954). We also know, as we will discuss later, that a vast amount of undeclared or badly treated, and thus persisting, disease can be found in random surveys of women, which suggest that 'greater readiness to consult' cannot be a full explanation. A further factor, rarely considered, may be that general practitioners, who guard the gateway to virtually all other medical care in Britain, behave differently towards men and women patients. For example, they may more often advise a return visit, more often initiate long-term, or less effective, treatment, or may less often refer for a second opinion when the person consulting is female. We will return to this point later.

## Women and hospital services

As noted above, women usually encounter doctors during pregnancy and delivery, and nowadays that almost invariably means attendance at and admission to hospital. By definition, too, women are the only users of gynaecological services.[2]

In Britain, the hospital admisson rates per year were, in 1972 (*Hospital In-Patient Enquiry*) 857 per 10,000 population and 847 per 10,000 population for men and women respectively (excluding maternity and psychiatric admissions). That is, men had marginally more admissions. However, if diseases of the breast and genital tracts are excluded, the rates become 816 per 10,000 population for men and 710 for women – a considerably higher rate for men. This seems paradoxical: women go more often to the general practitioner but less often become hospital in-patients. Of course, the individual has more control over general practitioner attendances, since he or she initiates the first visit. By contrast, doctors – the general practitioner, the emergency duty doctor, or the consultant – play a much bigger part in determining who will be admitted to hospital. One factor in such a decision is whether there is someone at home to care for a sick person, and one would expect more women to be admitted on these grounds, since their husbands would not be expected to look after them and far more women live alone. Other factors include the severity of the illness and its perceived need for specialist care – again as judged by the referring or admitting doctors.

It is not possible from the data available to judge whether men *need* to be admitted to hospital more than women, because of more, or more severe illness, or whether men's illnesses are likely to be taken more seriously by the men themselves or by doctors and hence regarded as suitable cases for hospital treatment. One light-hearted view of this from Margaret Dolan of the *Observer* was that there must be two varieties of flu, 'his' and 'hers'. The former requires one week's bed rest and two weeks convalescence, with peace and quiet, nourishing meals, and light entertainment; the latter can be survived with heavy doses of aspirin and one day in bed with fried sausages and cold tea to eat, and children playing all around.

A more serious view on a parallel matter came from Lennane and Lennane (1973). They noted that some common and troublesome conditions in women or children were long dismissed as psychogenic, and often still are, although there is clear evidence of organic causes. They document evidence for this in the case of dysmenorrhea, nausea of pregnancy, labour pains, and infantile colic (the latter being caused in children by their mothers, according to some doctors), and note that while such medical attitudes may help doctors to deter troubled women from consulting them, they are most unhelpful in every other way. They give no relief to individual sufferers (and even if the psychogenic theories *were* true, surely relief would be called for), and most of all they delay proper investigation and improvement of treatment.

## Doctors' attitudes to women patients

Barrett and Roberts (1976) have documented the specific ways in which both doctor and patient accept stereotyped definitions of the social as well as psychological causes of the problems of women patients. In middle age, women are often seen as neurotic, depressed, unable to cope with crises such as children leaving home, and constantly subject to vague complaints, and gynaecological disorders. In their study it was found that doctors were very willing to attribute their women patients' complaints to emotional or home and family problems. It seemed that the medical profession endorsed both explicitly and implicitly the prevailing ideology concerning sex roles – that women are 'naturally' concerned with their homes and families first and foremost (one woman whose illness consisted in an 'irrational' dislike of housework had been 'treated' by electric shock treatment), and that men 'naturally' want to work outside the home to support these families.

Of course, there are wide variations in how individuals respond to illness. Personal attitudes, willingness to complain, one's view of what doctors can do, 'being neurotic' – or just unhappy – and many other factors influence whether complaints are taken to the doctor or not – we are here in the wide field of 'determinants of sickness behaviour', as the sociologists say. But as the Lennanes (1973) have clearly demonstrated with common examples, such variables are not the factors causing the symptoms in the first place. So why do some doctors believe that they are? Partly because like other men, doctors have adopted the beliefs and attitudes which are deeply embedded in society. In addition, becoming a doctor involves an intensive period of professional socialization – learning in medical school, 'walking the wards' behind senior doctors, and reading medical textbooks. How does that affect the doctors' attitudes? Howell (1974) has described the processes whereby the student doctor in America learns the right approach to women. Women medical students are often left out of teaching situations by 'accident' (because there is no women surgeon's changing room, for example), or design, or are exposed to sexist remarks by lecturers. Women's health problems are denigrated with remarks like 'all women's illnesses are assumed psychosomatic until proved otherwise', and ignorance or embarrassment are hidden by jokes – often sexist ones. An analysis by Scully and Bart (1973) of references to female sexuality in recent gynaecological textbooks leaves no doubt of the books' predominantly male viewpoints. Few incorporate important findings by Kinsey (1953) and Masters and Johnson (1966) about female sexual responses. None index sex roles, but clearly they have a view, a traditional male view – Jeffcoate (1967), for example, says women want to acquiesce to the masterful.

The advertisements drug companies send to medical journals and to medical practitioners often show women unable to perform their domestic tasks because of illness. Very few portray women as working outside the home. One particularly good example is a picture of a man bedecked with apron, sweating over the dishes, whose caption reads: 'Do *you* suffer from menstrual pains?' In other words, give the wife drug X and she will be able to relieve you of the washing up (it's her job, after all).

These adverts only serve to reinforce a traditional view of women among doctors today.

At this point it may be illuminating to look back briefly to nineteenth-century medical beliefs. The prevalent medical theories of women's inferiority seem to have been based on two assumptions (Ehrenreich and English 1974b). The first was that middle-class women were 'sick' and defective, for their whole lives were ruled by their ovaries and wombs, and they therefore required bedrest and minimal brain stimulation in order to conserve all their energies for menstruation and pregnancy. This myth of middle-class female frailty disqualified women as healers but made them highly qualified as patients[3] (Ehrenreich and English 1974a). Moreover doctors found uterine and ovarian disorders behind almost every female complaint, from headaches to sore throats and indigestion. Treatments ranged from blistering the groin or thighs for diseases of the genital organs and applying leeches to the labia or breasts for amenorrhoea, to removal of the ovaries to cure 'troublesomeness, eating like a ploughman, masturbation, attempted suicide, erotic tendencies, persecution mania, simple "cussedness" and dysmenorrhoea' (Ehrenreich and English 1974b).

The second assumption was that working-class women were 'sickening', that is, dangerous and polluting. There was a great deal of concern among the upper and middle classes about what the poor were doing to the health of the cities, and working-class women were particularly feared because of their close contact with middle-class families, via the kitchen, the laundry, the wet nurse's breast, or the prostitute's vagina. There was also a fear that the working class bred too rapidly and might be stronger than the middle classes – even if 'genetically inferior'. The prejudices many women detect in their doctors today may be related to these nineteenth-century prejudices, albeit clothed in modern sophisticated disguise.

As Howell (1974) points out, it may well be easier to change behaviour than attitudes, and although women patients' demands may initially be resented and resisted they are more likely to produce change than are most other approaches. Legislative pressures can help to end discrimination in admission to medical school, for example, and in America students have tried collectively to point out to their teachers the sexism they detect in the course, some of which was genuinely unintended or had passed unnoticed before.

We hope that a systematic examination of women's health problems such as we will now attempt here, might also be helpful in drawing attention to and questioning underlying assumptions, although we are well aware that we rarely have simple solutions to offer to the problems we raise.

We will begin by discussing fundamental aspects of women's lives which, though perfectly normal, may lead to medical encounters. All of them are concerned with biological processes, but we will argue that the ways in which we experience and and interpret them are not determined by our biology alone, but are profoundly influenced by the society in which we live.

## Sexuality

The economic dependence of women on men impinges on their whole identity. It not only denies them economic self-determination but ultimately political and sexual determination too (Campbell, B. 1973) Woman is seen as a wife not a worker and her sexuality is defined by men. In men's eyes, she is a sexual object whose credentials are derived from her physical appearance, and she accepts this definition of herself. Her failure to be a successful sex object, measured according to the standards displayed on every hoarding, is important in her repression.

Whereas in the past woman would 'lie back and think of England', she now thinks of ecstasy, and waits in hope ... but passively – things are done to women, they are not supposed to take the initiative. Even the modern emphasis on the importance of foreplay in sexual arousal often reinforces the passive image of woman responding to clever things done to her. Sexuality is thus divorced from communication and mutual pleasing, and becomes the pursuit of endless sexual olympics, a dehumanized commodity.

To a considerable extent, alleged 'sex differences' in sexuality represent social stereotypes of behaviour which we consciously or unconsciously follow. These stereotypes define what is thought to be 'natural' and 'normal' in our society (Oakley 1974). Masters and Johnson (1966), however, have shown that male and female bodies respond in a virtually identical manner to sexual arousal: both follow excitement, plateau, orgasmic, and resolution phases. They found also that the development of sexual tension in males and females follows the same course, irrespective of whether the cause of stimulation is intercourse, masturbation, or fantasy. They also noted that women only have one sort of orgasm – not two as Freud and others contended – and that the orgasm is essentially clitoral, that is, located mainly in the clitoris.

To explain differences between male and female sexuality,

we have to look beyond the physiological to the social. When we read in the Hite Report (1976) that a huge proportion of American women do not have orgasms from sexual intercourse, we may look for an explanation in the behaviour of their partners (usually male), but we must also look at cultural factors. It is not simply that the most common position for intercourse, man on top of woman, as is well known, does not ensure direct stimulation of the clitoris, nor is it simply that women and men may be ignorant of female anatomy and its functioning. We have to go beyond this and examine the way female sexuality is defined and developed in our culture. One is not born but becomes a woman (de Beauvoir 1972).

Briefly the boy is regarded as inevitably sexual; manipulation of his penis in youth and sexual exploits in adolescence are expected. A man proves his masculinity by going to bed with a woman and is something of a failure if still a virgin when he marries. The opposite is true for girls and women. It is not long since Chesser (1956) found that one quarter of the women he studied had received the impression from their mothers that sex was something unpleasant which women had to put up with.

Small wonder, then, that it is very difficult for a woman to become aware that she possesses a very sensitive sexual organ, the clitoris, and a physiological capacity for sexual excitement and orgasm which is equivalent to that of the male. It is difficult both for her to get to know her own body and to have the confidence to tell her lover what she would like him/her to do. That would require her to accept and assert her own sexuality.

Cultural factors also influence the 'appropriate' personality for women; emotional instability, conformity, and lack of confidence, are all seen as endearing female traits and make self-assertion in the sexual act less likely. Moreover it is not with a view to pleasure, but only when the goals of marriage, children, and a home are in mind, that a young woman is supposed to show an interest in men and sex.

Thus differences in male and female sexuality which exist in our society are associated with differences in their roles generally. Other cultures which do not define social and economic roles in the same way as we do, do not necessarily perceive male and female sexuality as opposed and different.[4]

Nowadays a woman's inability to reach orgasm is seen as

equivalent to male impotence; both are common and both represent failure. Society expects men and women to make a sexual success of their lives, but at the same time it treats sex as something so completely private that little education or advice is offered to young people.

Most doctors' and nurses' involvement in sex education in a formal sense is marginal. Extremely few actually give talks in schools, or at meetings, or write for the media, although increasingly family planning doctors are being called on to extend this aspect of their work. Health visitors and midwives have been expected to give advice on family planning to individual women, usually women who have just had a pregnancy. Health visitors also give talks and films in some schools on topics such as venereal disease and sometimes contraception.

However, doctors are much more involved than they are formally required or trained to be. They are often consulted about sexual problems and find themselves having to accept a priest-like role of general moral adviser as well as being considered a sexual 'expert'.

In medicine emphasis has been on the anatomical, biochemical, and patho-physiological aspects of the patient. However, competence in these areas is insufficient to prepare one to confront sexuality, because while 'sex refers to a biologically and anatomically determined fact, described as "the character of being male or female" ', sexuality can be defined as the 'culturally determined expressive derivative of the biological state of maleness or femaleness' (Shainess 1968). In other words, no amount of orthodox medical training in sexual matters is going to help the patient overcome problems caused by social and cultural taboos.

The need for adequate training of the medical profession in the area of sexual counselling has been argued succinctly by Vincent (1968):

'The theoretical position that the physician cannot or should not engage in any marriage or sexual counselling becomes meaningless when the patients expect this role of their physician and when their illnesses have sexual or marital implications – if not origins. The majority of physicians literally have no choice; even to do and say nothing in response to the patient's questions and/or presentation of symptoms in the sexual and marital area, is, by default, one form of counselling.'

In 1971 a study by Pauly introduced the interesting question of doctors' capacity for self-deception. Whilst only 5 per cent admitted inadequate knowledge of human sexuality themselves, 40 per cent thought that 'most doctors' were deficient in this respect.

Doctors may have felt uncomfortable and been unwilling to take on the role of sexual counsellor, but nevertheless over the years they have sustained and contributed to a restrictive ideology of female sexuality in this capacity (Comfort 1967; Ehrenreich and English 1974b).

Today the medical view of women is tending to shift from a diagnosis of 'physically sick' to one of 'mentally ill'. It is now psychiatry as much as, if not more than, gynaecology which upholds the sexist tenets of women's fundamental defectiveness, which we saw was the generally accepted nineteenth-century attitude towards the female of the species. The ambitious woman, not content to be wife and mother, is 'neurotically rejecting her femininity and emasculating men', while the woman who is content to be with her family is 'infantile and infects her sons with guilt and dependency'. Psychiatry abounds in explanations which blame the victims for what has happened to them; female children whose fathers rape them are seen as 'seductive', or their mothers are blamed for secretly 'wanting it' (Rush 1971). Professional prostitution is seen as female 'revenge' and 'agression' – with no thought for the possible female victimization (Greenwald 1958).

Gynaecologists and general practitioners do, however, still hold the key to one door which is fundamental to women's sexual liberation. The control of women's fertility both in terms of contraception and abortion is still regarded by many doctors as legitimately theirs. When a general practitioner says that he is prepared to recommend one abortion but a second will be withheld, to prevent women from regarding abortion as contraception, and promiscuity from being rewarded, he is not making a purely medical judgement. He is using social 'norms' to control women's sexuality. Likewise, when a gynaecologist refuses an abortion unless the woman will submit to sterilization, he is not merely writing a *medical* prescription, he is implementing a social ideology.[5]

## Menstruation

Menstruation has been described as an iatrogenic disease – meaning a problem caused by doctors. What is being suggested is that recent changes in reproductive behaviour have led to a great deal more, and more troublesome, menstruation taking place, and this is true. It is not true to say, however, that doctors have caused these profound social changes; as we noted earlier, what they did was to observe and record (and even at times obstruct) processes which were the result of social change (McKeown 1976). Today we find that early sexual maturity, relatively late marriage, and small families, are characteristic of the conditions of modern urban industrial society. By contrast, the common pattern in many other parts of the world is that most girls expect to marry fairly soon after the onset of puberty is marked by the first menstruation. Subsequently they spend the best part of their adult life either pregnant or lactating, so that menstruation is not as important a feature of their experience as it is in our society. Thirty-five years or more of virtually uninterrupted menstruation is thus a recent phenomenon. This is particularly true of years of menstruation before a first pregnancy, which are often associated with the problem of primary dysmenorrhoea or painful periods.

Another problem which is only now beginning to be recognized is the occurrence in some women of pre-menstrual syndromes (Dalton 1969). These seem to be related to hormonal variations, probably causing changes in water and sodium retention in the body and various other physical effects, as well as affecting mood.[6] Considerable emphasis is placed by some people on the importance of the pre-menstrual syndrome and the disadvantages it has for women. This view is based on the argument that women are victims of physiological circumstances over which they have no control, and which dominate them and make them unreasonable. Of course everybody, whether man or woman, *is* subject to physiological variations in body functioning and these may often cause concomitant mood changes. We would argue that the circumstances in which these can make life a misery are particularly common for a large number of women in our society.[7] As Dalton has noted, many symptoms associated with the pre-menstrual syndrome are those which are often defined as 'neurotic'. She claims that her treatment cures the 'neurosis', but points out that

'Severity of symptoms month by month may vary with the stress. When a woman has had a particularly difficult month with domestic crises, legal problems or quarrelling neighbours it is likely that her premenstrual symptoms will be increased. On the other hand a good win at the pools may tend to alleviate the symptoms to a sufferer of the premenstrual syndrome.' (p. 67)

What we obviously need is more occasions when we win! Dalton goes on, quite rightly, to plead for the medical understanding of menstrual problems, but spoils it rather by seeming to assert that the main reason that menstrual disorders deserve attention is to help husbands who suffer from bad-tempered or inefficient wives!

The same author quotes many other effects of menstruation. For example, in one boarding school girls had cyclical falls in weekly grades and worse examination results during or just before menstruation. They also displayed greater naughtiness during menstruation and greater untidiness during the menstrual or pre-menstrual period than at other times of the month. In another study of adult women prisoners, it was found that 60 per cent of crimes of violence had been committed in the premenstrual period, and an unquantified but notable excess of arrests for alcoholism among women had occurred during menstruation. Accidents were said to be commoner and to lead to more injuries, and more serious injuries, around menstruation, because of slower reaction times.

Dalton's findings may well be true, although they are based on quite small samples, but her presentation and arguments are misleading. There is a great deal of evidence to show that girls are on average notably *tidier*, *brighter*, and *less naughty* than boys in school.[8] Dalton claims that they are a little less tidy, bright, and well behaved at their menstrual times. Similarly, women offenders are a tiny fraction of the number of men offenders, and when it comes to crimes of violence and drunkenness, they are an even tinier fraction – but they do a little bit more during or before menstruation. As far as accidents are concerned, if you are a woman driver and you are prepared to guarantee that your car will be driven only by women, the insurance company will reduce the insurance premium. We know of no research on clumsiness but have often been told that women are much better at jobs needing manual dexterity because of their nimble fingers.

The problems can thus be stated in two ways. Dalton implicitly asks how can we allow women to do all the sorts of things that men (i.e. normal people) do in society – when they have so many problems because of their menstruation. We would put it another way: some women behave a bit more like men, around their menstrual periods. Also some women have problems of pain, discomfort, and depression associated with menses, and these need investigation and relief.

It is important to sort out the physiological from the social aspects in the matter of menstruation, which has been in the past, and still is to some people, an excuse for discrimination against women. A century ago doctors threw their weight behind attempts to exclude women from higher education and entry into the medical profession, using the 'scientific arguments of physiology' and previously indelicate matters such as menstruation as evidence. In 1884, John Thorburn, Professor of Obstetrics at Manchester Medical School, had declared: 'This is a matter of physiology, not sentiment ... one body and mind capable of sustained and regular hard labour, and another body and mind which for a quarter of each month is more or less sick and unfit for hard work'!

Thorburn and the many other English and American gallant protectors of ladies[9] believed that study during the delicate years between fifteen and twenty-five would inevitably lead to amenorrhoea, chlorosis, nervousness, destruction of sensuality, infertility, and loss of femininity. Women should therefore be protected from their own folly and excluded from medical schools. As we have seen, these beliefs were acted on, too. The votes of male doctors who were prominent on the Court of Governors of the University of London helped delay the admission of women to the University for many years.

Most women have some discomforts with menstruation, at some time in their lives; a few women are intermittently quite disabled.[10] Medical responses have swung from pseudo-scientific nonsense to nonsense of the other extreme, which declares that the problems are all in the mind, that mothers who had menstrual problems themselves (and who probably had them because they 'rejected their own femininity') suggest to their daughters that they will suffer, with the result that they do. Both brands of male arrogance and ignorance can now be exposed for what they are. The achievements of women students dealt a fatal blow to the first; and the disappearance of dysmenorrhoea in women taking oral contraceptives, and the occasional onset of pre-menstrual tension in some women on high oestrogen pills, should have finally buried the second approach.

Women now have to demand that the basic research necessary for understanding be carried out, and non-harmful treatments be made available meanwhile for sufferers. Monthly menstrual extraction which we will discuss later may well prove to be the answer for many women.

### The menopause

Like other matters already discussed, the menopause will be experienced by all women who live long enough, and this means the vast majority of women. The suggestion that the menopause is a recent phenomenon is not correct however, since there has not been any great change recently in the expectation of life for those who reach adulthood. The great population explosion among the elderly is the result of the decline in mortality in childhood which began at the end of the last century and beginning of this. In fact for as long as records have been kept, most women who grew up lived beyond the end of reproductive life. Various euphemisms were and are used to refer to it – for example, 'that certain age', and 'change of life', but until recently relatively little attention has been paid to it by anyone, except perhaps by the 'old wives'. Even 'women and health' groups seem rarely to have focused on this aspect of women's health, probably because of the comparatively young age of activists, to whom it would seem less personally significant than such matters as abortion, contraception, and childbirth. However, writers such as Cooper (1975) have stimulated a growing general interest by expressing the views of women who are no longer prepared to grin and bear it. This has elicited a certain response from doctors, and has received what might be seen as ominous encouragement from a few very interested parties, namely drug companies (Veitch 1977). We will return to the implications of this factor later.

The menopause is essentially a period of hormonal change, the most obvious feature of which is the cessation of menstruation. There are various varieties of normal menopause. Some women experience a sudden end to what had been up to then normal monthly periods. More commonly, irregularities occur; periods become less frequent, sometimes sparse and sometimes heavy, or are totally unpredictable, in timing and quantity. Any of these sequences can be alarming, with, for example, queries about pregnancy or disease often crossing the mind. Not infrequently there are other accompanying features too, which aggravate the problems, and which we can consider under two headings, physiological and social.

*The physiology of the menopause*

It would be easier and perhaps more honest to leave this section blank for there is little agreement among experts as to what is going on, and less as to what causes the discomforts which some women suffer. But perhaps we should try, at least, to look at some of the theories available.

The hormonal cycles of reproductive life have recently attracted a great deal of attention in the development of oral contraception and treatments for infertility (sometimes the need for the second following the first), but very few studies seem to have been made of detailed hormonal change around the time of the menopause. The drug firms are now moving into this field, but they seem to be working on the assumption that menopausal symptoms are due to oestrogen deficiency, and that these can be remedied by oestrogen replacement.

We agree that there is evidence to show the success of this remedy (for example, Coope, Thomson, and Poller 1975) but doubt if their explanation covers all symptoms; and we are also not happy with the proposed solution for other reasons, which we will go into later.

It seems that hormonal changes can often be detected several years before the cessation of menstruation. Levels of the three natural oestrogen hormones fall with age, and as the menopause approaches, the levels of the two hormones produced by the pituitary gland, known as the gonadotrophic hormones, start to rise.[11] All this can occur before changes in menstrual patterns, and before the classical symptoms of the change of life, that is hot flushes (called hot flashes in the US) and sweats, appear. Surgical removal or irradiation of a woman's ovaries before the menopause usually precipitates dramatic hormonal change. Reports have shown that almost *all* women who have had an artificial menopause experience flushes and sweats, and some of them continue to do so for years afterwards. Obviously this is a different matter from the gradual changes of a naturally occurring menopause, but hot flushes were also reported by three quarters of a random sample of London women passing through a physiological menopause, and three fifths of the older women were still having them six years after the menopause. Interestingly enough, only one in five of the sufferers had consulted a doctor. This was in 1965 – we suspect the proportion would be greater today. Numerous other symptoms were reported but none so frequently, nor so closely following on the cessation of menstruation, as hot flushes (McKinlay and Jefferys 1974).

Other changes in body structure and function are believed to follow the changes of the menopause; loss of skin elasticity is one, which has led to the use of oestrogen skin creams, with no proven effect. Loss of bone strength is another possible effect, and here the evidence looks sounder, if only because broken bones (unlike wrinkles) are so much more common in elderly women than in elderly men. Moreover X-ray and other studies seem to show an acceleration of the bone loss due to ageing after the menopause, which ceases if oestrogen pills are taken (Lindsay *et al.* 1976). Local changes in the sex organs occur; the uterus becomes smaller, and the lining of vagina may become drier and less elastic, that is atrophic, and this can lead to penetration becoming uncomfortable. In this case, oestrogen cream is very effective in restoring the vagina to its earlier state.

A wide range of psychological symptoms have also been described, including depression, anxiety, sleeplessness, loss of energy, and loss of libido. These are all more or less common in women of all ages, and, as noted earlier, they vary with hormones in the menstrual cycle in some women. Obviously they may also be related to the existence of physical, family, or social problems.

A recent study of psychological symptoms in women, before, during, and after the menopause, suggests that some women experience an increase in symptoms starting before the menopause, and lasting until about one year after the menses cease (Ballinger 1975). The author speculated that changes in hormones other than oestrogens – e.g. the luteinizing hormone, may be playing a part in this. There are also suggestions that the experience of women who have borne children differs from those who have not, and that bodily build may make a difference to post-menopausal hormone levels (fatter women continue to produce more oestrogens). But we remain very ignorant as to which particular hormonal changes cause which particular symptoms, and how they do it. It is true that the hot flushes problem can be controlled for most women, most of the time, by oestrogens, and that suddenly stopping taking oestrogens usually leads to their return, when they are often worse than before (Coope, Thomson, and Poller 1975). But that is as far as our knowledge goes.

Before we go on to discuss hormone replacement therapy (HRT), or 'the happiness pill' as the press has dubbed it, let us look more closely at other aspects of the menopause which might be included under our second heading, that of 'social'. We proceed in this order because we think many discussions of HRT are based on assumptions which are value-loaded but rarely challenged, because of the belief that the menopause is purely 'biological'.

*Social aspects of the menopause*
As they grow older, women may find ever more irksome the constant reminders of the desirability of the physical characteristics of (some) young women, whose more prominent features jump out at them from hoardings and newsstands. They are bombarded with advice as to how to be attractive and remain young, most of it requiring at the very least a great deal of time and money, and even if they follow the advice to the letter, they may not be satisfied with the result. Those who have centred their lives around their children find that as children grow up and leave home, the image of devoted mother becomes just as elusive for them as does that of sex symbol for the ladies of fashion. In our society many girls and young women are brought up to believe that 'attractive woman' and/or 'mother' are the only careers they need prepare for. No wonder that many women in their forties, far from believing that life is just beginning, think on the contrary that the only life they know how to lead has ended. The crisis that this can represent may

have some components of regret at the loss of the child-bearing function (though many – nearly half in the London survey – are relieved at this loss), and may have physiological symptoms of hormonal change described earlier; but a major component is social, derived from women's restricted opportunities and consequent poor self-image.

It seems to us that some of the exponents of HRT, especially American doctors who claim to be offering 'the solution' to the problem of the menopause, are in reality part of the problem themselves. They seek to confirm the restricted sexist image of women that stresses 'femininity' as their only worthwhile characteristic, which must therefore be preserved by continuous medication unto death, otherwise women are nothing. This appears to be the same sort of reasoning that leads a woman to undergo surgery in order that she might conform to pin-up norms. There *are* powerful arguments in favour of HRT, but for us the 'feminine or worthless' line is not one of them.

There are also powerful arguments against HRT as well as vast areas of ignorance. On our reading of the evidence on long-term HRT, the only verdict possible at present is *not proven*. The case for hormonal treatment on a short-term basis to relieve distressing symptoms is stronger however.

*Hormone replacement therapy (HRT): the pros and cons*
The effect of specific treatments on symptoms which are subjective and which come and go are very difficult to assess, because most patients report some improvement, whatever the doctor does. This is partly out of kindness, because it seems rude and ungrateful to tell him his efforts have been useless, but in addition one can really feel better just because it seems that help is at hand, that someone is interested and trying to give relief. This is known as the 'placebo' effect, and to allow for it, proper testing of treatments must involve a comparison with some other substance, whose effect is known. Either the same patients take first one, and then the other, or there are two groups of strictly comparable patients, one taking the treatment and the other the placebo. A 'double blind' procedure is used, so that when the results are recorded neither doctor nor patient know which is which.

Many reports of treatments for menopausal symptoms have not been carried out in this way, and may therefore be suspect

(Mulley and Mitchell 1976). Nevertheless rapid, marked, and sustained improvement in flushes and sweats has been shown, in well-conducted trials, to take place only in women receiving active treatment, i.e. oestrogen therapy (e.g. Coope, Thomson, and Poller 1975). The success of this therapy is particularly important, for, in the past, many women have been dismissed without help, or given sedatives, and suffered miseries, sometimes for years; indeed this is still the response that many get from their doctors. The case seems to have been established that, unless there are other complicating problems, this treatment should be available to women in distress, particularly if the dosage is kept as low as possible and intermittent, as we shall explain later, and is gradually reduced. Much more work needs to be done in comparing the different oestrogen hormones which have varying effects, some of which may be safer than others. In addition, alternative drugs which act on the blood vessels and have been reported to relieve hot flushes without side effects (Clayden, Bell, and Pollard 1976) merit further investigation.

However, many advocates of HRT would go very much further than this. Drug companies, who see a prize of a '10 million market' glittering ahead of them form a major pressure group, of course; they are joined by specialist doctors who are consulted by a number of older women with troubles which have been attributed to the long-term results of low oestrogen levels – for example, easily broken bones, and atrophic vaginas. Then there are those women who have tried it and like it, some of whom stress the femininity argument mentioned above. Other supporters have maintained that HRT reduces the chances of heart disease, but the evidence for this is unconvincing. These assorted allies see the menopause as a deficiency disease, for which the specific prevention/treatment is hormone therapy from the age of forty onwards – like replacing thyroid hormones, or insulin, in those lacking their own supplies. This view seems prevalent among affluent American women and their doctors, and undoubtedly has something to be said for it – but the menopause seems to be a very peculiar deficiency disease indeed. Few, if any diseases afflict 100 per cent of the population at risk, and last for ever, as the 'disease' menopause is seen as doing, and a certain disquiet about 'the medicalization of everything' must strike any serious thinker. But unfortunately there are other grounds for worry too.

Hormone replacement therapy resembles 'the pill', that is, oral contraceptives, in that some of the same synthetic compounds are used. Other mixtures used in HRT, however, are composed of hormones extracted from the urine of pregnant mares and not totally synthesized in a factory, which their makers therefore call 'natural oestrogens'. The hormone dosages used are lower than in most contraceptive pills, which some find reassuring; but on the other hand, older women on the Pill are the ones most likely to suffer complications and HRT takers are mostly even older, of course.

What are the 'complications' that arise from taking hormones? Among them are changes in the blood, including increase in blood clotting factors with the possibility of clots reaching the lungs, heart, or brain, and increases in blood triglycerides; also raised blood pressure, liver tumours, gall bladder disease, and breast cancer. Another suspected danger of HRT is cancer of the uterus. The suspicion arose because the lining of the uterus develops changes which some think are precancerous, if oestrogens are taken continuously for any length of time. Up to now follow-up studies have produced conflicting results. To reduce the possibility of uterine cancer, most English doctors prescribing HRT insist on regular shedding of the lining of the uterus; they manipulate the pill dosage to ensure this, so that the taker has at least one period every three months. Not all women welcome perpetuating menstruation for ever, even if only four times a year. Breakthrough bleeding may occur in between, as well, and then the woman and her doctor cannot be sure that there is no other disease present. This particular problem does not arise, of course, for women who have had a hysterectomy.[12]

Up to now there is not enough information available to enable us to say whether or not all these risks are real ones, and if so, what the chances are of any one person suffering complications. Studies are under way that may provide some answers, but meanwhile we advocate caution in attempting wholesale drug solutions to what we think are partly social problems.

We believe that the changes we advocate in the position of women in our society would contribute to the reduction of some of the symptoms attributed to the menopause. Women with full lives, interesting jobs, and time for active leisure, who see themselves and are seen as human beings, not sex objects or family slaves, are less likely to get depressed and sleepless, or to experience rapid thinning of their bones than many of today's women. Support for this view can be found in anecdotes which suggest that older women in some other societies are less prone than we are to 'post-menopausal symptoms', which at once suggests that societal factors are important. We think this approach deserves as much research effort as HRT – but we doubt if it will receive much attention in our society.

This is one of the fields in which doctors seem to go to extremes. On the one hand the menopause, with all that goes with it, is regarded as 'natural', and thought to require no attention at all. This attitude sometimes goes as far as dismissing almost any symptom in a woman from forty to sixty years as something that is 'only to be expected at her time of life'. At the other extreme all menopauses are treated as illness, with automatic medication. Another variant is to offer psychological explanations wholesale – it is all because you see yourself as unsexed etc., with psychoanalysis or tranquillizers as the final solution. Each of these approaches can flourish in the field of ignorance which surrounds the menopause, and each of them, intentionally or unintentionally, amounts to a repression of the woman concerned.

## FIVE

# More women's conditions – the results of fertility

**Unwanted pregnancy**

Our foremothers undoubtedly knew ways to prevent pregnancy and to cause abortion. Inevitably some methods did not always work, and some were dangerous – just as they are today. The information was not – as it is still not – always available to those who needed it. But big changes have taken place, in moral attitudes, in technology, and in the sorts of methods used, as well as with regard to who controls them.

Early Christianity seemed to find no objection to abortion in the first months, and it is only in recent centuries with the rising tide of male domination that the State and Church, by forbidding abortion and contraception, developed the policy which in effect made pregnancy compulsory for women who engaged in sexual activity. Sisterly and commercial interests ensured that the policy was never wholly successful, but many women have borne unwanted children time and again, feeling helplessly that nothing could be done to prevent it.

Radicals and feminists in the last century and this fought hard to popularize methods of preventing conception, usually euphemistically called family planning, and later to legalize abortion. They were joined paradoxically by the eugenicists, who sometimes seemed to be far from endorsing a woman's right to choose; rather they reserved for themselves the right to prevent certain people – inferior stock – from reproducing. Their descendants are very active today, on an international scale, as we shall see.

In the past, orthodox medicine was firmly opposed both to making contraceptive advice widely available and to legalizing abortion. In both instances 'scientific evidence' was (and is) given by medical experts to justify their stances. As so often happens, personal prejudice and unfounded beliefs masquerade as expert medical advice, which women may have little option but to take.

## Contraception

Probably the oldest way of preventing conception was by avoiding ejaculation within the vagina, called withdrawal or coitus interruptus.[1] The use of a penile sheath made of animal intestine, or of a plug or pessary of crocodile dung placed in the vagina, are two other well-known ancient methods. In this century, withdrawal and the use of a rubber or synthetic sheath were probably the means by which the birth rate fell in the industrial world (unreliable though they sometimes are). Another barrier method, the rubber diaphragm in the vagina, aided by chemicals, was the method most often advised by the Family Planning pioneers at their clinics. Although the sheath and the diaphragm are quite effective, and do not carry any risk of damaging the user's health, they have the major disadvantage of being intrusive and inconvenient, requiring an unwanted interruption in love-making.

Another approach, the only one acceptable to some is the safe period. An egg is released (i.e. ovulation occurs) only once each month, at about mid-cycle, and if intercourse is avoided for the few days before and after ovulation, conception cannot take place. There are numerous problems here – including increased libido in many women precisely at the dangerous time of the month. In addition, some women have irregular cycles, and the methods of pinpointing ovulation are inaccurate and complicated, involving recording temperatures, or inspecting vaginal secretions. However, reports have shown that some people can make it work.

But these are all dark-age methods, in some eyes, for there have been several major developments in the last two decades which have rather overshadowed them. The first is the Pill (oral contraceptive) consisting of synthetic compounds which resemble female sex hormones. If swallowed regularly, it prevents ovulation taking place, and makes conception very unlikely indeed. The second, the 'coil' (IUD, or intra-uterine device), is a plastic wire which is inserted in the uterus and which in some way prevents conception. It is less reliable than the Pill, but still relatively effective. Recently additions, such as copper or hormones, have been incorporated into the coil, and are believed to make it more effective. The third way is new and controversial, and we will look at it in more detail later in the book. It is called menstrual regulation (or extraction), and involves a mini vacuum clean of the uterus. Not much has been published yet about how effective this method is.

The other methods are not really new, but have newly become fashionable – the so-called permanent methods of sterilization, male or female. For the male, this involves tying off the tubes which carry sperm from the testes (by means of two small cuts in the groins), and for females, tying off the ovarian tubes in the pelvis, which is a bigger surgical job.

As we have seen, many doctors traditionally opposed contraception. It is only recently that the prospect of extra payment and the ease of simply picking up a pen and writing out a prescription have encouraged doctors to take a greater interest in meeting the contraceptive needs of the population. Some of the profession have even become enthusiasts. The report of the Royal College of General Practitioners (1974) on oral contraceptives, no doubt rightly impressed by their effectiveness, seemed to display a missionary zeal in advocating the consumption of the Pill, but also tended to discount the numerous complaints of side effects which led many women (e.g. 27 per cent of takers within one year of starting) to give it up. The truth is, of course, that if oral contraceptives had no immediate unwanted side effects, like depression, weight gain, and loss of libido, then many women would refuse to consider giving them up under any circumstances. Many do put up with some side effects for the sake of the convenience and contraceptive efficiency, but we all know of people who, in spite of the advantages, had to come off the Pill, just as we know of some who have never been better than when on it. Women are individuals, with variable physiologies, hormonal levels, and responses to hormones; the varying effects of pregnancy and of the hormonal changes of the menopause should make that clear enough. But some men, including men doctors, seem to have the view that women are standard issues. If the maker says a pill is good, and it does suit women, then any woman who says it doesn't suit *her* is neurotic, subconsciously wants to get pregnant, is manipulative, unco-operative, etc., etc. We are back to the approach to dysmenorrhoea of days gone by: 'it is all in the mind'.

All this would be annoying even if we knew all there is to know about the effects of oral contraceptives – but we don't. Some of the things we know are reassuring – for example, it seems that women who have taken oral contraceptives have less breast disease than those who have not (Vessey, Doll, and Sutton 1972). But there remain a number of worrying indications that blood clots of superficial veins, of the lungs (pulmonary embolism), and the heart (coronary thrombosis), are more common in pill takers (Beral 1976), as indeed are all diseases of the vascular system (Royal College of General Practitioners 1977); liver diseases including cancer of the liver are also more common in takers. These diseases are still rare, but women have only been taking oral contraceptives for a relatively short time, and such diseases usually develop slowly. Bland reassurances cannot legitimately be given, and we cannot be satisfied that oral contraceptives are the answer to the problem of contraception.

The reported adverse effects would be less alarming if we were convinced that all possible steps were being taken to ensure that the women most likely to experience complications are not prescribed the Pill, and that those taking it were regularly checked for warning signs. The evidence is that this is not the case, particularly for women receiving pills from their general practitioners (Cartwright 1970). Pill sales over the counter, as advocated by some enthusiasts, might increase their consumption, particularly by young women most in need of informal easy contraception, but might also increase the risk of complications. A compromise proposal (DHSS 1976) that nurses should be able to prescribe oral contraceptives may be more acceptable, if nurses want to take on the job; they may be more likely to take it seriously and do the necessary investigations beforehand. But now that the general practitioners are paid extra for family planning work, we doubt if this proposal has a chance of being implemented, at least not until the health structure has undergone many changes. Problems also arise with other modern methods. The intra-uterine device, a plastic revival of an old idea,[2] has much to commend it, but it may drop out without being noticed. It often causes very heavy periods and is associated with an increased risk of pelvic infection, salpingitis (inflammation of the fallopian tubes), and sterility, as well as with an increase in tubal pregnancies.

Modern female methods are therefore not ideal, and recent surveys show that couples in Social Class I and II (professional/ managerial), who were the first to take up the Pill, are now turning away from it and going back to the sheath (Cartwright 1976). Contraception is still, as an American feminist once said, a matter of 'pick your poison'.

Female sterilization, or tubectomy, is a method for those who want no more children, but the cost of this is high too, for some women. It involves an operation, usually with a general anaesthetic and abdominal incision, although it can be done by puncture under a local anaesthetic. But it is now being reported (e.g. Neil *et al.* 1975) that for reasons not fully understood,[3] many women (between 20 and 40 per cent of those operated on) who previously had trouble-free periods, subsequently have heavy painful periods. This often leads to further surgery, a hysterectomy or removal of the womb, which is a major operation – all for want of a better method of contraception!

Sterilization is beloved of the eugenicist/population control lobby, for the very reason that causes people to hesitate before embarking on it – that you can't change your mind later.[4] Women for whom sterilization is probably not a good idea therefore are those whose marriage is in danger of breaking up. Later, in a subsequent partnership, the sterilization may be bitterly regretted. Many such cases figured in a recent study of women seeking to have the operation reversed (Winston 1977).

In many instances this could not be done because of the type of operation performed, and the women could not be helped.

In Asia mass campaigns have been organized for sterilization, carried out by sub-doctors in mobile camps. Reports suggest general satisfaction all round, but the operators usually move on, and perhaps do not become aware of later difficulties. The effect which heavy periods after the operation may have on the health of women on the edge of malnutrition, makes us doubtful about the medical wisdom of such mass campaigns. They may have unwanted social effects, too. Asian villagers often consider children useful for their own futures, and therefore do not want to restrict the size of their families (Mamdani 1972). The attempt by the Congress Government in India to resort to compulsion when persuasion failed to shake this logic was widely resisted, and this may have been the final straw which broke the people's backs, and led to Indira Gandhi's defeat in 1977.

In Britain, a pernicious but quite commonly reported misuse of sterilization is the 'package deal' approach – that is, a woman is granted an abortion, on condition that she is sterilized at the same time. No doubt this combination, if voluntary, is sometimes ideal; but at other times it forces an urgent decision with long-term implications on a woman already under stress. In our view, this represents a deplorable example of blackmail. In addition, the small risk which abortion carries is increased when sterilization is done simultaneously.

Male sterilization seems easier and safer, with very few reported unwanted side effects, but it is still not very popular. Perhaps doctors (mostly men) don't advise it, or husbands don't fancy it, or health service planners (mostly men) don't make it sufficiently readily available. Only 3 per cent of couples use it, currently, in England.

It is interesting to note the common medical response to requests by young or unmarried people for sterilization. Usually the requests are rejected, however certain the applicants, as if it were right for the doctor to be the final arbiter. This reluctance to take seriously the choice not to have children seems to reflect a medical endorsement of 'the family' as an essential way of life for everyone, and a disbelief that a young person could permanently reject it.

It should also be noted that there is still a very needy group, most of whom are not being reached at present with contraceptive advice and aid, that is teenage girls. Conception is welcomed by some unmarried women, but more commonly it is unwanted, and yet it occurs all too often, especially among very young women. Health services seem not to reach them until too late, often much too late; the very young are late attenders at ante-natal clinics too, according to McKinlay and McKinlay (1972). Increased medical involvement in contraception has in no way solved their problem.

## Abortion

Abortion is an emotive topic, but a most informative one for those who are fascinated by the interplay of doctors, women patients, and the social framework.[5] As we have suggested earlier, abortion has probably been practised since ancient times, when from necessity women have taken desperate measures in desperate situations.

Until 1803, abortion prior to 'quickening' – when the woman begins to feel foetal movements at about sixteen weeks – was not a crime in English common law. An act in 1803 continued to make a distinction between early and late abortion but punished both. Those convicted could be sentenced to transportation, whipping, or imprisonment for abortion before quickening, and to death for abortion after quickening. This distinction was subsequently dropped, and the 1861 Offences Against the Person Act confirmed that abortion at any stage was one crime, with the 'procurer', who performed the operation, liable to life imprisonment, even if it was the woman concerned. Later an exception was made for abortions carried out when the life of the mother was at stake.

During the century leading up to the British Abortion Act of 1967, the Law decreed that women had no right to use abortion to control their fertility, but in spite of this abortions did take place. Some few doctors and nursing homes grew rich, doing abortions in fairly sterile conditions for those who could afford to pay (in pound notes). The 'back-street abortionists', usually women, did it more dangerously and more cheaply, and the hospitals were kept busy dealing with the ill effects. Occasionally a total disaster, leading to death, caused an outcry and those involved in procuring the abortion were prosecuted. Most women with an unwanted pregnancy were unlikely to get any help at all, since both sorts of abortion of necessity were shrouded in secrecy.

Feminists who demanded the right to prevent unwanted births by contraception later came to see that, in the absence of universally available and effective contraceptive measures, abortion was necessary, at least as a last resort. After a legal test case in 1938, when a gynaecologist aborted a girl pregnant after a mass rape and was acquitted in the subsequent trial, some doctors began to interpret the Law as allowing them to abort cases where the woman was likely to become a 'physical or mental wreck' if the pregnancy were allowed to continue. Some few thousand women had abortions, under this clause, in NHS hospitals each year up to the 1967 Act, and an unknown but probably much larger number had semi-legal surgical abortions in the private sector.

The growth of the campaign for change in the abortion laws, spearheaded by the Abortion Law Reform Association (ALRA) was part of the liberalization wave of the 1960s (see Greenwood and Young 1976). In several instances behaviour which had been seen as deviant was reclassified, transformed from crime into sickness and was thus placed within the scope of medicine, which was expanding to take in more of society's problems. Abortion was no exception; some unfortunate, or feckless, or mentally unstable women were considered suitable to join those with severe physical ill-health as candidates whom the doctors would see to decide whether to recommend for abortion. Abortion was regarded as medically dangerous (as well as socially dangerous) and so had to be carefully controlled – and who better to do it than the doctors?

A major stimulus for the abortion law reform campaigns prior to 1967 was the concern about the effects of back-street abortion; an important argument in favour of legalized but controlled (or rationed) abortion was the belief that it would be merely replacing the even more dangerous back-street version. It was expected that only desperate women would resort to either, so better have it done in the operating theatre than on the kitchen table. To provide the best safeguards, it was laid down that abortion could only be carried out when the danger of continuing the pregnancy would be greater than that of termination.

Events did not turn out exactly as the reformers expected, and some of them came to regret the day they supported the Act. What went wrong?

Firstly, 'too many' women tried to get abortions. In the first full year after the Act, 1968, about 5 per 1,000 of the fertile women of England and Wales had an abortion; by 1971, it was 10 per 1,000, reaching 11 per 1,000 in 1973, with a slight fall in numbers since then. If these weren't all fallen women, misfits, or inadequates, then 'normal' women must be asking for, and getting, abortions too. And indeed they were, in spite of medical control, and in some places downright medical obstruction. About half of the abortions performed on women resident in England and Wales are being obtained outside the NHS in the profit and charitable sector, into which many women are forced by NHS refusals – but one way or another, a lot of abortions are taking place. (In 1973, about 57,000 abortions were done for non-resident women, almost all outside the NHS.)

Is the Law being flouted, as some claim, or are all these abortions justified, within the Act? The fact is that they are legal, and so is any abortion, because of the clause mentioned above, which allows abortion if it is considered that the continuation of the pregnancy would be more dangerous than the termination. Pregnancy and delivery can lead to death; relatively few do in Britain now but nevertheless the maternal mortality rate (excluding deaths due to abortion) is, at 11 per 100,000, *higher* than the death rate for abortion, which has fallen rapidly since the Act. In 1973, there were only four deaths associated with 110,000 legal terminations and two of these were among the 12,000 women who had been sterilized at the same time (Registrar General 1974a and b). The myth that the doctors must judge, because a dangerous operation is at stake, can no longer be sustained.

Abortion could be even safer if it were always done early, by vacuum extraction. This method has less possibility of damage than the traditional D and C (dilatation and curettage, or scrape), because the neck of the uterus (or cervix) does not have to be stretched much, if at all. It can usually be done on out-patients, without a general anaesthetic, and so avoids other dis-advantages too. Goldthorp (1977) points out that if done as menstrual extraction, even earlier, the procedure need take only ten minutes. Unfortunately the delay that women experience in getting an abortion, even under our supposedly liberal Abortion Act, means that many arrive at the hospital too late for vacuum extraction, which can only be done up to about twelve weeks. (In 1973, 32,000 abortions were done after the thirteenth week of pregnancy.) However, although the National Health Service uses the vacuum method on some women, it seems very loath to develop out-patient abortion, in spite of the shortage of cash and beds. It would be interesting to speculate why this should be so.

## Why are so many women having abortions?

The factors seem to be several; years of economic difficulty and the growth of the women's movement have made unintended pregnancy less acceptable to women themselves; and general practitioners have become increasingly aware of and sympathetic to the burdens of unwanted motherhood. Some private practice gynaecologists have found themselves with their fingers in a gold mine – and acceptable, safe, and effective contraception for all still lies in the future.

A remarkable change has taken place. Before 1967, 'straight' family doctors would have nothing to do with bringing about an abortion – such an offence was 'morally repugnant', and ranked with sleeping with patients as a sure way of getting blackmailed or 'struck off' the Medical Register. This is an interesting example of the Law helping to change widely-held attitudes. But in general, medical control remains. It may be nominal in parts of the private sector, and some doctors are seeking to end it,[6] but most cling to it, not just because they believe they know best, but because it might be a dangerous precedent if 'the patient were allowed to determine what was to be done' – and indeed so it might!

The *Lancet* (1977a) thinks that increasingly, the doctor's role in fertility regulation will be to assist someone else's choice, and feels unhappy that the term' patient' is still used for women who want to make use of the doctor's technical or administrative skills to meet their own, self-defined needs. 'The user of family planning has stolen the medical practitioner's magic robes', as they put it. The family planning doctors, mostly women of course, have not felt naked without these robes for many a year. We think that women doctors may need them less, and this is another link between two of the themes of this book, that is, the contribution that women health workers can make, and the need for the demystification of medicine in the modern world.

Several attempts have been made to put the clock back since the passing of the 1967 Act. Frequent scare stories of 'abuse' led to the setting up of a Select Committee, under Mrs Justice Lane to investigate the workings of the Act. After hearing many expressed opinions, and collecting available facts, the Committee took the most unusual step of commissioning research on the subject, and this was published as an appendix to their report (Cartwright and Lucas 1974). The Committee found that there was some racketeering and exploitation in the private sector that should and could be (and subsequently has been) controlled by administrative means. Otherwise they documented inadequacies and delays in getting an NHS abortion in many parts of the country. The opponents of the Act were disappointed but undeterred, and two Private Member's bills – the James White Bill and the Benyon Bill – have been promoted since then in an attempt to curtail the availability of abortion for women in Britain. Both of these failed to make the Statute Book, but their sponsors are still trying. The struggle against these bills has led to the establishment of National Abortion Campaign Committees all over the country, and to ALRA's emphasis on 'a woman's right to choose'. These bodies have helped increase support for feminists' demands for the right to have access to abortion, as we shall see later. Even the British Medical Association Annual Representative Meeting in 1977 defended the Abortion Act and opposed the Benyon Bill's attempt to undermine it.

Elsewhere things have turned out differently. In parts of Eastern Europe and in Japan the accessibility of abortion is being curtailed, because with very high abortion rates there is a fear of future falls in population. These are retrograde steps. One wonders how much they are due to medical politics, as well as population policies.

In New York in 1970, the pendulum swung the other way, with abortion becoming freely available to all in the first twelve weeks of pregnancy, a remarkable step forward for women's self-determination.[7] But it also seems to be related to a commitment to population control on the part of powerful interests, expressed through such groups as AID (the US Agency for International Development). This and other bodies have become unpopular in many countries of the Third World for allegedly forcing their population policies on unwilling black peoples. This is certainly the light in which some US Black Power groups' spokesmen (largely male, of course) view abortion policies at home, that is as a form of genocide.

Who is right? Clearly, we oppose pressures being brought to bear to force abortion, contraception, or sterilization on unwilling people. But this is not the only alternative to no legal abortion, or to medical control of abortion. The new demand, *a woman's right to choose* brings sanity into the confused picture. Of course, that choice may be strictly limited by social circumstances. Many women would like a child, but cannot provide the means to give her a full and happy life, and so 'choose' abortion. Others have no real desire for motherhood, but feel it is expected of them, and 'choose' to have a baby. Neither society's problems, nor those of any one woman are solved simply by making abortion widely, safely, and freely available. But this one fundamental right is nevertheless essential, as one step on the road towards women gaining control of their own bodies, which is necessary before we can realize our potential in society at large.

### Pregnancy and childbirth

The one indisputable difference between men and women is the fact that the female of the species conceives, bears, and gives birth to offspring. This biological fact has become both modified and challenged in the modern world.

It has been modified because the occurrence of childbirth has become rarer, and can be and is prevented altogether by some women, perhaps by an increasing number of women. Of those who do give birth in modern urban society, most usually do so only once or twice, and often from choice. They expect to survive the experience, and expect their children to survive too. The biological fact has been challenged, in the sense that, in the eyes of some 'experts', the ability of most women to give birth unaided is no longer accepted, so that the activity has to be taken over, as a medical, or surgical, emergency. Labour now has to be 'actively managed' by the doctors.[8] The justification for this takeover is the need to ensure safety, particularly for the child, although the evidence for improved safety resulting from some of these interventions can be said to be equivocal, at best.

It has always been difficult to evaluate the part medical intervention has played in reducing maternal mortality. Much of the decline must be attributed to healthier mothers, better-fed in childhood and so better-grown, and with reserves to carry them through pregnancy and make them able to survive haemorrhages and infection. Reduction in family size has contributed too. Mothers having their first babies run relatively high risks, compared with those having second and third babies, but after that, the risks rise again, and if many women have large families maternal mortality is likely to be high (McKeown 1976). The probable contribution of ante-natal care, mainly due to the midwives' careful work, should also be acknowledged. Thus the successes may not all be due to medical intervention – and further, not all the results of medical intervention may be successful. But, before pursuing this, let us take a look at the experience of the modern mother-to-be.

## Pregnancy

Pregnant – the word is used in general parlance to indicate great future possibilities, and the condition itself is sometimes described by euphemisms such as 'expecting', or an 'interesting condition', which indicate the social importance of the event that lies ahead. Many women enjoy some if not all of the physiological changes involved, as well as the special attention they receive. In the first pregnancy, the coming transition to motherhood is a matter of great concern to the psychological state and social position of the woman (Hart 1977), and if she is part of a couple, of the man too. But the outcome is not certain, and the status passage has its dangers, so appropriate steps must be taken to ensure that all goes well – in other words, experts must be consulted. In the modern world, this means the doctors. Now doctors are mostly concerned with sick people, that is, with people who do not welcome their condition, and want to be relieved of an unnatural and unwanted disturbance in their lives. Some of the sick are incapacitated, and, particularly in the case of hospital patients, are cut off from other social roles and from their families outside. Their main business is to be a patient, until they can, they hope, return to their previous state.

The situation of the pregnant woman is quite different. Ideally, her condition is welcome, and the minor physical discomforts are happily tolerated because of the immense significance of what is happening to her, and the future social transition that it foretells. She is not 'sick', she is 'normal', and she is not abandoning social roles so much as preparing to undertake major new ones. But in the ante-natal clinic and maternity ward she is called 'a patient', and subject to a variety of medical procedures; she is often processed without much communication except for a few mysterious comments or instructions – as if she had any ordinary illness. She is 'taken over' and indeed many a woman has accepted this to the extent of having to ask a doctor if she is pregnant in the first place, and not announcing it until it is 'confirmed' by a doctor (Oakley 1975) – even though she really knew it herself from the time her period was a few days overdue.

As we shall see there is an increasing tendency for the woman in labour to be in effect a patient. When she is in hospital, the appropriate behaviour for a patient, from the staff's point of view, can be enforced fairly effectively, since the individual's life is observed and controlled. Pregnancy is altogether more ambiguous, for how we are supposed to behave when pregnant is ill-defined, and in most instances the ordinary jobs of everyday life have to be continued. But, in the eyes of medical personnel, the pregnant woman too is a patient, to be examined, investigated, advised, and treated (Comaroff 1977). Confusion may be confounded by the fact that what are often the most incapacitating aspects of pregnancy – nausea and sickness – occur early on, before the condition is noticeable.

Although confirmation of pregnancy is often wanted at the earliest possible time, early ante-natal attendance may seem not worthwhile.[9] Unexplained routines, interspersed with long delays, and marked by very little communication, do not always seem a good reason for spending several hours at a hospital and more travelling to and from it, particularly if time is lost from work, or if small children have to be farmed out, or kept quiet in the waiting room. The experts who advocate early attendance to establish base-lines for weight, blood pressure, general health, etc., have not found a way of ensuring that all women know this is thought to be desirable, or if they do know, that they accept it and co-operate. Some countries, such as France, make it indisputably worthwhile from the woman's point of view by having a maternity benefit payable from early in pregnancy to those who are attending clinics (Wynn and Wynn 1976). Modification of the regime in the ante-natal clinic might also encourage attendance. Women would appreciate greater staff willingness to answer questions and offer practical advice on current problems, as well as greater preparation for what lies ahead. Comaroff (1977) notes that the physiotherapist's ante-natal classes do already provide something of this alternative style of care.

Doctors and nurses will have to face the difficulty of dealing with a clientele who are not really patients and adapt their approach accordingly, recognizing that the pregnant woman may have competing commitments, to existing children, for example, or to her husband, and to her job. If a woman who feels well is to follow her doctor's advice then the proposed modification in her life pattern must be necessary, practicable, and convincingly argued – as when she is instructed to rest, for instance, because of raised blood pressure.

Ante-natal care may become more difficult to make effective as pregnancy gets rarer, and more of the potential users are in-experienced. Certainly lack of knowledge about what to expect is likely to be more prevalent, and the educational needs of users will probably increase. It is doubtful if the experiences of women who have had babies before, and who are thus an im-portant source of knowledge on the matter, will be more re-assuring now that many of them have been through 'active management', that is medicalization (or surgicalization) of labour. Hart (1977) found their stories most alarming.

### Delivery

The tendency to regard pregnant and labouring women as patients has now developed into actually turning labouring women into patients. The professed aim of the obstetricians is 100 per cent hospital delivery, and for many it seems to be 100 per cent active management of labour. In some areas, admission to hospital, 'preparation' – involving an enema, shaving pubic hair,[10] and the inevitable uncomfortable examinations have be-come the lot of every pregnant woman. Many of them go on to experience 'induction' of labour – that is to have a surgical rup-ture of the membranes, and a drip put into an arm vein, containing a powerful stimulant of uterine contractions. The increased severity of contractions that follows may then lead to a need for increased pain relief. As a result of the induction and the drugs, a larger proportion of women have forceps deliveries or caesarean sections, and a larger proportion of babies are found to be unexpectedly small and in an unsatisfactory condition at birth (Haire 1973).

Many women are distressed by the whole experience and report greater pain and discomfort than in 'normal' deliveries. In addition, babies may be at increased risk at birth – all as a result of policies designed to make labour easier and safer, according to their advocates! What is going on? Unfortunately the evidence is contradictory, and genuine differences of interpretation are possible. In our view, since the experts disagree, increased weight should be given to the views of the women who are themselves the subject of the controversy.

*Place of birth*
The fashion for hospital delivery is recent. Most people born before the last war were born at home, but during and since the war the percentage of hospital deliveries has risen, as a result of 'patient' demand on the one hand, and professional pressure on the other. When beds were in short supply it was repeatedly found that the 'wrong' women occupied them – that is, women with a low risk of things going wrong, and that 'high risk' women remained at home (see, for example, Butler and Bonham 1963, and Smith and Macdonald 1965). It was not clear whether this was a result of the women's own choice or unfair rationing, but many assumed that more maternity beds would solve the problem, and 70 per cent hospital deliveries became the target (Cranbrook Report 1959). Early discharge was adopted as a device for increasing turnover, and thus getting more women into hospital. At the same time, home emergencies were dealt with by obstetric 'flying squads' – mobile teams with basic equipment for resuscitating mother or child, and ever at the ready to speed out and provide life-saving care at home, or bring patients in, when needed, for hospital treatment. But doctors prefer to stay put, with patients coming to them, and the obstetricians persuaded policy-makers that an even greater proportion of hospital deliveries was desirable (Peel Report 1972). They produced evidence from earlier national surveys showing

how home or hospital confinements are often inappropriately chosen; they quoted from enquiries into disasters, that is, maternal deaths, some of which might have been prevented, given *good* hospital care. They pointed out that many homes were ill-equipped for childbirth, and that general practitioners had little practice to keep up their obstetric skills; they added, correctly, that 'normal labour' is a diagnosis that can only be made after delivery; however good the outlook, things *can* go wrong. It all sounds very convincing and only unreasonable women would oppose it.

*But* – there are other considerations. One is that in spite of the increase in the percentage of hospital deliveries (and inductions which we will come to later), Britain's position in the international league table of perinatal mortality – that is the proportion of infants dying around the time of birth – has deteriorated in the past ten years. Another is that one of the few countries of Europe which still has a high proportion (48 per cent) of home deliveries, the Netherlands, remains better in this measure than Britain – although other good performers, like Sweden, do have high hospital delivery rates. In cannot be a simple cause and effect matter, for, as we have implied historically, medical care is not the only factor influencing the outcome of pregnancy. In spite of the increase in hospital deliveries in Britain and the USA, opposition has also grown because of the whole hospital atmosphere, as well as the specific 'advances' in technique, which have made active management of labour commonplace.

What is wrong with having a baby in hospital? Well, as we have said, the usual function of hospitals is to take care of patients who are sick, helpless, and dependent, who do as they are told, and are given medicines and operations by those who know best. 'No thanks, I don't want an injection', 'I want my husband with me', 'Please give me the baby at once, and leave her here beside me', are considered unexpected, or even subversive, remarks in a hospital, and do not endear the mother to the staff. At home, on her own ground, the balance of power is different, the home team of husband and wife is in a majority and the expert is a guest; furthermore, the experience of the domiciliary midwife has often led her to see the sense of the mother's wishes for herself.

Numerous studies of women who have experienced both

home and hospital deliveries show a large majority preferring home (see, for example, Alment *et al.* 1967), although these are likely to be women with straightforward pregnancies and birth experiences. In addition, hospitals are still, or are once more becoming, dangerous places, as a result of the build-up of hospital bacteria resistant to antibiotics, with which many infants and some mothers become infected. It was recently suggested that some general surgery should return to the home to avoid operative infections – a bit far-fetched perhaps, but an indication of what some surgeons perceive to be a growing problem. So 'scientific medicine' begins to add some weight to our 'humanitarian' plea. We are not suggesting that home is a suitable place for all women to give birth; we are arguing that women with a low risk of complications should have a choice, which they no longer have in many areas, where domiciliary midwifery is disappearing. Not that this choice is a substitute for the necessary changes in hospitals, for many women should and will continue to deliver there; hospitals should try to incorporate the best aspects of home deliveries.

Dutch maternity hospitals seem to be good examples of places where specialist care, which is made available when necessary, is combined with a friendly and relaxed atmosphere. A visiting British doctor described informal wards where no masks are worn, husbands are in evidence, and, even more interesting, rates of intervention are very low. Only 2·5 per cent of women had caesarean sections, and 5 per cent assisted deliveries, mostly vacuum extractions, which, as an alternative to low forceps, help the baby's head through the last few inches of its journey down the birth canal. Teaching hospitals were said to have even lower rates of operations at delivery (Cavenagh 1968). The Dutch midwives, who are responsible for most deliveries, have three years' training, and when they work in the mother's own home, they are helped by the 'maternity aid', a woman with fifteen months' training who does maternity nursing, child care, and domestic work for the new mother.

Anyone who can remember a birth, at home or in hospital, will probably recall several differences – and may not be surprised that statistics confirm the superiority of this Dutch system over most others.

## Active management of labour

We have referred to this technique already, so let us see what it means in practice.

Normally at about forty weeks of pregnancy, a woman becomes more aware of contractions of the womb, and sooner or later they start to occur regularly, and get more noticeable and uncomfortable. When they are occurring strongly, every fifteen to twenty minutes or so, labour has started. This may happen at the wrong time. Labour can, and often does start too soon – 5 to 10 per cent of pregnancies end early and a small premature baby is born. Less often, it can start too late, and the baby emerges 'post-mature', the placenta not having given sufficient food and oxygen in the last days. The baby may look slightly shrivelled up, and sometimes does not survive labour, particularly with older mothers having their first baby. It was for such women, first time mothers over thirty years old, two weeks or more overdue, that a respected senior obstetrician, Dugald Baird of Aberdeen, introduced a policy of induction of labour – artificially starting labour in a healthy woman. He reported in the medical press that he believed that induction had reduced stillbirths in this group, and it probably had (Baird, Walker, and Thompson 1954). He used the technique which had been developed to start labour early in women who were ill and had to be delivered urgently, or in women whose babies had died in the uterus. This involved 'the artificial rupture of the membranes' by puncturing the amniotic sac with a sharp instrument, which usually led to labour starting in the next twenty-four hours. This was 'surgical' induction – in contrast to medical induction, a fairly ineffective but innocuous routine known as giving the 'OBE' (castor Oil, hot Bath, and Enema).

Unfortunately rupturing the membranes does not always start labour, but it is a procedure which must be followed by delivery in forty-eight hours or else the risk of infection of the womb becomes very high. So failed induction may lead to a need for caesarean section. An alternative and preferable policy is to use some additional means of making the uterus start contracting. Pitocin, a chemical which the body manufactures, but which can be made synthetically too and be given by injection, was developed, and several modified but similar products are now available. They can be introduced gradually into the body through a drip, and this is the usual way they are given, so if labour does not follow the artificial rupture of membranes within a given period, this can be added – and usually does the trick.

Some obstetricians, however, extended the use of these techniques in two ways. One was to accelerate labours which had started normally, and the other was to use induction for more and more women, at first with fewer indications of need, and eventually with no indications at all.

### 'Towards easier childbirth'

This alluring title was given to one of the early papers on the subject in the medical journals (Tacchi 1971) reporting the results of a policy of 'active management' of labour, including 'the liberal use of surgical induction, oxytocin infusion, analgesic drugs, epidural anaesthesia and forceps delivery' – although the author's surgical induction rate of under 20 per cent would not pass for liberal these days. The objective was short labour and this was achieved; the mean total length was eight hours. The author's impression was that 'today's woman appreciates this new approach to labour'.

A variation on this theme from Dublin (O'Driscoll, Stronge, and Minogue 1973) was that a guarantee of delivery within twelve hours for a first baby 'places the problems of pain in a new setting'. In effect, what they meant was that the need for analgesia was greatly reduced – 42 per cent out of a sample of 1,000 patients received none; however most of the labours were accelerated by oxytocin, which is known to cause powerful and painful contractions. Perhaps the reduced need for analgesia is less surprising when it is noted that every woman had a personal nurse, although the implication that pain is imaginary conveyed by the remark that 'women are sometimes influenced to expect pain for the purpose of having it relieved', makes us wonder precisely what the attitudes of these obstetricians are to their patients. Most other 'active managers' were more conscious of the increased pain that often goes with oxytocin contractions, and advocated more analgesia – usually pethidine injections and epidurals. The later are injections into the spinal column which remove all feeling from the lower parts of the body including the feeling of pain. Thus the escalation of the 'cultural warping of childbirth', which we will come to discuss shortly, proceeds.

The accelerators, however, are at least dealing with a going concern; the process of labour has started, by whatever mysterious and at present quite unknown mechanism by which the body decides it is time for the foetus to move on and become an independent being. They are speeding up what is already imminent, and are spared two errors that inducers fall into – trying unsuccessfully to start labour, or starting it too soon and causing the birth of a premature infant.

*Suitable cases for induction*
Richards (1975) has argued that the whole philosophy of modern obstetrics is mechanistic and leaning towards intervention, so that innovations such as induction were likely to be taken up quickly, although the evidence for any benefit has yet to be produced. The national perinatal mortality rate – stillbirths, plus deaths under one week per 1,000 births – was falling in the late 1960s, and some doctors concluded from the improved figures that inductions had saved lives. Other studies, on larger numbers, did not give this impression (Chalmers, Lawson, and Turnbull 1976) while further claims (McNay *et al.* 1977) on closer investigation, lacked conclusive evidence (Leeson and Smith 1977a and b; Chalmers, Newcombe, and Campbell 1977).

Most reports have noted that the number of mothers needing to have their babies pulled out with forceps increased following induction, and that the number of caesarean sections also increased – both of which the obstetricians could hardly fail to notice. Mothers noticed the increase in operations too, and also the increased rates of episiotomy – the cut made to enlarge the outlet of the birth canal, necessary for forceps to be used, and increasingly necessary as labour became more rapid and the time left for gradual stretching decreased. Episiotomies, say the doctors, are less painful, and heal better than tears, which they prevent; but Dutch midwives, delivering mothers at home, seem to avoid both.

The paediatricians also noted some results from active management; more babies were slow to breathe, and were in a poor state at birth. This was no doubt related to such things as pain-relieving and sedative drugs passing through the placenta, the use of the forceps, a precipitate entry into the world – and being born too soon, in some cases. This has led to increasing numbers of infants being placed in 'special care' facilities for their early days. Jaundice, a common complication occurring a few days after birth, is reported to be considerably more frequent, and more severe in induced babies. The causes of this are still in dispute.

It remains to be seen how many infants will be permanently damaged by these perinatal experiences and when we know, we can speculate on whether less intervention would have led to less damage.

What have the women who have experienced these major changes in childbirth felt about it? Very few exponents have told us and we can't tell if they know, or even cared. Tacchi (1971) 'had the impression' they liked it, O'Driscoll, Stronge, and Minogue (1973) thought they took 'a new view of pain that only lasted twelve hours'. But the women, who were literally lying down, their legs in the air, rarely figure as persons in the reports. However some at least were reacting; organizations like the National Childbirth Trust, the Association for the Improvement of Maternity Services and the Patients' Association all began to receive letters of anger, anguish, and despair from women who had felt alienated, tortured, and deprived of all human dignity by the process of being delivered under the control of a machine (Robinson 1974; Kitzinger 1975).

Obstetric care in Britain seems to be heading towards the American situation, expertly analysed by Haire (1973) in the 'Cultural Warping of Chidbirth'.

### The cultural warping of childbirth

Few examples are known of populations of active, strong, well-built, and well-fed women who give birth to one, two, or three children without the surroundings of modern obstetrics. Perhaps today's Dutch women are the nearest thing we have. Elsewhere, medical intervention is increasingly common, particularly in the US where midwives were gradually eliminated early in the century and the medical take-over is almost complete. A common result is depicted on the following chart (modified from Haire).

## How the pregnant woman becomes a patient

| Physical effects | | Psychosocial effects |
|---|---|---|
| | impersonal ante-natal care | |
| technically efficient (? does BP go up because of it) woman may 'default' sometimes | – different staff test urine, blood pressure, etc. | little preparation for childbirth or parenthood |
| | ⋮ | |
| | labour starts | |
| | ↓ | |
| noisy, confusing, isolating | admit to hospital | tense and frightened |
| | ↓ | |
| discomfort | preparation – shaving, enema | – as if for operation! |
| | ↓ | |
| horizontal position – probably inefficient for labour | put to bed, wired to machine, and left alone | – as if sick; no distractions, no support, no communication |
| severe pain dehydration | | distressed |
| | ↓ | |
| (foetus affected?) | given analgesics | feels dopey, can't co-operate, can't do breathing exercises – a complete patient now |
| | and | |
| woman has to be on back | put up drip | |
| | ↓ | |
| | no progress in labour | |
| big frequent contractions | put oxytocin in drip | 'taken over' |
| pain worse | | |
| can't move at all | epidural analgesia | |
| | ↓ | |
| can't feel when to push | second stage, still horizontal | |
| | ↓ | |
| | baby's head fails to rotate | |
| | ↓ | |

126

| Physical effects | | Psychosocial effects |
| --- | --- | --- |
| shocked baby | episiotomy and forceps | failed as a mother, didn't feel birth and couldn't hold baby |
| | ↓ | |
| | placenta delivered | |
| | ↙        ↘ | |
| can't sit comfortably | mother stitched        baby to special care | baby not seen or held for forty-eight hours |
| breasts engorged | ↓ given bottle | |
| | ↘  ↙ | |
| | baby brought to feed; won't suck | unsure of ability to handle |
| failure of breast feeding | suppression of lactation | failed again |
| | ↓ | |
| | mother + baby + bottle | |
| | discharged to father, who has seen them for half an hour a day, and other children who haven't seen them at all | |
| | ↓ | |
| | They all live happily ever after | |
| | (?) | |

This is a relatively straightforward labour! Complications such as caesarean sections, retained placenta, breast abscess, infections of the infant's cord are all common, and in some instances are the direct result of 'the process'. Caesarean sections are performed because induction or acceleration have failed, and powerful contractions may be damaging the baby's oxygen supply; retained placenta is more likely after forceps, and if the baby is *not* put to breast at once; breast abscess and nursery infections come from not rooming-in (that is leaving the mother and baby together) and not feeding on demand.

Let us stress here that we are well aware that obstetric intervention can be life-saving, for mother and for child. We believe it should be accessible for all pregnant women. But we suspect it would be much less necessary if many 'standard practices' were modified. Some *are* being modified in many hospitals: for example preparations are minimized, husbands or friends stay to support, dayrooms with televisions are available to help pass the time during the first stage, and radio telemetry can be used to monitor the baby, if necessary, by remote instruments without wiring the mother up (Flynn and Kelly 1976). Some places even encourage a more physiologically rational position, half sitting, in the second stage, or lay the mother on her left side in which the baby's route is at least not uphill. Many 'room-in' and allow mothers to care for and feed their infant as and when they choose. All these are welcome and long overdue – though not yet universally available. In 1961, the *Lancet* pointed to a need for changes in attitudes and practice in maternity services; in 1971, *Which?* published a survey which revealed that many of these changes had still not occurred. More recently Dunn (1976) feared that in some respects matters could be getting worse. We suspect the gains made may be threatened by the present enthusiasm for technology, for example induction or acceleration accompanied by 'epidurals' automatically rule out some of these practices.

On the other hand when some clinical interest would not seem amiss, it does not seem to be forthcoming. The painful post-partum perineum which has been stitched, attracts very little interest – even though it may be of overwhelming concern to the woman. The pain may interfere with her ability to sit up and feed the baby, regain bowel function, or move about, etc., but unlike the similar pain which occurs after piles operations, not much seems to be done about it.

Another serious but often disregarded after-effect is post-partum depression. Some depression comes to notice, but most of the 50 to 70 per cent of women who become very depressed about six days after delivery, find scant attention paid to them. There seem to be hormonal factors underlying the mood changes – but we suspect that the experience of being a modern maternity patient and the frustration that 'patienthood' brings to someone anticipating motherhood may also play a part, as may pain and discomfort, and a feeling of inadequacy in handling the baby, compared with the professionals. Jean Robinson's correspondence from mothers supports this (Robinson 1977). It would be interesting to have reliable studies of post-partum depression after home confinement compared to hospital confinements.

## Breast-feeding

Can I, can't I? Could I, should I? It depends who is asking whom, and when, and where. Until very recently, this century in fact, the choice was simple – ensure breast-feeding, or lose your baby. This is still the case for most of the mothers of the world, but in the industrialized countries we live in, technology has now made alternative ways of feeding babies available.

Those few women in the past who had a choice, that is, who could afford to employ a 'wet nurse', another lactating woman, usually seem to have opted out of breast-feeding. Such women were members of the aristocracy or bourgeoisie, and had social activities to which they gave high priority, and which were not readily compatible with being available to feed a baby. They did not look after their children very much at all, since nannies and governesses were employed to do this, and the wet nurse was just one more woman taken on to carry out another aspect of child care.[11] Cow's milk was a poor substitute even when available, although affluent mothers could use it. Elizabeth Garrett Anderson, who did not breast-feed because of her medical duties, decided that for one of her children 'milk from one cow' was an acceptable substitute, and sadly lost the baby from tuberculous meningitis, presumably from infected milk – at the time there was no knowledge of the nature of the infection, or the way it spread (Manton 1965).

But for the last fifty or more years, we have had the knowledge and the means to provide safe alternatives – cow's milk in various forms. Cow's milk, fresh, boiled and diluted, evaporated or powdered, and more recently 'humanized' (in other words, taken apart and reassembled with its constituents in different proportions, more nearly like human milk) is now widely available, together with a variety of feeding bottles, and plenty of instructions. Many instances of healthy babies, thriving on it in life as well as in advertisements, are known to all mothers.

At one time, it seemed that most doctors really favoured the benefits of 'artificial feeding'. There was a certain scientific satisfaction in calculating exact calorie needs according to the baby's weight, and dividing these up into a certain number of feeds to be given at regular intervals, each comprising so many calories. This was important knowledge for a hospital or other baby nursery to have, as a guide for busy nurses with a big turnover of babies all to be fed. But the trend extended to home feeding too, and it rapidly caught on so that for many years now, in Britain, most babies have been bottle-fed. It is *not* because most mothers of young babies go out to work, they don't; and it is *not* because physiology has failed and breasts can no longer produce milk, we are sure that they could do – we therefore need to look for other factors that may have been operating.

### Why has breast-feeding declined?

We have already mentioned that the wide-spread availability of a safe alternative is clearly a necessary, if not a sufficient reason for the decline. Medical and technical advocacy has also been mentioned. Without suggesting a medical conspiracy, we do consider this important, not just in what an individual mother is advised, but in the insinuation that the latest, most up-to-date product advised by doctors and used in hospitals is the one which must be best. But there must be more to it than that. We suspect that demographic changes leading to small families, who are relatively isolated from close relatives, have resulted in many children and young people never having close contact with a small baby, and certainly never seeing one breast-fed.

Now breast-feeding, especially a first child, is not always easy to start with. Modern obstetrics often makes it harder, as we have seen. A post-operative mother, sitting on an episiotomy scar, trying to clamp a baby who is still sedated from drugs received in the uterus, on to rather sore nipples fixed to engorged breasts, is a sad sight indeed, and a sad and painful experience, as both of us can testify. The chances of success are low if the mother is not determined to persist, and not very high if she is. If the baby has been crying in the nursery and is quietened with a bottle, then the chances must be nearly nil.

Further, the breast cult has made it more difficult for feeding to be done in public. (Incidentally, there is little or no provision of 'mothers' rooms' in towns or stations for it to be done privately either.) The isolated young mother, inexperienced but trying to cope with this strange little creature, her young baby, may be very relieved if father, friend, or relative can take over one chore, and give the baby a bottle sometimes – especially in the night. We would like to think that fathers' desire to play a bigger part, too, may have been a good aspect of the decline of breast-feeding. Another factor frequently mentioned by mothers is that 'you can see what she has taken' when bottle feeding. And of course, she is more likely to put on what is regarded as a satisfactorily large amount of weight, if filled up with good, sweet Brand X baby milk.

What we are saying is that there are real pressures operating on parents who are trying to get through the day, and even more, the night, and who want to do what seems to be the right thing for their baby, nearly all of which push towards 'the bottle'.

However, from time to time they are offered 'good advice' that bottle-feeding is a bad thing. Bottle-fed babies are described as being at risk from all sorts of dangers, which only heedless or selfish mothers would expose them to. For the 'medical experts' or some of them, have swung the other way, and are mounting a powerful counter-attack on behalf of breast-feeding, sometimes pressurizing unwilling women to conform. Some of the women's organizations, like the National Childbirth Trust, are with them, and mothers who don't want to, or can't breast-feed, are beginning to feel that they must be failures. What is the truth of the matter?

### Breast or bottle?

Although we must confess to being enthusiasts for breast-feeding, objectively it seems to us that for most babies growing up in a modern urban home with water, power, and fridge all available, and money to buy enough powdered milk or extra food for the mother, the differences between the two are very slight. Breast milk is the ideal food, in food value and safety, and gives some extra protection against infection, especially very early on. A well-nourished woman is probably more likely to regain her pre-pregnancy size if she breast-feeds, and her baby is less likely to get too fat. A few babies are allergic to some constituents of cow's milk, and do not thrive on it, and there is a greater risk of gastro-enteritis – an infection acquired through contaminated milk – for a bottle-fed baby. 'Cot deaths',

131

mysterious and as yet unexplained, though rare, are even rarer in breast-fed babies. So if other things are equal, health-wise, breast-feeding is definitely, but only slightly, better, although most infants thrive either way.

But other things are *not* equal. Feeding the child can be done only by the mother of the breast-fed baby, and this causes others to be excluded, and her to be very tied, especially because, as we have noted, there are few facilities away from home to facilitate breast-feeding. Mothers are also not expected to take young babies with them to work, or to social events (unlike in many parts of Africa, for example).

Our argument is for full and honest information, and a real choice, followed by help in fulfilling that choice. The medical 'evidence' does not justify a crusade to pressurize mothers into or away from breast-feeding. Such zeal might be better directed at obstetric wards in particular and society in general, persuading them to modify the circumstances which currently discourage mothers who would like to breast-feed. This alone would considerably increase the number of babies being breast-fed, and perhaps some of those mothers not so inclined at present would follow the trend, too.

Our general point is that in many instances, of which breast-feeding is one example, good medical advice is offered in a hectoring manner, and in social circumstances that make it difficult or impossible to follow. This has two likely outcomes : one is to generate guilt in those who fail to follow the unfollowable advice, and the other is to discredit medical advice. Neither outcome is going to help maternal and child health services to be effective.[12] It remains to be seen whether pressure from democratic sources outside medicine can lead us out of this impasse; we discuss this in Part III.

We must note however that we are certain that mothers in the underdeveloped countries of the Third World should be encouraged to breast-feed, and that firm social action must be taken to exclude 'The Baby Killer' as Muller (1975) has legitimately described the baby-milk firms pushing their products in Africa, Asia, and South America. It would be almost impossible to rear a baby on bottle-feeding in a village or urban slum, where the family has little money, no piped water, or expensive or troublesome fuel, and is living in an environment where many gastro-intestinal and other infectious diseases are common.

In summary, we are suggesting that the increasing use of technology in childbirth may lead to the call for even more technology, with little firm evidence that mothers and babies are deriving much benefit. We should like to see good hospital obstetric care available to all who 'need it or want it'. This should reproduce many of the desirable aspects of home delivery, such as comfortable sitting rooms for the woman and her companion, and a personal midwife, and only such intervention as has been shown to be clearly in the interests of the well-being of mother and child. Those women with no high risk of mishaps should be able to have their babies at home, with the back-up possibility of a 'flying squad' to carry emergency care to them if necessary. For them, and for those for whom hospital delivery is advisable, but who want to get home quickly, adequate home help services and domiciliary care for themselves and their child are essential.

# SIX

# Women's diseases

### The reproductive organs

Men and women are built to a similar pattern; even the sex organs are derived from the same basic structures in the embryo. But humankind gives birth to fully-formed young who have been nourished for nine months before they are ready to be born and the female of the species has to provide a home for them during those nine months and a passage through which they can enter the outside world.[1] The female reproductive tract is thus an addition to the basic human model[2] and is subject to the special processes we have already discussed, as well as to some associated diseases.

But before we discuss these, we should first mention 'the experts' in women's diseases.

*Gynaecologists, the specialists in women's diseases*

We should say straightaway that we personally have mostly experienced high standards of care and consideration from gynaecologists.[3] So we are not opening a complaints file, we are just noting the rather strange circumstances of doctors (mostly men) who deal exclusively with women. Gynaecologists were prominent in the efforts to exclude women from higher education in general and medicine in particular, and it seems likely that as well as their professional misconceptions about women's needs and abilities, they were driven by a fear of unfair competition. They need not have worried; although women doctors initially did attract women and children from far and wide, by the time there were large numbers of women in the profession, the routes of entry to specialties, and appointments to posts, were well under control, and there are still relatively few women doctors in obstetrics and gynaecology today. According to DHSS statistics there were eighty-nine consultant obstetricians and gynaecologists appointed between 1969–75, but only six of them were women.

It might seem bizarre if a woman doctor specialized in men's diseases, for example prostatic surgery, but our society seems to accept the parallel phenomena of male gynaecologists as natural. With the best will in the world they must labour under severe disadvantages. Jeffcoate (1967) recommends that they should be husbands, and fathers of daughters, if they want to be able to understand their patients, which prompts us to wonder if first-hand experience of womanhood might not be even better? We would not suggest that experience of every disease in the book is necessary before you can treat patients (though some experience of sickness may be a good thing) – but the gynaecologist knows he can never have the diseases his patients have, nor experience their normality either. This does not necessarily decrease his ability to sympathize, but it must make it more difficult for him to understand and interpret symptoms.

Of course he is also a man in our male-dominated culture, and often takes as given, or even as 'scientific facts', many male myths. This is especially true perhaps of those concerning female sexuality, such as the one about women's alleged desire to acquiesce to the masterful (Jeffcoate 1967). In a sense, even more than most other doctors, the gynaecologist is in the front line of the battle to define women's social position in our society as biologically determined. As a result he comes under heavy fire from feminists, particularly those involved in women and health movements, and particularly in the United States where gynaecology is the specialty most often indicted on the charge of unnecessary surgery.

But now let us look at the organs and diseases that together with the conditions we have already considered provide the gynaecologist's daily bread.

### The uterus

This is a really remarkable organ. From the teens until the age of about fifty, the lining of the uterus goes through a monthly cycle of building up, and then shedding (menstruation). In the event of pregnancy the cycle stops, and the uterus develops to accommodate its growing contents until towards the end of pregnancy it is about twelve inches long. After delivery, it is only a matter of days before it returns to its original size. The uterus is capable of doing this ten or fifteen times in the course of a lifetime, although it is two or three generations since that frequency was common in the industrialized world.

Not surprisingly, things can go wrong, in pregnancy or childbirth, and at other times too. We have already spent some time on menstruation, but we should remind ourselves here that disorders of menstruation are probably the commonest of the problems peculiar to women. The pre-menstrual syndrome and dysmenorrhoea are very prevalent, and dysfunctional uterine bleeding (menorrhagia, or heavy periods), are probably equally common in older women. Heavy periods can be due to the coil, or to some conditions we will discuss shortly, but often there is no cause detected, though there may be a predictable result, and that is anaemia.

### Heavy periods

Since we can only be aware of what is normal for ourselves, what most women mean by 'heavy periods' must be 'markedly heavier than I used to have'. Another component is probably 'inconveniently heavy', with floods which can hardly be contained by tampons and pads, or which make it necessary for them to be changed more often than circumstances allow. These are obviously 'subjective measures' and some gynaecologists have sought to show that certain women's 'heavy periods' are not really any heavier than those of other women, who do not complain. Research into menstrual loss is done by arranging for the collection of all used pads and tampons, and then extracting the blood from them, and estimating the volume lost. But what is important is that women do not complain of loss in measured amounts of blood, or of loss which is significantly more than that of other women. They complain of losses which are excessive and inconvenient for them. Perhaps it is the relative ineffectiveness of most treatments which leads some doctors to resort to denying that the women have a real problem – in cubic millilitres. Objective measures are desirable in medicine, but they must be reliable and must measure relevant matters, and even then they are no substitute for responding to patients' problems, as they experience them.

Sometimes possible explanations for excessive periods can be found. The commonest, sometimes also causing secondary dysmenorrhoea (period pains starting later on in life), are fibroids. These are tumours but not malignant ones. They are very common, and mostly cause no symptoms, but some near the inside of the uterus give rise to pain and heavy bleeding and others are thought to prevent conception or cause miscarriage. It is really only worth having them removed if they are causing troublesome symptoms.

*The position of the uterus*

Hippocrates and many of his successors thought the uterus was prone to wander around and cause trouble in remote parts of the body; the term hysteria means just that.[4] In the last century, and perhaps more recently too, local malpositioning of the uterus has been a frequent concern of gynaecologists, who sometimes found the cervix pointing the wrong way in women who were consulting them (Baird 1969). It was often assumed that retroversion (bending backwards) was a common cause of various symptoms and should be corrected by a pessary (an instrument put in the vagina) or by surgically tying it down. This was done for women with a variety of complaints. Many gynaecologists now realize that treatment of retroversion is seldom necessary, and women and health groups have provided detailed information to confirm this. Many women find that the direction of their cervix varies spontaneously from time to time, without any symptoms at all.[5]

Another problem to do with the position of the uterus is more troublesome however – that concerned with prolapse.

## Prolapse of the uterus

The uterus is suspended in the pelvis by a sort of sling of ligaments which, together with muscles, make up the pelvic floor. Repeated pregnancies, clumsily applied forceps, poor general health and muscle tone, and perhaps heavy work during and immediately after pregnancy, probably contribute to the pelvic floor sometimes ceasing to do its job properly, and allowing the uterus and vaginal walls to sag. In extreme cases most of the uterus can be hanging outside the vaginal opening, but the problem is usually less serious, and the main trouble may be due to the bladder sagging with the front vaginal wall, so that urine sometimes leaks, when coughing for example (stress incontinence). Quite a good surgical repair job can be done to tighten up the tissues – although overdoing it may lead to new problems, sometimes making intercourse difficult because the vagina and its opening have been made too small. The importance of post-natal exercises in helping these muscles regain their tone is often ignored, and is a subject that the National Childbirth Trust has emphasized.

## Cancer of the uterus

Fibroids are non-cancerous growths and are common. Cancers are less common and are divided into two classes, depending on which part of the uterus is involved – cancer of the body and cancer of the cervix, or neck. Cancer of the body of the uterus is much less common that that of the cervix. It usually occurs in older women, and is a cause of post-menopausal bleeding which should therefore always be investigated. It requires a 'scrape' (D & C) for diagnosis, and is treated by removal of the uterus.

Cancer of the cervix,[6] however, is quite common, and is curable if treated early. It is believed to develop gradually over many years from diagnosable pre-cancerous conditions. It can, for all these reasons, probably be prevented and is certainly curable if it is detected in screening programmes before the symptoms begin. Cervical screening is now widely practised at special clinics, family planning clinics, general practice surgeries, and hospital out-patients departments. The cervix is scraped with a wooden spoon and surface cells collected.[7] The cells obtained are examined under a microscope. If any of them are abnormal or pre-cancerous, part of the cervix can be cut off, removing the diseased area, and that should be the end of it. If the cells are already cancer cells, then the whole uterus may be removed (hysterectomy), but the outlook should still be good.

It seems obvious that such screening must be a good idea, and should be employed everywhere. We believe that almost certainly this is the case, and so do many people who have looked at the evidence (e.g. the Canadian Ministry of Health 1976), but there remain some queries and doubts (Knox 1966). It is not certain that all pre-cancers become true cancers, or that all cancers have been through a detectable pre-cancerous stage. So there may be some unnecessary operations for 'false positives', as well as some misleading reassurances that 'you have no chance of cancer for five years'. And smears can be misread, too. But there are two bigger, perhaps related problems. One is the controversy over the actual results obtained from practising screening. The death rate from cervical cancer has been falling.[8] The question is whether the fall has been any greater in areas where there has been screening. The evidence is equivocal, but is beginning to suggest that the answer is 'yes, somewhat'. The second problem is why the results are no better. Cancer of the cervix is more common in some categories of women than in others; for example, it is more common in women with husbands in manual occupations, in women who had early sexual experience, and in women who have had multiple partners.[9] Such women are not, on the whole, keen attenders at clinics; in fact, the women who do turn up for screening tend to be 'low risks'. We have yet to solve the problem of drawing in, or going out to, the women most likely to get cervical cancers.

However, in spite of the verdict 'could do better', which we might be implying for some existing programmes, some are already doing well. In Aberdeen about 85 per cent of the target group of women have been screened, and it seems that death rates are falling there faster than in the rest of the country (MacGregor and Teper 1974). There also are many side benefits of cervical screening. All sorts of other troublesome things, such as vaginal infections and persistent cervical erosions, are being found and treated. Cervical erosions do not always need treating, they may be present without symptoms and they often disappear spontaneously, but erosions which last for months and are associated with discharge are worth treating. We should like to see cervical screening as just one facility of comprehensive well-woman clinics, such as we shall discuss later, but we still think that even cervical screening alone is a positive asset.[10] It remains to be determined at what age it should be started, how often it should be repeated, and most of all, how to ensure that 'high risk' categories of women participate.[11]

*Hysterectomy*

Many of the conditions mentioned above lead to surgical treatment – a D & C to investigate first, and then quite often a hysterectomy.[12] Removal of the uterus may be total or partial, that is leaving the cervix behind. Many gynaecologists prefer to carry out the former, as a means of preventing later cancer of the cervix. This does not seem a very good reason since relatively few women will develop that cancer anyway, and cervical smears can be used to prevent it. It may be that removing the cervix sometimes interferes with intercourse – but this is rarely if ever mentioned in the discussion of the pros and cons.

Hysterectomy is a very common operation. In Britain, figures from Oxford suggest that, in the early 1960s, between three and four per 1,000 adult women had a hysterectomy each year (Fairbairn and Acheson 1969). In the USA, the rate in 1968 was 6·8 per 1,000 women, rising to 8·6 per 1,000 in 1973. The reasons for the difference between Britain and the USA are unclear (*Lancet* 1977b). It is said that American women are choosing to have hysterectomies to avoid cancer, pregnancy, menstrual, and menopausal troubles, but it could be that they were being persuaded by some hard selling.[13] Some American doctors have advocated *routine* preventive hysterectomy for all at thirty-five! Cole (1974) notes that in the USA about one million women reach that age each year and that to operate on them all would cost about 1,500 million dollars net, to save 17,400 women from dying from cancer, whilst causing 600 operational deaths. This may be good for business, but it is not our idea of preventive medicine.

Hysterectomy is undoubtedly a life-saving operation for some women, and a blessing for many others. But it is not without a cost beyond that of expense. It is a major operation and often has a debilitating effect lasting some months. It may affect sexual function. It is commonly followed by depressed feelings, which may be due to unknown glandular effects. These occur whether or not the ovaries are removed too. Richards (1973, 1974) found evidence that women who had undergone other operations also had a tendency to depression, but fewer of them suffered as much as those who had a hysterectomy, and their depressions did not last as long. Some of the women without a uterus who were under forty-five and who still had ovaries, suffered post-operative hot flushes and other features often associated with the menopause. They seemed to be relieved by oestrogen replacement. This study reminds us of the great areas of ignorance that still exist in our knowledge of the functioning of the female reproductive organs, and of the shortcomings of the 'take-it-all-away' solution for many of our problems.

*Vaginal discharge*
Many of the conditions we have just mentioned can cause excessive vaginal discharge, as do the sexually transmitted diseases we discuss later. Like heavy periods, 'normal vaginal discharge', and 'excess vaginal discharge', can only be personal assessments based on our own experiences. Many women find they vary during the month, that they have more discharge after childbirth, and that it lessens as they pass the menopause. A sudden or marked increase, especially if it smells and is accompanied by other symptoms, should certainly be investigated – although a clear explanation is not always found. It seems that we still have much to learn in this field.

Cystitis, which we discuss later, can also be an associated symptom. Another often associated problem is what is called 'pruritus vulvae' – meaning itching round the vaginal opening – which is particularly likely with some sorts of discharge (e.g. thrush). It is an agonizing and embarrassing problem, and one that is not likely to be cured without the precise cause being found and treated. Doctors sometimes omit taking a swab and just give a prescription in the hope that it will be the 'right' drug. Sometimes the medicine given is a combination of drugs. The only problem with this blanket approach is that it entails the possibly unnecessary use of the drug metronidazole which, although the correct treatment for trichomonas, is not needed for thrush (which is cured by nystatin). Metronidazole has some occasional adverse side effects and should not be used unnecessarily.

Another mistake made by treating without investigation is that gonorrhoea or other diseases may be missed. Finally, very few doctors give the kind of practical advice which can be read in *Our Bodies, Ourselves* (Boston Women's Health Book Collective 1971) or *The New Women's Health Handbook* (MacKeith 1978). This includes avoiding nylon pants, irritating soaps and vaginal deodorants, making sure sexual partners have washed, and keeping down sugar intake.[14]

### Other 'women's diseases'

Things can go wrong with the other female sex organs, too. The ovary, like any other part of the body, can develop a cancer for unknown reasons,[15] and this seems to be an increasing occurrence, nearly as common now as cervical cancer. It does not usually give rise to early symptoms, but when it is detected it is usually removed together with the tubes, the uterus, and the other ovary. Non-malignant tumours are more common, particularly cysts, and these, like fibroids, can sometimes grow to an extremely large size if not removed. Troubles may arise from the infection of the ovarian tubes (salpingitis) and can lead to a blockage preventing the ovum from reaching the uterus, which eventually results in infertility. Using the coil increases the risk of salpingitis. The infection can be due to various viruses or bacteria, a common one being the gonococcus, and can give acute pain which, if on the right side of the abdomen, may be mistaken for appendicitis. Symptoms can also include pain during intercourse, fever, and irregular bleeding. Such symptoms should be investigated urgently, with a proper examination and vaginal swabs taken. If salpingitis is confirmed, it should be treated by antibiotics and rest in bed.

### The breasts

Until very recently, satisfactory functioning of the breasts was essential for a child's survival, and lack of breast milk was a death warrant to an infant. Natural selection presumably favoured the offspring of women with well-functioning breasts. Paradoxically, it seems that the importance of the breasts in sexual attraction has increased at the very time when the survival value of lactation has become less important, for, as we have seen, it is now technologically possible to obtain adequate and safe substitutes for breast milk. The fetishism of breasts is a central part of the view of woman as a sex object, and it is not remarkable at all that groups of women who had realized and rejected this view of themselves, ceremonially burned their bras. Nor is it surprising that such an action outraged the gutter press, as it challenged much of what they stood for – and all their circulation depended on!

Medicine has become involved in this view of woman as a sex object in various ways. The most amazing is the role played by plastic surgeons in designing and constructing breasts of the size and shape men are supposed to require. Women have wanted to have bits taken out, or have silicone implanted, in order to get nearer to *Playboy* norms. And doctors have wielded their knives for this end – usually for a fee, of course. Many customers have come from the ranks of bunny girls and topless waitresses requiring a sort of industrial rehabilitation service perhaps.

Is this kind of operation any different from straightening noses? Some nose straightening has an undeniably worthy purpose – to enable people to breathe through an organ which is especially designed for breathing, but which is not able to function because it is bent or blocked for some reason. It is true that some breasts may be so large as to be uncomfortable, but breast function seems quite unrelated to original shape and size. When the whole purpose of nose or breast surgery is cosmetic, we would argue that, except perhaps for a few extreme instances of Cyrano-de-Bergerac noses or equivalent breasts, society should be able to accommodate them in all shapes and sizes, and if it can't, better change society than start carving people into standard shapes. This feminist stance has substantial conventional medical backing. All operations carry a small but definite risk, and noses can be ruined by intervention. Similarly lactation would probably be impaired by surgery, and breast implants can go wrong, go septic, or lumpy, and possibly cause cancer (Marchant 1975, 1976). We have trouble enough from cancer of the breast as it is without creating more.

*Breast cancer*
This is a very important topic and is surrounded by controversy.

Each year in England and Wales, 11,000 women die from breast cancer, which is by far the commonest cancer in women, causing about one fifth of all female deaths from cancer. Unfortunately the treatment is usually drastic, and cannot always guarantee cure, although up to half of all early cases can expect to be cured. The death rates from breast cancer have risen recently in spite of many new approaches and attempts to persuade people to seek treatment at the very beginning for any lumps in the breast. Why?

First, we should admit that no-one knows the cause or causes of breast cancer. It is most common in women who have not borne children, and there are big differences between breast cancer rates in different countries. In Japan, the rate is only one quarter of that of the United States, but women of Japanese ethnic origin born in the USA have rates which are much higher than Japanese women in Japan, although lower than for all USA women.

Of course there may be many separate causes or causation may be multifactorial – that is, numerous factors may pile up together to produce a cancer in a particular woman. But up to now we have no idea of how to prevent the disease; all we can hope to do is detect it early, and treat it effectively. Controversy, however, surrounds these areas too.

Early detection, at the very least, requires rapid response when a lump is noticed in the breast. The woman who notices it should go at once to her doctor, who should refer her immediately to a specialist surgeon who is expert in breast cancer, and has all the necessary apparatus for special examinations, like X-ray mammography. Then, if necessary, she can be admitted to hospital without delay for a biopsy – the surgical removal of a small piece of breast tissue for microscopic examination.

At present it is by no means certain that this chain of events usually takes place. Women themselves may delay, either because they don't think it important, or on the contrary, because they immediately suspect cancer, and therefore put off having their suspicion confirmed. General practitioners often delay too, not being sure that they can feel the lump, or not thinking it is cancer. The hospital services are often inadequately equipped and have waiting lists for appointments and admission; many surgeons see few breast cancers, and so are less experienced than is desirable. All these features were evident in a recent survey of the organization of breast cancer services in the West Midlands (Bywaters and Knox 1976). The authors pointed out that remedying these defects should surely preceed any network of extra services for the dectection of breast cancer – in other words that effective management of women who know they have lumps in their breasts is necessary before one starts going out to look for women who may have lumps, but don't know it.

This searching-out of cases, also called screening, is ardently advocated by some as a means of reducing the terrible toll of breast cancer. A simple form of this is self-examination – all women can palpate their own breasts thoroughly and regularly and initiate medical action at once if they find a lump. An additional possibility is for every doctor who examines a woman patient for whatever reason, to examine her breasts too. At first, this may discourage some women from being examined at all, but sensitive explanations would overcome this reluctance, and the practice could and should become standard medical procedure.

The controversy arises over more ambitious screening. The earlier a cancer is treated, other things being equal, the better the chance of cure. But in various parts of some breasts lumps have to be quite big before they can be felt. There remains the possibility that they can be detected by other means. The most hopeful is X-ray mammography which can pick up many cancers missed by the hand. So why not establish a routine examination of all women from middle age onwards, and find cancers earlier? There seem to us to be several reasons for not doing so, at least yet:

1 We are not yet dealing adequately with those lumps which women have already felt, and, as we have seen, it is first necessary to improve this aspect.
2 Studies to date have shown that five out of six women, who are suspected of having breast cancer on screening, are found not to have it on biopsy; so five out of six of the operations and scars are unnecessary.
3 The use of people and equipment for this screening, if applied, say, to every woman over fifty, every year, would cost a great deal of money, and would require a lot of time from radiologists and surgeons who are already in great demand.

It might be more feasible if other specially trained staff, for example nurses and radiographers, were to perform the examinations. Preliminary studies by Sellwood and his team (George *et al.* 1976) suggest that this can give equally good results (although it may be regarded by some as just another example of regrading a job, giving it to women, and paying them less).

4 Mammography uses X-rays; X-rays, especially repeated X-rays can occasionally *cause* cancer and if done frequently to the whole female population could noticeably increase the occurrence of breast cancer, whilst trying to diagnose it early! This problem is also being tackled by the same researchers who have developed techniques using very low doses of X-ray, which should be relatively harmless.

5 Some women delay going for examination even when they know they have a lump – so it may not be easy to persuade all middle-aged women to go regularly for screening.

6 We need to be sure that we will really improve the chances of cure by this means – which makes it desirable to do careful studies before universal application.

7 The only outcome of screening is to be told either 'you haven't got breast cancer at present – come again in one or two years', or 'you need an operation, although the chances are five to one against your having a cancer'.

Unlike cervical screening, there are no likely side benefits. Undoubtedly some women will go for screening, or will go initially anyway. Some pioneer breast screening clinics have found a surprisingly high proportion of lumps – a very interesting circumstance. It seems likely that women may think perhaps they have a lump, but may not be sure enough to 'bother' their own doctor, but will go willingly to a special breast clinic. This suggests that screening clinics, even if not aiming to cover the whole population, may play a useful role. They could be even more useful if they became part of a well-woman clinic, as we discuss elsewhere. But the real question is how much improvement in outlook can we hope to achieve by screening – how good are the results of early treatment, and is it worth the effort? Up to now we cannot answer this question, and careful monitoring is needed for an extended period before we can begin to answer. It does seem certain that the earlier the lump is detected, the better the result of the treatment, particularly in older women. This is the argument put forward by the increasing number of people who advocate universal breast screening for women over fifty.

## Treatment

This involves removing the lump if possible. What else should be involved? Surgeons disagree. Some do only that (i.e. local resection), others remove the whole breast (mastectomy) but no more, and yet others remove more, all the lymph glands in the area and under the arm, and some muscles too. These may be accompanied by X-ray treatment, or not, and more recently cytotoxic drugs have been introduced to try to reach any cancer cells that may have spread to other parts of the body.

The more radical the treatment, the more unpleasant it becomes. This would not matter so much if cure were certain, but for those who are not cured, the side effects of treatment may increase the miseries of the end of their lives considerably. In short, medical experts are not agreed about the best way to treat breast cancer when it is diagnosed, and the treatments have a lot of unpleasant features, too.

There are other aspects of the treatment of breast cancer which concern us too. As noted earlier, many women have breast biopsies, and most of these prove negative. The period of waiting for the operation and then waiting for the report is a very anxious time, and in some hospitals the anxiety is compounded by asking the patient to sign a consent form for mastectomy just before the biopsy operation – often the first time such a possibility is mentioned. Some women go to the operating theatre not knowing whether they will wake up to find that they have two breasts or one.

Trevor Griffiths' moving play, *All through the Night*, said more about mastectomy from the patient's point of view than we can hope to convey here. We wish it could be shown to staffs of all surgical units every few months! The woman in the play who has a mastectomy is fortunate enough to meet a young house surgeon who is prepared to talk to her (although even he does not seem keen to *listen* to her), and she is able to learn something about what has happened, and about what the future may hold in terms of life and death. However, the young man could hardly help her with the less dramatic but nevertheless important problem of facing life again, with part of herself physically missing – brought sharply home to her when she opens the *Daily Liar* to be confronted with two large breasts and a girl standing behind them.

A person's self-image is damaged by the loss of any visible part of the body, of course, and the loss of even a finger or an ear would be distressing and significant to some degree, particularly if an ugly scar remained. In our society, as we have already noted, there is a fetishism of breasts and mastectomy may be felt to interfere significantly with an essential sexual attribute; it certainly involves the loss of an erogenous zone for many women. As the woman recovers from a major operation and often other distressing treatments too, and faces the possibility that she may not live to the end of her expected life-span, she may also have to come to terms with feeling that her own body is repulsive, as well as with the possibility that others will share her feeling. Few doctors, nurses, or other hospital workers feel able to take on the task of trying to help. Consequently she may well have to cope alone, unless she is really lucky and comes into contact with the Mastectomy Association, whose members have been through the tunnel, have emerged at the other end, and hence are able to offer some practical and warm support of the kind needed. There are, of course, prostheses – well-designed replacements sewn into a bra – which can restore a woman's public image, at least. Some surgeons try to preserve most of the breast and replace the removed parts, with silicone for example. This has much to recommend it, but if it carries the risk, in some instances, of causing another cancer, it may not be worth it. We just do not know yet.

*Other breast problems*
These are many and varied, and can mostly be put under the heading of 'very little known about them, and very little done for them'. During the reproductive years, the breasts undergo cyclical changes, that is in the course of a month they vary with the stage of the menstrual cycle. For some women the swelling that often occurs pre-menstrually is acutely painful; other women have painful breasts all the time. These pains, called mastalgia, have been of little concern or interest to medicine, since it was assumed that most patients had a psychological basis for their symptom. It is only recently that the first serious

study of breast pain has been published (Preece *et al.* 1976). It concluded that psychological explanations for the complaints were not, after all, necessary, since thorough investigations found causes in the vast majority of cases, and better still, appropriate and effective treatment was found for most of the women. So mastalgia could be added to the list of diseases afflicting women, described by Lennane and Lennane (1973), which are often dismissed by doctors as imaginary, but can be shown to be due to underlying pathological causes, and can be effectively dealt with.

We have put forward the case that women are subject to particular problems, related to their anatomy and physiology, and to their life situation. We have also suggested that doctors have often been unsympathetic and unhelpful to women suffering from such problems, partly because of gaps in medical knowledge in these areas, but also because of a tendency to devalue women's conditions and diseases. Strategies need to be devised to overcome this neglect, and the well-woman clinic is one such strategy.

## Well-woman clinics

Whenever an open access medical service has been offered specifically to women, a great number of problems have come to light (e.g. Edwards 1974; Marsh 1976). Usually the service has concentrated on one or two specific areas, such as screening for breast or cervical cancer, family planning, or the menopause, and the attenders have been self-selected, and thus drawn from among those women who are most mobile and most likely to be aware of new trends in medical services – in other words from the upper and middle social classes. This has not always been the case, though, and when serious attempts have been made to invite all women, and to make services convenient for them, for example by taking a well-publicized mobile clinic to factories or localities, the response has been good. A particularly attractive approach has been to offer women an examination done by other women. When Marsh provided a choice, almost all respondents preferred to see the practice nurse rather than their own general practitioner.

General practices are well placed to offer screening services to all the women in a locality and some have done so, successfully, but it seems to be the exception rather than the rule for this to happen.

We would like to see the extension and development of the sorts of services mentioned above into comprehensive well-woman clinics. They should open the door to any woman who chooses to go, as well as regularly inviting high-risk groups to come for particular tests. These would include screening tests for diseases such as anaemia, urinary infections, raised blood pressure, cervical cancer, and other genito-urinary problems. There should be day-time and evening sessions, and creche facilities for the children of attenders. The problems dealt with would be any that a woman wished to raise; we would expect all the issues we have dealt with in this book to arise. Traditional health education topics, like sex, sexuality, menstruation, contraception, pregnancy, childbirth, child-rearing, smoking, obesity, and the menopause, should be the subjects of exhibitions, discussion groups, and personal counselling, as well as medical investigation. Many women, some professionals like doctors, nurses, and teachers, and others, such as mothers with particular interests or experience in some aspect, could contribute to the functioning of the clinic.

We believe that group discussion and mutually supportive action could make a major contribution to the relief of the common problem of distress, hopelessness, and isolation in young women, which at present goes unhelped, or leads to the prescription of psychotropic drugs.

A service like this could easily be created now, building on existing cervical screening and family planning clinics, and general practice screening programmes.

However, we would like to see developments which go beyond these, towards the self-help and self-examination concepts of the women's movement, with the women users themselves playing an increasingly important part in examining their own bodies, and deciding what is to be done to them. The most obvious area of application is in the control of fertility, the choice of contraception, and decisions about abortion. We think that a well-woman clinic would be a good place to develop services for menstrual extraction.

In our view, well-woman clinics will only really meet the needs of local women if these women are involved in organizing and planning the clinics and if the clinics are under the control of users' committees.

Others may have different agenda for the well-woman clinics. Some feminist groups want no health professionals involved, and we differ from them in valuing medical and nursing skills. We think these skills will provide information on which women can base decisions about their own bodies, and the expertise with which those decisions can be carried out.

We differ even more from the approach of the commercial well-women clinics, so common in the USA, where the definition of a healthy woman is one who has not yet been thoroughly investigated. Such clinics are cynical institutions, in the business of medicalizing everything – or rather, everything from which a profit can be made.

The model we propose could begin to develop now, within the NHS, and perhaps within some of the pre-paid insurance schemes elsewhere. Community participation and user control in this and other services will have to be fought for, but in our view it is only in this way that acceptable and effective services can be ensured.

## SEVEN

# Diseases common in woman

We now turn to some diseases which are not unique to women, but which either present particular problems for women or are more commonly found in women.

We are resisting the temptation to launch into a health education polemic on two particular problems which might be included here – obesity and smoking. We regard them both as conditions which are very dangerous to health and yet are fostered by the special circumstances in which we live. Medicine has been ineffective in dealing with them as individual problems, and it seems to us that social decisions, such as national food policies, national facilities for physical activities, control of advertising, and prohibition of smoking in public spaces, would be more likely to produce results. Obesity is already more of a problem in women than in men. Smoking, which seems to have reached a plateau in men, is increasing in women, and the smokers' diseases, especially lung cancer and bronchitis, are increasing one step behind it. In both instances, it is predominantly among working-class women that the major risks are occurring. We do not intend to say more about these conditions in this book, except to hope that any group or organization concerned with women's health, whose members may read this book, will before long add them to the agenda for investigation and action.

This chapter will look at two topics not unconnected with some of the 'women's diseases' discussed earlier, and these are sexually transmitted diseases and cystitis. We will also consider two others which seem to be major problems for women, anaemia and neurosis, and will conclude with some diseases that women have been accused of causing in others.

## Sexually transmitted diseases (STD)

This has nothing to do with telephones, but is the new term which has replaced VD (venereal diseases) in official terminology; doctors in the STD clinics have also been renamed as specialists in genito-urinary medicine. These moves are attempts to improve the image of the service, and reduce the stigma for the user. Perhaps they help. They might help more if the premises and procedures were all brought up to date too, although we do appreciate that for a service where contact tracing and follow-up of patients who have not completed treatment are central, it is inherently difficult not to appear unnecessarily prying.[1]

### Syphilis and gonorrhoea
Historically, syphilis was one of many diseases which were rampant in Europe from the sixteenth century onwards, but were clearly declining both in prevalence and severity before effective treatment was widely available. It is relatively rare in Britain now though not declining, and most clinic cases (82 per cent in one London survey) are in homosexual men. In other parts of the world it seems to be increasing, for example, in the United States and much of Africa and Asia. The control which Britain has maintained may be due to the network of clinics which give better coverage, and make a bigger attempt to trace and treat contacts, than most services elsewhere.

Because syphilis has a longish incubation period of about three weeks, contact tracing can be much more effective than in a disease like gonorrhoea, in which the newly infected person can rapidly pass it on to others within two or three days. Gonococcal infection is the prime example of an infection in which the 'ping-pong effect' occurs, as it can be passed to and fro between a couple unless both of them are treated at the same time.

Our Victorian forefathers were very concerned about venereal diseases; at that time there was no effective treatment, and there were many historical and literary reminders of the disasters which could follow infection. In an era of double standards the solution seemed simple – fallen women must be prevented from infecting our youth. After a report by a Royal Commission, the Contagious Diseases Acts were passed (1864–9) to permit the compulsory arrest and medical examination of prostitutes. The Acts were implemented in garrison towns, where police could apprehend any young woman 'suspected of being a prostitute', and submit her to gynaecological examination. This was akin to police regulation of prostitution, and was vehemently opposed by many feminists in a campaign led by Josephine Butler. Eventually in 1883, the inspections were dropped and the Acts were repealed in 1886. The reasoning behind this experiment in police medicine was the belief that there was a pool of infection among women, and that each woman might infect many men.

It was certainly true that, until recently, there were many more men than women seeking treatment (this seems to be changing towards a one-to-one ratio now). But in the case of a woman, infection with syphilis may pass unnoticed, because the chancre or sore is painless and may be inside the vagina out of sight. Gonorrhoea, too, is often symptomless in women in the early stages. Men are much more likely to be aware of these infections, since their sores will generally be visible, and gonorrhoea usually gives them pain and purulent discharge. As we shall see, when other sexually transmitted diseases are included, the picture changes somewhat.

*What do we include under the term sexually transmitted diseases today?*
STD consist of infections transmitted by sexual activity, and

traditionally this used to mean mainly syphilis and gonorrhoea. Today in many countries the clinics see more of other diseases than they see of those two – the figures for new cases treated in clinics in England[2] for 1974 (DHSS 1975a) were as follows:

|  | Total | Women |
|---|---|---|
| Syphilis | 2,278 | 372 |
| Gonorrhoea | 58,139 | 20,778 |
| 'Non-specific genital infection' | 84,627 | 14,928 |
| Trichomoniasis | 19,011 | 17,591 |
| Candidiasis | 32,457 | 27,221 |
| Genital warts | 18,733 | 6,282 |

Together with about 50,000 people (32,000 women) suffering from various other diseases or conditions, and 84,000 (31,000 women) not requiring treatment, these add up to nearly 350,000 (140,000 women) new cases in a population of 29 million people (15 million women) between the ages of fifteen and sixty-four. (It is, however, rather misleading to put it like that, because one person may have more than one disease at a time.[3]) We may therefore conclude that most women who go to STD clinics have some condition other than the diseases listed above, or do not have any diagnosable disease at all. Many are probably 'contacts' of infected men who have luckily escaped infection.

When a diagnosis of STD is made, it is most likely to be candidiasis (thrush), followed by gonorrhoea (clap), trichomoniasis, and non-specific genital infection. This order of likelihood is different for men – why? Part of the explanation is that some diseases are asymptomatic, or more difficult to diagnose in one sex than the other. For example, non-specific genital infection,[4] and gonorrhoea are much more commonly found in men. By contrast, thrush is more common in women. In both instances the tendency to relapse may mean that the apparently uninfected partner may actually be a carrier, who reinfects the sufferer later. This is not widely known. Often thrush is treated by family doctors and others without examining or treating the sexual partner, and, for this reason, many women suffer the agonizing itch of thrush for years.[5] Trichomoniasis is another cause of irritation and vaginal discharge which may persist for a long time, especially if there is an infected partner. Vaginal discharge or cystitis often takes a woman to a general practitioner or to a gynaecologist, neither of whom detects the underlying infection, or even takes it very seriously. The woman is deterred from going to the special STD clinics because of the stigma and she therefore does not have the thorough investigation she needs.

As in most other infections, the body's resistance may vary, and other factors may encourage or discourage the micro-organisms. This is particularly true of thrush, and hormones probably play a part here. So does the local environment, and nylon pants and tights have been indicted as preventing sweat from evaporating, thus keeping the skin moist, just as the fungus likes it. People with diabetes are particularly prone to fungal infection, and in others it may be influenced by diet and especially by taking antibiotics. Sometimes the sufferer has thrush in her bowels too, and this can be a source of reinfection. The organism is often also found when there are no symptoms complained of.[6]

Venereal diseases were once known as 'social diseases', because their prevalence is determined by many social factors. Wars have always caused great increases, as did the slump in the 1930s. It has been seen as paradoxical that an affluent era should also be one of increasing STD, and much ink has been spilt discussing it. Perhaps there have been changes in sexual behaviour, particularly in young women, which have contributed. Another factor is that the sheath did really seem to protect against the spread of infection. Antibiotics have played a part too; indiscriminate use, as in the US Army in Vietnam, has led to the development of resistant strains of gonococci, so that treatment is not as easy or as certain as it used to be.

## Cystitis

Cystitis means inflammation of the urinary bladder. The commonest symptoms are pain and burning, and frequently wanting to pass urine. It can occur in both men and women, but is much more common in women, probably because of the comparative shortness of the urethra, the passage which connects it with the outside world, for much infection ascends by that route into the bladder. Cystitis is more common in women who are sexually active than in those who are not.

Urinary infection is yet another paradox. Studies of random samples of normal women have found that many of them have bacteria in their urine – 4·7 per cent in one study (Gaymans *et al.* 1976). In some women, attacks of cystitis occur again and again; in addition to all the pain and distress they involve, there is a risk of infection spreading backwards into the kidneys and doing serious damage there.

*What causes cystitis?*
Some of the sexually transmitted diseases, as already discussed, can cause cystitis, but more commonly the organisms are bacteria that live in the gut without doing any harm, but which can cause symptoms of infection if they reach the urethra and the bladder.

Once more we must note that this woman's problem has not attracted much concern and interest in the past. It lies literally on the borders of specialists' interests, sometimes being considered as the province of the gynaecologist, and at other times being the business of the urologist, general physician, general surgeon, urological surgeon – or nobody at all. Coverage in medical education is brief, and most general practitioners limit their activities to reaching for their prescription pad when faced with a woman with cystitis.

The condition has been put more prominently on the medical map recently by Kilmartin (1973) and the U and I Club, which we will mention later. Bitter personal experience has taught Kilmartin how to deal with recurrent cystitis, and she in turn is teaching other sufferers and their doctors. The points she makes include the simple ones mentioned in connection with vaginal discharge, such as avoiding irritants and maintaining hygiene in the area around the openings of the urethra, the vagina, and the rectum. She also stresses the value of drinking plenty of liquid, and of taking bicarbonate to stop the urine being acid, both of which can prevent cystitis in those who are prone to it, in the early treatment of attacks.

**Anaemia**

We are including anaemia in our discussion, although of course it is not restricted to women. This is because the commonest form is much more likely to occur in women than in men, and it has been subject to queries in recent years as to whether it is a 'real' problem.

The anaemia we are concerned with is iron deficiency anaemia, in which the red cells in the blood are too few and too small. It is an inevitable result of less iron being absorbed into the body than is being lost from it. The main sources of iron are meat, peas and beans, wholemeal bread, eggs, oatmeal, and iron cooking pots. Fruit and green vegetables have little iron in them, but their vitamin C helps iron to be absorbed. The body loses little iron except by bleeding, for instance from ulcers or piles, and by menstruation, pregnancy, and childbirth. Anaemia is rather difficult to define precisely. The measure used is blood haemoglobin level in grams per hundred millilitres, and an arbitrary decision has to be made as to where to draw the line between normal and abnormal.

The use of the idea of 'normal' is difficult. It can mean several quite different things, but is commonly used in the sense of 'as it should be' or 'healthy', that is, in comparison with some abstract ideal state of affairs. Although the level usually fixed as the lower limit of normality of haemoglobin is lower for women than for men (12·0 gm per 100 ml, as compared with 12·5 gm per 100 ml), studies repeatedly show many more women than men who are below this level, and can thus be called anaemic (roughly 15 per cent and 3 per cent respectively). It seems very likely, however, that heavy menstrual loss is frequently a major factor in women's anaemia (Elwood, Rees, and Thomas 1968). An increase in iron intake[7] (by tablets[8] or in food) usually results in a rise in haemoglobin, and eventually in the restoration of low iron stores. But if subsequently loss continues to exceed intake, obviously the anaemia will recur.

*Does anaemia matter?*
Textbooks describe the symptoms of anaemia as pallor, tiredness, lack of energy, breathlessness, palpitations, and, in severe cases, swelling of the ankles and angina. This description immediately gives rise to problems. Many of the 'symptoms' are very common in people who are quite fit, as well as in people who have other diseases but not anaemia, in other words, they are not specific to anaemia. The symptoms are not easy to quantify, and are relative and often insidious and gradual.[9]

All these difficulties are relevant in considering whether anaemia matters. Most clinicians would assume the answer was yes, and treat it. Many women who have had adequate courses of iron and felt significantly different afterwards (although of course still tired, etc., sometimes) would say yes, too.[10] But a survey in one community in Wales has caused several doctors to doubt it (Wood and Elwood 1966; Elwood and Wood 1966). The women's answers to questions about 'symptoms' of anaemia did not correlate closely with their haemoglobin levels, and iron treatment for eight weeks of those with low haemoglobin levels did not significantly reduce the number of symptoms recorded. To us, the survey says more about the difficulties of measuring non-specific symptoms, than it does about whether the quality of life of many of the 15 per cent of women who appear to be anaemic could be improved if their haemoglobin levels were higher.[11]

We think the whole matter needs further investigation, but meanwhile, any woman who feels shattered for no very good reason, or has less energy than usual should have her haemoglobin level tested, and if it is low, take a long course of iron tablets. The chances are that she will be better for it, although in some instances, further investigation may be needed too.

### Women's neuroses

From the way the term is used, you might think it is not so much a diagnosis as a moral failing – and we suspect it is often used like that. The psychiatric textbooks (e.g. Curran, Partridge, and Storey 1972) usually describe mental illness under two headings, the psychoses and the neuroses, with many sub-groups in each.

Under 'psychoses' come the 'organic mental states', with known causes like injury, infection, and senile degeneration, and the so-called 'functional psychoses', which include schizophrenia and manic-depressive psychosis, the causes of which are not understood or agreed. The sufferers from psychosis, in British terminology at least, are characterized by distortions in their perceptions – for example, hearing voices that others do not hear – or by misinterpretations of reality, or delusions – such as believing that they are responsible for causing an earthquake.

In contrast, sufferers from neurosis do not have hallucinations or delusions, but are incapacitated by their feelings. Curran's textbook now calls this latter category 'personality problems'. The most widely used sub-groups are 'anxiety neurosis' and 'neurotic depression' (and some would add 'hysteria' to the list), but many patients show features of more than one sort. When it is noted, further, that 'depression' appears under both psychosis and neurosis, and we add the information that many authors claim depression cannot be divided into two distinct types but should be regarded as one continuum, it is obvious that these terms and classifications lack precision, although they are widely used and useful to psychiatrists who are faced daily with ill people seeking help. The first task in any science is to construct a classification of the phenomena studied, and all classifications are unsatisfactory in some ways, and hence provisional, but have to be used until better ones are devised. Almost everyone would agree that the psychiatric classifications outlined above are limited, but are the best we have. A minority view (Szasz 1961) that there is no such thing as 'real' mental illness, that it is a label attached by malevolent authorities is yet another approach.

For what it is worth, our standpoint is that mental illnesses really exist but that a large proportion of the neuroses diagnosed are simply due to practical problems people are experiencing, which they find intolerable but which they cannot solve. They are in situations in which anxiety or depression may well be a reasonable response – and they can see no way out that is conceivable for them, or which would not be a 'frying pan into the fire' escape (we will return to this later). Although the range covered by the legitimate use of 'neurosis' is wide, the truth is that many people, including doctors, use it even more widely, and apply it to people – often women – who are causing inconvenience in some way.

If we restrict ourselves for the moment to medical encounters and the use of the diagnosis 'neurosis', it seems to us it can be, and sometimes is, used unhelpfully in the following ways:

1 People who have a physical illness which a doctor has failed to diagnose are told that there is nothing really wrong, with the explicit or implicit addition of 'you must be neurotic'.
2 People who behave in a way which is seen as unnatural, or unacceptable may be accused of being neurotic.
3 People who are unhappy and dissatisfied with a life that by any reasonable standards *is* intolerable are told that, since others do tolerate it, they must be neurotic.

4 People whose life experiences are so distressing that they have become profoundly anxious or depressed are diagnosed, perhaps correctly, as suffering from neurosis and are given drugs, without much attention being paid to the persistence of the situation which is making them ill.

All these circumstances may and do apply to men as well as women. The diagnosis 'neurosis' is given to women much more often than to men, however, and we suspect that this is partly due to the greater likelihood of women falling into one of the above categories – which we shall now examine in turn.

1 *'There's nothing wrong, you're just neurotic'* As we have noted before, Lennane and Lennane (1973) have documented the dismissal of many female ills as being psychogenic or neurotic. Dysmenorrhoea, sometimes alleged to be due to a rejection of the female sex role, is one example. The allegations have persisted in the face of irrefutable evidence of the physiological, hormone-related nature of the pain which often disappears in the absence of ovulation, as women on the Pill have been happy to discover. Dalton (1969) has found that many 'neurotic complaints' of vague discomforts, pains, and depression, disappear on her hormonal treatment of pre-menstrual tension. It may be that of all women with menstrual troubles, only a few, some of whom are particularly anxious people, consult a doctor about them. We cannot see, however, that this absolves the doctor from taking their complaint seriously.

2 *'Normal women don't behave like that, you must be neurotic'* The woman who aggressively refuses to conform to the female sex stereotype is a prime recipient of this diagnosis. (In some instances she may be compelled to feign 'neurosis' – for example, in order to persuade doctors to terminate an unwanted pregnancy.) Many professional women know that if they behave like men by being concerned with their own careers and earnings, and not being prepared to run around filling in the gaps in the services to pupils, patients, etc., this is likely to be unexpected, deeply resented, and even penalized by many of their male bosses. Sometimes the sin is further compounded by a failure to find his charms irresistible, and by the expression of views which challenge his own – behaviour not usually displayed by women surrounding 'big men'. The 'double-bind' aspect of this

is that the women who do conform, and spend time giving caring help to others around them, may jeopardize their chances of promotion by not meeting professional standards. These concentrate on 'male' characteristics and do not generally include caring about people (Simpson and Simpson 1969).

Choosing to be unmarried or childless clearly indicates neurosis in some eyes, as does any relationship with a man which is not subservient. In fact, commonly-held conceptions of normal behaviour for 'people', unspecified, and for 'men' are very similar, and differ notably from the norm for women (Broverman *et al.* 1970). Medical and psychological experts have played a prominent part as agents of social control in this field, consciously or not, by defining any changes in women's roles as dangerous to the women themselves or others; they are often apparently unaware that the majority of women, from choice or necessity, are *de facto* changing their roles, for instance, by going out to work. Lesbian women of course are prime subjects for the label too, since they are a challenge to the 'normal' heterosexual family model. (The recent controversy over whether lesbian women are fit to be artificially inseminated, in which doctor Shirley Summerskill intervened to say 'no', illustrates the way doctors illegitimately use their medical status to make essentially social judgements.)

Thus the symptom of 'neurosis' in this group is failure to be proper women.

3 *'You have a lovely home, a good husband and two beautiful children, everything a woman could want, and you're not satisfied. You must be neurotic.'* 'All that a woman could want' is defined as resting within the four walls of the nuclear family home, and should be totally fulfilling. All the other residents of the home may have major interests and commitments outside, and come home just to be serviced, as it were. Their social statuses are achieved outside, at work or school, and their satisfactions gained there. The woman remains 'just a housewife', as she may apologetically put it. Oakley (1976a) has analysed perceptively what that involves, and what it means to many women, even those who do have 'a beautiful home'. Isolation probably weighs heaviest on those with young children at home (Gavron 1966), and those who have moved away from their home areas. More complaints of frustration and boredom may

come from women who have had enjoyable jobs in the past. But even the grind of working in the supermarket or in the jam factory had compensations in the form of a giggle with your mates and a wage packet at the end of the week, both of which 'the housewife' lacks. This group of 'neurotics', young married women, cannot be accused of failing to *be* proper women – their sickness is that they don't *enjoy* being 'proper' women.

4 *'You feel miserable because your husband has left you, the children are always crying and your landlord won't repair the leaking roof – well, you've got depression, take a pill.'* 'Reactive depression', as it is called, is extremely common as we shall see. Doctors don't see it all, by any means, and when they do they often prescribe an anti-depressant drug. In truth, they may follow this course after due consideration, believing that it is the only approach they are competent to take. But in so doing, they effectively define the problem as existing in the woman herself, and thus reinforce one basis of her depression, that of self-blame for her predicament.

At the same time they may dampen her responses, making her less likely to be able to take any steps to break out of the trap. Some doctors may have just adopted the attitude of one of their student textbooks (Curran, Partridge, and Storey 1972), which after a sympathetic discussion of the depressions which can be caused by living away from friends in uncongenial climates, or being obliged to 'toil at exacting work' to 'support ungrateful relatives', says, by contrast:

'On the other hand, the development of depression may depend more on the individual qualities of the patient; an unintelligent housewife with few resources of her own and small capacity for satisfactory relationships, may become worn down into depression through her anxieties over bringing up what for her become too many children, and through her inability to do things to her own or her husband's satisfaction through muddleheadedness which, through imprudent expenditure, prevents her from ever having anything to spare for such amusements as might otherwise be beguiling.' (p. 252)

This reminds us of the joke about the psychiatrist who says, 'Inferiority complex? Nonsense, you just *are* inferior.'

*Depression, helplessness and hopelessness*

It may surprise some readers to find that in affluent Britain there are many women bringing up children in poverty and deprivation, but the problems have been well documented by Child Poverty Action Groups (Field 1977) and many others. The impact that such lives may have on women has been described in detail for an area of South London, by Brown, Bhrolchain, and Harris (1975). They carried out a small survey of women living in randomly selected households, asking questions concerned with mental state and life history. Of the 220 women, 16 per cent gave answers that, in the view of psychiatrists, indicated they were psychiatrically ill. (We should prefer to say that they were severely distressed.) For example, they were feeling depressed, anxious, and short of energy, and they were sleeping badly and losing weight. For 10 per cent, the troubles had begun in the last year, while for 6 per cent they had lasted longer. Forty-five (20 per cent) other women had some of the same problems, but to a lesser degree.

The writers found that many of the women had experienced recent crises such as the death of a loved person, and that many lived with continuous major difficulties, such as housing problems and poverty. By no means had all those with such experiences become depressed; working-class women both had more problems, and seemed to be more vulnerable to depression as a result, than did middle-class women. Further, the authors found that those with young children at home, those without a close relationship with anyone, those who did not go out to work, and those who had lost their mother in childhood, seemed to be more vulnerable to sinking into despondency than other women who were also living through death and disaster. Very few of the women had seen a doctor about their distress.

There are several important points to make about the study. The first is to note the high prevalence of problems, acute and chronic, which press upon many women, particularly working-class women. Some of these, such as confronting death and disease in others, are inevitable aspects of life; but many, like having to bring up children without social support, in bad housing conditions, with an inadequate income, should not be.

The second point is not unexpected. When enough of these problems pile on top of each other, some women become depressed and develop symptoms which make it even more difficult for them to cope. What is perhaps more interesting is the finding that some things seem to protect against breakdown – in particular, having a confidante (in every case in the sample who had one, it was a man – husband or boyfriend) and having a job. The researchers noted that most of the women were not being treated by a doctor for their depression, and seemed to think that this was a bad thing. This is open to doubt. A 'super-doctor', who organized social support, pressed successfully for rehousing, advised on social security, listened sympathetically, arranged a convalescent holiday for the woman and a summer camp for the children – or anyone else who could do all that, would be a great help, but we suspect that few doctors provide such 'treatment'.

What other approaches might help? Mutual support – community groups, play groups, and the like – may be preventive, but would have to go out to find women already feeling hopeless and persuade them to join in. Social changes profound enough to transform the quality of life for ordinary people, particularly for ordinary women, will reduce this sort of problem but in the meantime what should be done?

We find Seligman's (1975) model of depression, and his reports of how others have used the same model to find a successful treatment (Taulbee and Wright 1971), very attractive, though we have no first-hand experience of its application.

Seligman suggests that depression can be regarded as 'learned helplessness'. He believes he can produce a similar condition in laboratory animals by giving them problems they cannot solve, or unpleasant circumstances from which they cannot escape. All the responses the animals try are futile; eventually they give up trying altogether, even in different situations. They become passive and slow to move, they show no aggression, lose their appetite and sex drive, and lose weight. The parallels with depression in humans are clear.

Based on this analysis, treatment programmes have been devised for depressed people, which involve such things as setting tasks which *can* be achieved and then rewarding the achievement, thus breaking the 'negative cognitive set' and rebuilding the low self-esteem of the depressed person. Other approaches include rewards for the expression of anger when it is appropriate, and give assertive training, decision-making training and practice, and relaxation training – in a word, turn 'born losers' into 'sure winners'. That sounds fine for those who *can* win, but what about the rest, who cannot? In therapy, winning can be arranged, so that at least the possibility of fighting and winning can be encouraged. Once you turn to face the outside world, when in a fit state to do so, the prescription becomes:

Take positive action to change what can be changed.

Accept what can't be changed.

Learn to tell the difference.

Treatment for depression along these lines might avoid the negative aspects of labelling and drugging, which we have already mentioned but will look at more closely next. We would like to see Seligman's approach tried out systematically and evaluated. (Perhaps all women should have assertive training anyway – it seems lacking in most girls' education.)

But prevention seems to us to be the obvious way to tackle the mass problem of distress and unhappiness that Brown has documented. It requires social measures to break down the isolation of women, particularly of those with young children, and to relieve the economic and practical burdens that press upon them.

Some remedies can be achieved by legislation and the creation of better community services; others require changes in relationships. Priorities should be given to both sorts of remedy, for example the abolition of family poverty and the sharing of parental and domestic responsibilities by men. When both parents work, creches and out-of-school care facilities are essential, and when women are at home, they and their children need community centres with play groups and a range of other facilities.

We believe that developments such as these are much more appropriate, and likely to be more effective, than attaching medical labels and prescribing medical treatment for ills which are caused by social problems.

*Women – suitable cases for psychotropic treatment*

We have already looked at some of the reasons why doctors and society may be encouraged to label a woman as neurotic, but we have not yet taken account of a factor of increasing relevance – the explosion of psychotropic drugs.

The story of the brilliant scientist who invents a cure for a disease that hasn't even been discovered yet, is not at all far-fetched. A drug firm would soon solve the problem of inventing suitable cases, drawing on its existing experience in marketing, which involves extending indefinitely the range of patients for whom its latest drug is the right treatment. If the drug should be a bit addictive, so that the user once started will want to continue taking it, so much the better. Selling psychotropic drugs has been so profitable precisely because of the possibilities in both these respects. One firm produced a series of booklets about stress in the modern world, covering in turn every possible circumstance from the cradle, via examinations, promotion, parenthood, widowhood, etc., to the grave – each one with an advert for Brand X tranquillizer. As patent rights run out, of course, a subsequent campaign has to be mounted for the next generation tranquillizer: Brand X plus 1.

Doctors are snowed under with drug advertisements; Stimson (1975) estimated that the average general practitioner receives thirty-five issues of various free (drug-firm) magazines each month, fifty adverts through the post, and four or more visits from drug-firm representatives. Together with journal advertisements, there pass before his eyes about 1,300 advertisements per month. These contain some information in writing of course – names, dosages, indications for use – but they also show plenty of pictures with perhaps more subtle messages. As Stimson points out, many of these messages convey stereotypes of women, as women and as patients. The advertisers seem well aware of the high prevalence of distressing pressures on working-class mothers. Their solution is simple – 'prescribe a pill'. The same formula goes for the stresses of young women and old women too. The doctor does not even have to wrestle with diagnostic problems such as whether anxiety or depression predominate. Many pills are mixtures, poly-pharmaceutical offerings to be used as cure-alls.

Most doctors claim that they pay little attention to adverts, that none of the 15,600 or so put before each doctor each year have any impact. But does that make sense? Drug firms monitor the effects of particular campaigns in particular areas, build up detailed dossiers on each prescriber, promote representatives if sales go up in their beat, and spend £30 millions per year on advertising. Is this all for nothing? Three thousand million doses of psychotropic drugs were prescribed in 1971, and the numbers continue to rise. We think that drug companies have a very big vested interest in medicalizing everything, in turning people with problems into patients, and we know that women are most often on the receiving end of this as far as psychotropic drugs are concerned. Almost identical findings have come from studies of drug advertising in the USA (Prather and Fidell 1975) and Australia (Mant and Darrock 1975). Probably some people, with the sorts of problem we have been discussing, sometimes benefit from a short course of psychotropic drugs, although there seems little objective evidence of this (Porter (1970) discussed this in relation to a popular anti-depressant).

There is also another important consequence of the widespread prescription of psychotropic drugs, namely the modern epidemic of 'over-dosing'. The diagnosis of self-poisoning is recorded for more than 50,000 hospital admissions each year, most of whom are women (Alderson 1974).

We are convinced that most of the millions of pills prescribed each year are not merely unnecessary, but are bad for the individuals concerned and for society as a whole. They cost a lot – more than £20 million a year – and they sedate many people whose performance when driving, for instance, is therefore less efficient. They also reinforce the process of labelling individuals as mentally ill, when in reality they have social problems, demanding social action. In the case of the 'over-dosers', the drugs have literally transformed someone with a problem into a patient, sometimes with fatal results.

### The epidemiology of mental illness

We have already said enough to make it obvious that the diagnosis of at least some sorts of mental illness is so dependent on social attitudes that variations in time and place have to be interpreted very cautiously. It is not uncommon for researchers in the USA to report that half the adults in a survey area are neurotic (e.g. Leighton *et al.* 1963). Usually such high rates are associated with an excess of women. Conversely, areas with very few psychiatric facilities, as in developing countries, tend to have more men than women in their few mental hospitals.[12] As well as aspects already discussed, we should also consider what sort of behaviour is not tolerated and leads to official action, and whether such behaviour is more likely to be displayed by men or by women who are mentally ill.

For example, violence and setting fire to huts was often recorded in the notes of male in-patients in the Lusaka psychiatric hospital, Zambia (Haworth 1968). On the other hand, it may be more socially acceptable for a woman to describe feelings of sadness, fear, and inadequacy than for a man (Nathanson 1975). Men with similar problems, may either interpret their feelings differently, and put blame on others rather than on themselves, or may respond by acting them out, or by drinking, or fighting, and so on.[13]

How 'inherent' is this tendency for women to have more mental illness diagnosed? We have already noted that it seems to be localized and recent. Gove and Tudor (1973) suggest it derives from changes for the worse in the role of women in modern societies, as they have become more isolated from other women and from economically rewarding work; their child-bearing roles have been reduced, while their uncertainty about alternatives has grown. Gove (1972) has noted that various studies of the relationship between marital status and mental disorder suggest that it is only among the married that this large female excess is found. Studies of the never married or no-longer married were not conclusive, but showed a tendency for the women in each category to have rather less mental illness than the men. Of course, there may be other societal factors operating as well as those related to sex roles.

## What about the psychoses?

It is worth noting that the female excess in mental hospitals is by no means entirely due to neurotic or depressed young and middle-aged women. Nearly half of all psychiatric in-patients are elderly, that is over the age of sixty-five, and the proportion of women over this age is more than half (DHSS 1975). Some of these are very old, and suffer from degeneration of the brain related to ageing, and it is not surprising that women predominate heavily, since they form the majority of the older age groups in our society.

The dividing line between neurosis and psychosis in depression is ill-defined, if it exists at all, and women predominate in the psychotic depression group too. For schizophrenia it is rather different, and the admission rates for men and women are nearly equal.

Chesler (1972), has drawn attention to the types of delusions that women with psychoses commonly experience. Many identify with one or other of the few powerful women in history or mythology, such as Joan of Arc, and Chesler feels this is a response to powerlessness in the real world. She also notes that sexism permeates many mental hospital regimes, where women are required to show that they are recovering by doing womanly things, like washing floors, putting on make-up, and being docile and obedient to their husband-surrogates, the doctors. She suspects that return to the hospital of the discharged patient, or even first committal may sometimes be a punishment for not being properly womanly. However ill the woman is, if she can make the dinner and please her husband, that will do – but if she looks slovenly and sits reading a book – back to the ward.

Chesler quotes a report by a male psychiatrist, Dr Herbert Modlin (1963), on how he managed to bring a group of 'paranoid' women back to 'feminine' health. He felt his patients needed strong male control and demonstrated to the man his wife's need of him, helping him assume a stronger position for her sake. He instructed psychiatrists in the hospital to be firm and authoritarian.

It would be interesting if a total sample of women ex-hospital patients could be followed up to see what seems to influence their survival in the world outside. Brown et al. (1966) did this for men, and found that the expectations of those around them were important; those in an indulgent parental home survived longer, even if their symptoms recurred, than those who returned to a spouse. The best outcome seemed to be associated with living in lodgings, where there was limited independence, and low demands put upon the men. How do women with schizophrenia make out in such different settings, we wonder?

This brings us to the end of our consideration of conditions and diseases which pose particular problems for women. Others could have been included too, if space permitted, but we have tried to look at some of the main ones. We seem to have documented a rather depressing scene, with vast areas of ignorance, plenty of misconceptions, and little indication that medicine is about to solve all our problems for us. But we have mentioned glimmers of light here and there, provided by women who have combined personal experience and determined study in attempts to document the need for, or to suggest alternatives to, some of the situations we have described. In our final section we will examine in more detail how women are organizing for change in health care, but before then we have one more matter to consider which has been assumed by many over the years but rarely challenged, and that is: are women to blame for the illnesses of others?

## It's all her fault'

As Ehrenreich and English (1974b) put it, medical mythology has often gone along with the notion that not only are women sick, but they are also 'sickening', in other words dangerous to the health of men and children.

There is still a fair amount of this approach about. Feminists are often accused of 'emasculating' men and making them impotent, just as witches used to be. According to some, wives try to push their husbands, or overfeed or misfeed them, giving them ulcers and heart attacks. Other husbands are driven to drink. But it is really in the role of mothers that women do the most damage, as the mental health 'experts' never cease to tell us. Although the role of mother is instinctive, so totally dependent on biology that only a woman, and almost only the biological mother, can fill it, she is obviously very bad at it. In fact men are always having to write books telling women how to do it. Left to themselves it seems mothers either neglect it, or overdo it, or do it all wrong, and are therefore responsible for a vast range of troubles in their children. It is really surprising that since women have made such a mess of it, and it is so important and so difficult, that men do not take it over and do it themselves. They would do, of course, except that nature, or biology, or instinct, or something, has ordained that only women can do the mothering.

We intend to look at just a few of the indictments against mothers and to examine the evidence. Others are discussed by Lennane and Lennane (1973). We will start with what are probably the most persuasive and damaging accusations for women everywhere.

### Maternal deprivation.
As we have seen, until very recently, the newborn child without a source of breast milk did not survive. If she survived at all she

must have been puny and sickly, suffering from many gastro-intestinal infections and very unlikely to have an adequately balanced alternative diet. This is no longer the case in the developed world, but this folk memory, together with the Oliver Twist-type life which the older workhouse or orphanage child used to suffer, are probably the earth in which theories of maternal deprivation took root.

The connection was closer than was generally admitted, in fact, for the main works on which the theory was based were concerned with orphaned or abandoned children and/or severely generally deprived children (Bowlby 1946). Bowlby (1951), in a very influential monograph which was published by the World Health Organization, translated severe general deprivation into 'maternal deprivation'. This theory was then used as an excuse to close down facilities for child day-care in England, and was a stick to beat working mothers with for years. Its ideas linger on, remarkably resistant to the evidence which confounds them, no doubt because they are so convenient. The final intellectual death knell to the theory should have been rung when Rutter (1972) wrote *Maternal Deprivation Reassessed*, which we warmly recommend.

There have been many good developments in child care derived from focusing on children's needs, but there have also been bad ones which have stemmed from the translation of observations about deprivation, and privation too, into an ideology which was falsely presented as a freedom charter for children. Neither mothers nor children benefit from hypothesizing a mystical link which in early life must never be broken for one minute. Cross-cultural and historical evidence immediately calls it into question. Mother and child have never before been tied together continuously like this; in large families and small scale communities there are always willing arms, old and young, often male as well as female, to share in the care of babies and young children (Mead 1962). The isolated mother working alone in her home, and with sole responsibility, most of the time, for rearing her one or two children, is a new and extraordinary phenomenon, not a natural and inevitable feature of human reproduction.

Yudkin and Holme (1963) found that working mothers who make adequate arrangements for the care of their children are no more likely to have delinquent, neurotic, or backward children than are mothers at home. If they have to use a nursery which is badly run and poorly staffed, then of course this may damage or retard the child – just as a bad home may do, too.

Many women themselves have been taken in by the notion that their child must not be left, and have stayed at home for that reason. As we saw in the work of Brown, Bhrolchain, and Harris (1975) on depression the result may have serious effects on the mother's mental state. Other women have gone out to work from choice, or more often from necessity, and in addition to all the other problems they have to solve to do so, they have been made to feel guilty by diatribes about the latch-key children. Governments and local authorities have excused themselves from providing adequate pre-school, out-of-school, and holiday facilities for children, by citing 'scientific evidence' that they should be looked after by their mothers alone.

This may be the place to remind ourselves that 'science' is rarely neutral. The questions it addresses, the focus of the studies, the conclusions that are stressed, and the use to which they are put, are all chosen in particular ideological and material environments, by actual people. Since these people are usually men, and the ideological and material environment is one which undervalues and underuses women, many of the findings deserve careful examination before they are accepted.

*Other maternal sins*
Most of us are only accused of turning our children into potential young delinquents; other mothers are accused of worse offences.

Childhood autism is a form of mental handicap in which the child seems unable to relate or communicate with other people and has most bizarre behaviour patterns often indulging in very repetitive acts, and is almost unmanageable. Sometimes the child seems normal at first, and often she looks normal. One school of child psychiatry thought they detected a coldness in the way some of the children were handled by their mothers, and so advanced the explanation that the child's condition was the mother's fault! (Kanner 1943). It is amazing to us that any of those mothers in the 1940s carried on with the wearing, impossible task of trying to cope with a completely unresponsive but often hyperactive child, in the face of such an insult. Fortunately this prejudice has been more or less laid to rest, in Britain at least, partly as a result of parents' action through the National Society for Autistic Children, helped along very forcefully by Lorna Wing (1976), who has a deep understanding and knowledge of the condition.

Another disease with a postulated maternal cause is schizophrenia. As in any disease, physical or mental, circumstances surrounding the sufferer may influence the severity, the outcome, and in schizophrenia more than in many other diseases, the sort of symptoms. Manifestations of the disease include thoughts and interpretations of the actions of others, as well as behaviour in relation to others. So all in all it is not surprising that other people often come into the story, and since the onset is early in life, the parents may be the main actors in the drama. A range of authors have taken this up, and numerous studies have been carried out, purporting to show abnormalities in the families of schizophrenic patients (Bateson *et al.* 1963; Laing and Esterson 1970).

Unfortunately none of these studies meet modern scientific standards, as they do not make comparisons with suitably matched families. Hirsch and Leff's (1975) careful examination of the evidence, notes with some surprise that when 'the family' is attacked, actually it is the mother who is the target. Very little interest has been shown in fathers, it seems. Schizophrenogenic families (i.e. mothers) have been described as over-protective and intrusive, aloof and rejecting, having 'atypical dominance patterns' (i.e. mothers have too much influence), experiencing conflict, or just being peculiar. Apart from the known small increase in schizophrenia in parents of schizophrenic children, as compared with the rest of the population, Hirsch and Leff found little evidence of their being different from 'normal' parents. Those few that were, may have been so because they had a schizophrenic child.[14]

So once more the smear will not stand up to the evidence, but unfortunately our mass media are much more likely to take up and sell ideas which slander women, than they are to refute these ideas. So added to the pain of having to cope with a mentally-ill child is the stigma that, in the minds of many members of the public, mental illness is the mother's fault. Scientific refutation is not enough; organized woman-power is called for, and it is to the developments in this field that we will turn in Part III.

# PART III

# Women get organized

In the first section of this book we looked at the position of women workers, the major providers of health care, and at their difficulties as health professionals and as workers struggling for their own rights.

In the second section, we discussed the problems of women as patients or users of health services, the specific conditions which affect women, and the way the treatment of women is related to their position in society as a whole.

This third section deals with women organizing to improve women's health.

First we examine the role of the trade unions and labour movement in the struggle for better facilities for women; then we look at voluntary bodies' activities directed towards enhancing women patients' rights and facilities for health care; and lastly we come to the 'women and health' movements which started in the United States and are now active in Britain.

In conclusion we discuss how we see the way forward for women's rights both as health workers and health consumers, for we believe the two to be inextricably linked.

## EIGHT

# The trade unions, the labour movement, and women's health

## The trade unions

In general, until the early 1970s, women's health issues rarely figured in trade union activity and policies. The Trades Union Congress (TUC) Reports for the 1950s and 1960s contain only three references to health issues specifically pertaining to women. One was a report of an attempted investigation by the TUC National Women's Advisory Committee into the prevalence of tuberculosis among women workers, which it was admitted (TUC Report 1950) had been handicapped by an inability to produce adequate information either from affiliated organizations or from the Ministry of Health. The second was a report of representations made in 1964 by the TUC General Council to the Minister of Health for the establishment of a nation-wide cervical cancer screening service. In the following year a motion urging the Government to provide funds to make

the cervical cytology service available to all women was successfully moved by the Health Visitors' Association.

Only in recent years with the increase in women's membership of and participation in trade unions, the greater public
prominence of the issues of abortion and contraception, and
with the establishment under the Employment Protection Act
of minimum rights of maternity leave for women workers, have
trade unions begun to give more attention to women's health
matters. In 1972, the Women's TUC passed a resolution calling
for support for Family Planning Clinics, the availability of contraceptives on prescription and without charge, and stricter
control of pregnancy testing services. Another resolution called
for nation-wide publicity campaigns about the effect of venereal
disease. Commenting on these resolutions, the TUC Women's
Advisory Committee believed them to have been 'the first on
these subjects to have been carried by a TUC Conference'.

Since then the pace of trade union activity on women's health
has accelerated. Provision for maternity leave has been a regular
item on the agenda of the Women's TUC. In 1975, a resolution
on this subject was accepted which encompassed paternity
leave as well. Both the TUC and several individual unions
monitored and publicized maternity leave agreements, which
were negotiated nationally and locally, with a view to spreading
'best practice' arrangements. The TUC has also been active in
pressing for an extension of the Family Planning and Abortion
Services within the NHS, and in resisting the two successive
Private Member's bills which followed the Report of the House
of Commons Select Committee on Abortion, seeking to restrict
the grounds on which abortions could be obtained. The
Women's TUC is now firmly committed to the concept of a
woman's right to choose whether or not to have an abortion,
and the TUC itself carried a resolution of the Tobacco Workers'
Union in 1975, in favour of the principle of abortion on request,
within the NHS.

Many individual unions have adopted similar policies and
have supported the activities of the National Abortion Campaign. In 1975, the National Association of Local Government
Officers (NALGO) carried a resolution supporting abortion on demand, calling for family planning clinics to be established in
every locality, and urging the TUC General Council to amend
its 'Aims for Working Women' accordingly. The Association

of Scientific, Technical, and Managerial Staffs (ASTMS) has sought to influence the attitudes of their sponsored Members of Parliament on this issue. The ASTMS National Women's Advisory Committee set up a working party in conjunction with the union's Medical Practitioners' Union section, to maintain a watching brief over changes in legislation and existing practice on abortion.

These developments and also the growing body of support for the Working Women's Charter were reflected in its revision. The TUC's Charter of Aims for Working Women was originally adopted in 1963 when it contained only six points covering the issues of equal pay, promotion, training, and the protection of the health and welfare of women workers, but was revised in 1975 and again in 1977 to include a wider range of women's interests. The Charter now contains fourteen points. Items 8, 9, and 10 cover respectively health and safety at work, family planning and abortion, and maternity. Similarly, individual unions are beginning to adopt programmes of aims for their women members, which explicitly include demands relating to health and safety at work and family planning. The ASTMS programme was adopted in 1975 as a result of activity around International Women's Year and discussion of the Working Women's Charter. It declares its opposition to moves to allow women to work on jobs or with materials which might endanger their health or the health of an unborn child, and advocates special steps to protect particular high-risk groups of employees such as radiographers. It goes on to oppose proposals for the abolition of protective legislation for women in industrial employment, as the price to be paid for legislation against sex discrimination, and calls for the expansion of the health and safety inspectorate, and the inclusion of more women on workplace safety committees. It upholds the principle of free contraceptive advice and prescriptions without regard for marital status, and the principle of abortion on demand through the NHS. Finally, it calls for more expenditure on research into methods of contraception.

Other individual unions can also point to records of action on specific aspects of women's health. The Transport and General Workers' Union (TGWU) moved a successful resolution at the 1971 Annual Conference of the Confederation of Shipbuilding and Engineering Unions (CSEU), pointing out that the International Labour Organisation (ILO) Conventions Nos. 89 and 90, prohibiting the employment of women and young persons on night work, had not been ratified in the UK. It also called on the CSEU to give a lead by negotiating such a prohibition with the Engineering Employers' Federation. In 1976, the same union called for mobile units to visit places of work to make cervical screening more widely available. Several unions have supported the Women's National Cancer Control Campaign (WNCCC). The Eastern Division of the Union of Shop Distributive and Allied Workers (USDAW) has worked for ten years to raise money for the WNCCC, and have obtained enough to buy a mobile clinic. Members of NALGO have been active in the campaign to prevent the closure of the Elizabeth Garrett Anderson Hospital and to set up a well-woman clinic there.

However, apart from concern with abortion, contraception, maternity leave, and such well-recognized women's problems as cervical and breast cancer, unions are only just beginning to come to terms with the full range of issues involved in women's health. A pointer to the future directions which could be pursued was provided by a resolution to the 1976 Women's TUC, moved by the Tobacco Workers' Union. This called on the General Council to negotiate with the Government on provisions under the Health and Safety at Work Act, whereby women workers can receive, either at the place of work, or by being granted time off, regular medical attention. This would include precautionary screening for known women's complaints, and advice and guidance to offset the problems and effects of the menopause. The mover was clearly projecting a wider and more socially aware concept of occupational health for women, than that which has until recently informed trade union policy.

It is of course difficult to proceed far along this line without confronting the issue of how women's differences from men should be regarded, an issue which is posed most clearly by protective industrial legislation and the Health and Safety at Work Act. On the one hand, women can be seen as more 'delicate' than men. Whether for this reason or because of their 'essential' role in child-breeding, child-rearing, and caring for the family, it is suggested that women need to be protected from heavy work, or night work, or various work hazards. Thus protective legislation comes to be defended in order to 'protect' women from doing all kinds of jobs, many of which they are in fact perfectly capable of doing.

On the other hand, it could be said that it would be better, whilst defending existing levels of protection, to seek to extend them to men. This would avoid having to accept the image of the frail mother-woman, and meanwhile individual women could opt out of protective legislation if it stood in the way of their individual promotion prospects or job opportunities. The stance would be modified to show that although women do have special health problems requiring special provision, this should not be used as an excuse for employers or male workers to exclude women from certain kinds of work.

The ramifications of a broad concept of women's health, which connects with the social roots of women's oppression, are explored more fully in a document submitted by the National Joint Committee of Working Women's Organisation in evidence to the Royal Commission on the National Health Service, under the title 'Health Care for Women' (1977). The document is comprehensive and detailed, makes careful use of available evidence, and, above all, places women's health issues in their social and ideological context. It stresses the importance of preventive medicine, the promotion of medical self-knowledge among women, and the democratization of the health service to make it more responsive to the patients' needs. It also discusses a whole range of issues which have not yet been taken up by the trade union movement; these include the over-prescription of tranquillizing drugs which, to some extent, contributes to rather than relieves the stress from which women suffer, the male domination of the medical profession, the institutionalization of childbirth, and the need to extend the concept of health and safety at work to embrace the health hazards experienced by houseworkers due to long hours and insufficient rest.

## The Socialist Medical Association

The SMA is a body affiliated to the Labour Party which consists of members working in, or otherwise involved or concerned with, the NHS. They are committed to an NHS free at the time of use, and financed out of general taxation. The SMA was the architect of the Labour Party's 1945 health policy, although unfortunately not all its proposals were embodied in the 1946 NHS Act. Over the years it has discussed many aspects of people's health, and has issued leaflets and pamphlets on many issues, from private practice to lead pollution in Birmingham. However it has not produced any pamphlets on subjects specifically relating to women's health.

At its last conference (1977), the SMA passed three resolutions on women's health. The first registered its concern about induction and other aspects of childbirth today. The second and third resolutions urged MPs to oppose the passage of the Benyon Bill on abortion, and called for abortion to be available for all who want it, and for adequate provision of day-care abortion facilities. They called on the Parliamentary Labour Party (PLP) to mandate all Labour MPs to vote against attempts to restrict abortion, and to support A Woman's Right To Choose campaign.

We can conclude that as a result of the pressure of women themselves, within the Labour movement and outside it, many hitherto neglected issues relevant to women's health are beginning to be recognized. Labour organizations always have very many issues before them competing for attention : it will only be to the extent that women play their part, and insist that women's issues must be considered and acted on, that the impetus achieved partly as a result of International Women's Year, can be maintained and developed.

**Voluntary organizations**

*Community Health Councils*

These are statutory bodies set up after the reorganization of the NHS in April 1974 – but since their members are all volunteers, giving their time and energy to matters concerned with health, we include them here. They are required to represent the views of the consumer to the administrative authorities. Women form 43 per cent of their members (Klein and Lewis 1976). They have the power to secure information, to visit hospitals and other institutions, and have access to the Area Health Authority (AHA). It is their duty to bring to the notice of the AHA potential causes of local complaint (other than those complaints coming under the jurisdiction of the AHA complaints machinery, or that of the Health Services Commissioner!). They are also supposed to be consulted by the AHA about plans for health service developments.[1]

Community Health Councils have such a range of approaches that it is difficult to generalize about the degree to which CHCs have taken up women's health issues, and we can only give a few examples.

The lack of publicity about family planning services prompted Medway CHC to discuss the issue with the Kent AHA, but Islington CHC had a different solution. Together with some women from the Trades' Council, the local National Abortion Campaign and Essex Road Women's Centre, they organized a survey of women. This showed that not many women used the existing services. As a result, the Health Education Officers of the Area and District collaborated in the production of posters, pamphlets, and a mobile exhibition on women's health.

Barnet and Finchley CHC was requested by the Barnet Branch of the National Council of Women to press the AHA to set up 'women only' advice centres in health clinics. The idea was that women should be able to discuss frankly their own problems with other more experienced women. It was felt that this advice would be better than that offered by some male doctors. It was said that some doctors were more ready to offer antidepressants rather than investigate women's problems.

Liverpool Central and South District CHC has pursued three women's health issues: abortion, family planning, and home confinements. Their secretary was previously working for the British Pregnancy Advisory Service (BPAS) in Liverpool, and so had considerable experience of Liverpool women's problems in trying to get NHS abortions. The CHC has produced an excellent report on *Abortion Services in Liverpool* (1976) which 'exposed the grossly insensitive, inefficient and inadequate NHS services and particularly the variation in facilities within Liverpool itself' (Liverpool Central and South CHC Annual Report 1975–6). The report's finding have been well published, and the detailed recommendations on how to improve NHS facilities – by establishing a day-care unit – are under discussion by the Regional and Area Health Authority, and will probably be implemented soon. The CHC also opposed the proposed closing of an existing family planning clinic – a view with which the District Management Team later agreed. In response to complaints from women wishing to give birth to their babies at home, the CHC, in consultation with district midwives and general practitioners, has produced an information leaflet about home confinements.

CHCs have been described as toothless watchdogs, and their powers are indeed very limited. However, they have the right to obtain information about present health services and proposals for the future, and to express opinions on these. It seems to us that they can, and in some cases already do, provide another valuable forum through which the particular interest of women health service users can be expressed.

But to turn to voluntary bodies proper, the Patients' Association lists seventy-seven organizations concerned with particular diseases and handicaps (including childbirth!). Out of these, the Women's National Cancer Control Campaign, National Childbirth Trust, Association for Improvements in the Maternity Services, Mastectomy Association, and the Pregnancy Advisory Service, could be selected as being concerned exclusively with women's problems. In addition, some others may well be dealing with diseases which concern women predominantly. Some groups have been omitted from the list: the U and I Club, the National Abortion Campaign, British Pregnancy Advisory Service, and Women's Abortion and Contraception Campaign, to name but four. There are many more voluntary bodies not specifically concerned with women's health, but which have policies on the issue and have campaigned for them. Examples of the latter are the Women's Institute, the Patients' Association itself, Women's Liberation groups, and the National Council for Civil Liberties, among many others. It would be impossible to deal with each in turn, besides which this book does not set out to be a handbook. All that can be attempted is to pick out a few organizations which seem to have contributed in a major way to improving women's health.

### The U and I Club

This was founded in 1971 by Angela Kilmartin, who was a coloratura singer until she was afflicted by repeated bouts of cystitis, which eventually forced her to abandon her singing career. The Club produces a bi-monthly magazine. In the first three years this went out to 10,000 sufferers. Angela Kilmartin has subsequently written a book on *Understanding Cystitis* (1973), and the U and I Club runs weekly self-help classes in London.

The magazine contains case histories described by the patients themselves, letters, general articles, questioner's forum, and medical articles and practical hints on the prevention of cystitis, and how to deal with an acute attack as soon as it starts. Regular readers will almost certainly have acquired more knowledge than most doctors have about cystitis. A survey of reader/ sufferers found that 89 per cent had a substantial improvement, 93 per cent were 'cheered up', and 18 per cent were completely relieved of their cystitis after following the U and I Club's advice.

## The Women's Institute

The Women's Institute movement was started in Canada in the last century by women concerned to improve rural life, and it spread to Britain during the First World War.

From the start an interest was taken in welfare and health affairs, and particularly in children and childbirth. In the 1930s, it campaigned for improvements in the maternity services in Britain, and for better ante-natal care.

In the 1960s, the Institute was campaigning for cervical screening to be more widely available. More recently, in the 1970s, it asked for breast cancer screening units to be made available and for family planning services to be provided free of charge. A recent central concern has been the accessibility of doctors, chemists, and other health services in rural areas, and the particular problems of elderly people and women without private transport, for bus services have declined at the same time as services have been centralized (NFWI 1976).

## Women's National Cancer Control Campaign

This seeks to promote and extend facilities for the detection and prevention of cervical cancer; to co-operate with the medical profession, to educate the public in all matters concerning it; and to act as an information and co-ordinating centre, directing the attention of the public to the facilities available. (In some areas, they have close links with USDAW.)

## Mastectomy Association

The Mastectomy Association brings women who are about to have, or who have had, a breast removed into contact with other women who have themselves had a mastectomy. From them they can obtain reassurance and encouragement, as well as practical suggestions. A newsletter is sent out three times a year, giving information about organizations and literature, and developments in the management of breast disease.

## National Childbirth Trust

In 1956 a number of women joined together to form the NCT. Mostly they were mothers who felt that all was not as satisfactory as it might be for women giving birth. They considered that women were kept too much in ignorance of what was happening. As a result, and often because of the way they were treated, they had very unpleasant experiences which left them with the feeling that their dignity had been assaulted. They could not, under these circumstances, achieve any real satisfaction from something they were convinced should be one of the great moments of their lives.

Some of the founder members had used Grantly Dick-Read's relaxation method (Dick-Read 1963) and found it beneficial, so they decided they would like other mothers to be helped in a similar way. They were enrolled as 'helpers', and started handing on their knowledge to expectant mothers around them. This snowballed and some of the new mothers in turn became helpers.

There are now ninety branches with helpers and teachers throughout Britain; the work has spread overseas as well. A formal training process has been developed for NCT teachers, and their education committee seeks to extend NCT's work into school courses related to childbirth and parenthood.

Although it is a charitable organization, and therefore cannot be a directly political pressure group, it is able to make representations to select committees on 'issues connected with childbirth'.

The NCT hopes to enable women to have greater opportunity to decide for themselves whether to have home or hospital confinements, whether to breast-feed or bottle-feed, and whether to have painkillers during childbirth. The way forward, as they see it, is by increasing information, giving support to individual parents, and offering advice to hospitals, doctors, and midwives, to enable them to help give women real options.

*Association for Improvements in the Maternity Services*
This body was formed in 1960, following letters to the national press written by Sally Willington (currently AIMS president), as a result of her experiences and observations during a ten-week stay in hospital before the birth of her second child. She asked if others felt as she did, and had a large response from people offering support, money, and asking her to do something. A public meeting was arranged and AIMS was launched as a voluntary organization whose objective, as the name suggests, was to bring about improvements in the maternity services. (It was originally suggested that the group should be called the Society for the Prevention of Cruelty to Pregnant Women!) Groups were established in various parts of the country, composed mainly of lay-people, with a scatter of midwives, and one or two obstetricians. Many are mothers who have been led by their own experiences to seek out AIMS, as a way of trying to ensure that the maternity services will improve.

What have AIMS done? In 1970 members conducted a nationwide survey on mothers' attitudes to maternity care, which involved 2,312 women and is still quoted, although of course the respondents were self-selected and were not necessarily representative of all mothers. The Farnham group has conducted a national survey of mothers' attitudes to induction, in collaboration with *Mother and Baby* magazine. About 1,500 women responded and a full report is now being prepared. AIMS has in the pipeline an investigation of hospitals' attitudes to the presence of fathers during delivery, and the Leeds group has prepared a one-page questionnaire designed to discover some factual information and some personal views of childbirth. Locally, AIMS has members on Community Health Councils, and has prepared a leaflet on maternity care which has been distributed to all CHCs.

AIMS produces material for the press, and has become involved in a large correspondence on all kinds of subjects, ranging from offers of advice to women who are keen to have a home confinement, to helping schoolgirls writing 'projects'. Contact is maintained with related organizations, such as the NCT, and the Society to Support Home Confinements, and 'official' involvements in the last year or two have included providing a speaker for the DHSS one-day conference on infant feeding, sending along a group to give evidence to the Working Party on Foetal and Perinatal Health of the Court Committee, and submitting evidence to the House of Commons Select Committee on Violence in the Family.

AIMS carries on in the hope that with the growing recognition that women are people, the increasing interest in women's health, and the greater involvement of consumers in medical matters, it can help promote an interest in childbirth both as an important event in the life of the individual and the family and as a physiological phenomenon.

### British Pregnancy Advisory Service and the Pregnancy Advisory Service

These were set up as non-profit making charities in order to offer women safe and relatively cheap abortions. They offer a very good service, including abortion and birth-control counselling. Their aim is to inform the woman of all her options so that she is in a position to make up her own mind.

They now offer day-care abortions done by the vacuum extraction method to women who are less than twenty-one weeks pregnant, and who fulfil other conditions. If it is difficult for a woman to raise the £65, they will help with an interest-free loan. They have made films on abortion counselling, and on the regional disparities in the NHS provision for abortions. They see their organization primarily as a necessary stop-gap, but hope that the NHS will soon make their existence redundant.

### Abortion Law Reform Association

ALRA has been a powerful fact-finding pressure group since the 1930s. It publishes an action guide for campaigning and also keeps an up-to-date list of publications on abortions. It is now working on a model bill to replace the 1967 Act.

### The National Abortion Campaign

The NAC was formed to fight the James White Bill and has local branches all over the country. It sends out a regular newsheet on both local and national activities. It is now campaigning against any attempt to restrict abortion, and for the abolition of regional inequalities in the provision of abortion facilities and the setting up of out-patient abortion clinics.

### The Women's Abortion and Contraception Campaign

This arose directly out of the Women's Liberation Movement

several years ago, and has been campaigning for freely available abortions evenly distributed across the country. It also publicizes the harmful side effects of commonly used contraceptives such as the Pill and the IUD and opposes any population policies which ignore individual desires and relationships. Their policy is that women alone should control their own fertility.

*The Patients' Association*

The Association was founded in 1963 as a result of concern about reports of unethical experiments on patients without their knowledge or consent, and about the tragedies following the use of the drug thalidomide. Since then its campaigns have led or contributed to action in such areas as the appointment of an NHS ombudsman, a code of practice for the medical profession in using patients for teaching, improved hospital visiting hours, improvements in drug safety, and action on reducing hospital waiting lists. It produces information leaflets on using the NHS, getting information, sorting out difficulties, making suggestions, making complaints, and patients' rights.

The PA is an advice service, as well as a collective voice for patients. On specifically women's issues, the PA has given advice on family planning, maternity services, abortion, the health of women at work, and hysterectomy. It has been active in advocating a woman's right to choose home or hospital confinement and to have a say in the management of her own delivery, to refuse induction, and to extend the rights of husbands and friends to attend delivery.

On abortion, the PA literature explains the legal side, and gives details of how to go about getting an abortion through the NHS or charitable organizations. It also puts women wanting to have their babies in touch with organizations which help unsupported pregnant women.

One issue of the PA magazine *Patient Voice*, in 1974, carried an important article drawing attention to the fact that in mortality statistics married women are classified by their husbands' occupation. This meant that there were no routine data available for analysis in order to connect women's occupations with their health. Since then such information has been made available.

Under the energetic leadership of Jean Robinson, who was formerly involved in AIMS, the Patients' Association has come a long way in recent years, and has played a most valuable part in calling attention to the concerns of many women patients.

## Women and health groups

For the past seven years in the USA, there has been a growing women's health movement. This has taken many forms – fund raising, information and referral groups, home birth and birth-centre movements, women's clinics, mutual help and women's self-help groups. Although the developments of the health movement were a response to the very particular health-care system in America, many of the ideas have been taken up and modified by women in Britain over the past five years.

The women's health movement in the USA was nourished by the rapid growth of the Women's Liberation Movement (WLM) in that country. Our own WLM in Britain lagged behind in its formation, as has the growth of our women's health movement.

## 1 The American experience

### The broad movement

Over the past twenty years groups like the March of Dimes (concerned with polio), the Heart Association, and the American Cancer Society have been raising funds on a voluntary basis to promote their areas of interest. Groups like this do not challenge the system of health care or the profit motive in USA medicine, nor are they particularly concerned with women.

In addition, various information, referral, and counselling groups or agencies have been set up to help guide consumers through the medical maze. They are often based on a very medically oriented approach and geared to private patient care, or offer counselling on an individual basis focusing on personal problems. One of the most radical of these groups has attempted to counteract the differences between the individual state laws on abortion, by referring women to suitable places. Planned Parenthood has provided birth-control information and clinics, as well as telephone information and referral. 'Hot lines' have evolved to try to prevent suicides and help in drug dependency.

Another group of organizations which operate more as a focus of pressure, locally or nationally, are those concerned with the environment. Units of Environmental Concern have been set up to oppose the dangerous use of pesticides and herbicides, and industrial air pollution, and have campaigned to close or restrict nuclear power plants. They often lobby for legislation and create watchdog committees to ensure enforcement of current laws. Some of these groups are specifically woman-oriented. One such is Urban Planning Aid in Cambridge, Massachusetts, which has focused on the health hazards of certain work environments where females predominate. Local women's centres, too, are working on environmental issues.

Many mutual help groups have been formed by people who have experienced similar diseases or treatments. They try to offer each other the kind of support only another sufferer could provide. Many of these groups have challenged some of the more destructive practices of the medical and socio-legal system. All use the principle of group support.

Groups of women have come together over issues such as childbirth and breast-feeding. There seems to be a marked difference in their approach, when compared with that of many of the 'patient' groups, in that they see the process of birth as a 'natural' one, and therefore put much energy into opposing medicalization, or the 'intervention of technology' into an essentially 'normal' or 'natural' process. It seems to be easier for women to challenge the present power and mystification of medicine in these areas, because they can deny that they are 'patients' at all, by asserting that birth is natural and therefore something we can all understand. Whether one agrees with this approach, (and we don't totally), its value indisputably lies in the possibility of cracking open the medical encapsulation of human experience at its weakest point.

Another aspect of this movement in the USA, which we have already touched on is the growth of the home birth and birth-centre movements, as a result of the 'escalating intervention of hospital childbirth'. The movement is a response to both the increased technology and the perceived dehumanization of hospital delivery.

So on the one hand women are deciding to have their babies delivered at home or at birth centres, and on the other, groups are teaching women how to survive in the hospital system.

On the west coast of the USA there are several birth centres where women give birth in a communal setting, with friends and a 'lay midwife' in attendance. In some mid-western and eastern cities, groups have been forming round the willingness of one or two doctors to deliver at home, usually within a limited geographic area surrounding the hospital. Often these programmes have a feminist perspective, in contrast to the usual implicit or explicit dependence of women on male doctors.

Women and health groups proper have been set up all over the USA. Some base a course on women's health on the book *Our Bodies, Ourselves* (Boston Women's Health Book Collective 1971). These groups have not been limited to women in the WLM but have extended their work far beyond this to adult education classes, high schools, town Boards of Health, Young Women's Christian Associations and to many other associations.

Self-help groups have grown partly out of the tradition of mutual help groups, but partly out of a much older tradition. There is nothing new about self-help. People have always come together to help one another deal with everyday problems. Perhaps what is new about the self-help groups of the 1970s is that they have arisen in spite of the proliferation of the helping professions, including medicine, precisely because these professions fail to meet needs adequately. In particular, they have formed in response to the failure of modern medicine to provide acceptable services for many sectors of the community, and especially for women.

The Women's Community Health Centre (Cambridge, Mass.) defined self-help as:

'... women sharing experiences, knowledge and feelings – women supporting each other and learning together. Self-help begins by working from a practical base, starting with learning from physical self-examination, finding out what we *do* know and exploring from there.

Self-help groups are action orientated. One self-help group might investigate the menopause, another human sexuality, another lesbian health issues, another might train as paramedics and health counsellors. The possibilities are endless, depending only on our own creativity and needs.

Self-help is women relating to ourselves in order to demystify health care, the professionals and our own bodies; it involves being able to make personal choices based on our own very valid experiences and knowledge. Self-help is a positive action

192

by which we can change our own lives and those of our sisters.

Self-help is a political act. It is deeply challenging to the existing health care system. Through sharing our knowledge collectively we have developed skills – we, not only "the professionals" will know what is done to us medically and why it is done. We do not take the place of the doctor but we *do* reverse the patriarchial-authority-doctor-over-patient roles!'

Self-help thus involves: self-examination and self-education; original research into health issues; group support for specific problems; and attempts to analyse and change aspects of the health-care system locally.

*The women's health movement*
The challenges to the health care system in the USA thus fall into two categories. One directs itself to consumers, helping patients as individuals or in groups to try to gain knowledge and alter their individual experiences, or to reform the system. The other is influenced by a perceived failure of the first approach, and believes that women will have to take over their own health care in order to effect real change.

Both approaches recognize the pervasive male bias and control of social institutions. Both feel this to have damaging consequences for women's health care. The deep feeling linking all these groups together is partly due to a rediscovery that healing is traditionally a woman's role (Ehrenreich and English 1974a).

Developing an alternative health system by setting up women's clinics has been one of the main ways in which the second category mentioned above finds expression. The growth of these women-run clinics[2] has revealed the need for a new type of training, geared to this setting, and a new type of hospital care directed by women for women. Some clinics have begun more formal training programmes. These efforts have resulted in serious conflicts with the medical profession, and arrests and legal charges have been made because of self-help and lay midwifery.

The women's health movement in the USA is fighting strongly for a future when health will be 'a full time responsibility for the patient, but not health as identified today, which is really synonymous with disease. The tools for prevention belong in the hands of the patients.' Such a perspective, however, has a rather disturbing emphasis on the individual. Whilst this has been sadly lacking in some of the traditional left-wing analyses and programmes for health, and in that sense is welcome, it does seem to accept and even to embrace the competitiveness of the private system as providing levers for change.

In *Our Bodies, Ourselves*, the authors write: 'The campaign of the 1960s for prepared childbirth ... progressed because consumers could pit one hospital against another and drain off desired clientele....' This approach can only be described as a middle-class, individualistic one. At best, it ignores the thousands of people in America for whom health care is not a matter of choice because they haven't the money to pit one hospital against another, or have no accessible medical care at all. There is no clear strategy for advancing health care for *all* women in the USA, unless it is by a spreading of women's clinics until all women go to women with their problems. There seems to be no linking of the best aspects of feminist demands and practice with demands for an American national health service free at the time of use, or at least an extension or improvement of the state sector of the health service in existence.

## 2 The British experience

The experience of women and health groups in this country has been an illustration of the difficulties of transposing an essentially individualistic, alternative approach from America onto a health system which is already nationalized.

The birth of the women and health movement took place in 1973 as a result of imported enthusiasm from the USA in the form of Carol Downer, one of the most experienced women from the American self-help movement. She came to Britain in October 1973 and visited several towns and cities, including Manchester and London. She gave talks accompanied by slides of self-examination, showing how to insert a speculum[3] into the vagina, and how a woman can then see her cervix for herself with a mirror. There were various slides of the cervix (the mouth of the womb) showing healthy and unhealthy ones as well as pregnant and non-pregnant ones. She then demonstrated on herself how to insert a speculum and the women present at the meetings were invited to have a look at their own cervices with a mirror and torch. She talked about her experiences in America, including her court case. (She had been cleared of the charge of practising medicine without a licence. This followed her inserting yoghurt into a woman's vagina, a well-known treatment for thrush.)

She told the gathered women of the invention of the Del-EM by Lorraine Rothman, which incorporates the Karman plastic cannula (tube), attached to a syringe and an airtight bottle. She explained how this device is used in self-help clinics for 'menstrual extraction' – the process of sucking out a woman's menstrual blood and womb lining at the time her period is due. Carol Downer in a *Nova* article by Carolyn Faulder, in August 1973, is quoted as saying:

'We are totally unconcerned with the question of whether or not a certain menstrual extraction would be classified as an abortion. We simply want to control our own bodies, to regulate our reproduction at whatever point we are in our reproduction cycle, or to relieve menstrual cramps, or to ensure a menstrual period will not spoil a vacation.'

As a result of the enthusiasm felt by many women in London, Leeds, and Manchester, women and health groups were set up using the book *Our Bodies, Ourselves* as a guide, and armed with the specula obtained from Carol Downer.

The first things that had to be discussed were attitudes to the NHS. In Manchester there were several meetings devoted to this question, where women also began self-examination. The Manchester group included several women working in the NHS, who felt that they did not want to develop into an alternative medicine group outside the NHS. They believed that, although the service had many faults, the main emphasis should still be on putting pressure on the NHS to change for the better. At the same time it should be defended against attacks from those wishing to erode the principle, 'paid out of taxation and free at the time of use'.

How did they plan to pressurize the NHS? The first step was to educate themselves by reading about their own bodies and discussing the information, and by examining themselves and getting rid of fears and taboos. Then it would be possible to begin to challenge medical mystification. The next was to support each other, for example, by discussing their problems before going to doctors, or by accompanying one another; they would challenge injustices, and fight for women patients' rights through all the legitimate channels of the NHS. To do this it was necessary to learn how the NHS works, both in theory and in practice. Finally, if the legitimate channels failed to acknowledge the wrongs, the failure would have to be publicly exposed.

Somehow, out of all these different strands emerged a fluctuating but continuing group, which has engaged in a wide range of activities. Self-examination progressed, and records were kept of observations. Herbal medicines, yoga, and massage were studied and used. The relationship between diet and health was discussed. Some were already vegetarians, and others decided to join them.

Instances of injustice experienced by patients were taken up, and support was given to women having problems with their doctors. Some of the group went to an STD clinic (still known as the VD clinic) and wrote an article criticizing the way they were handled, others went to a family planning clinic and wrote about that, suggesting improvements. Many aspects of women's health have been discussed and regular articles written for the *Manchester Women's Paper*. Leaflets were produced on various illnesses, suggesting what women should do about them, and these were given out from market stalls. A play was written and performed for various women's organizations. Free pregnancy tests were carried out. Some women gave talks in schools on sex education, and on women and health generally.

Several members helped form the Manchester National Abortion Campaign group, and others took part in activities to oppose the James White Bill to amend the Abortion Act. A member was nominated for the Community Health Council (and was turned down). Some women attended the Nurses Action Group at a time when nurses were campaigning for better pay, and thus formed some links with a group of women health workers.

At that point, the model for change that the group held was: first, find out about ourselves; second, find out about the NHS; and then, third, put pressure on the NHS for change. There was little conception, however, of how health trade unions fitted into this if at all, or of how to reach other women and involve them in putting pressure on the NHS.

Over the last four years, many women have come into the women and health group, and many have left. Some entered because of their own health problems, and later broadened their interests. Others came because, from the start, they wanted to explore *new concepts* in health. Many felt it was not enough just to challenge little bits of the system like visiting times, and not being given information, when what was at fault was the whole system of health care. They felt it necessary to challenge on a broad front, opposing such matters as wrong priorities, neglect of prevention, and the definition of women as mentally ill if they do not fit in with female stereotypes.

A very different set within the group were those who felt they should have nothing to do with the NHS but should try to set up an alternative structure of health care for women by women, along the lines of the women's clinics in the USA. Other women felt the group should be mainly concerned with going out towards working-class women, and sharing experiences and new-found knowledge with them.

Women and health groups have also been functioning in London, Leamington Spa, Birmingham, Glasgow, Swansea, Leeds, Sheffield, Bristol, Cambridge, and York. In the main, their activities have been similar to those of the Manchester group, but some groups have also been involved in menstrual extraction.

Menstrual extraction has raised certain problems. The first relates to its legality. Some legal advisers have expressed the opinion that since pregnancy cannot be tested at the time the period is due (you have to wait until two weeks after this), you cannot be performing an abortion since you don't know whether or not you are pregnant; the provisions of the Abortion Act therefore do not apply. It could also be argued that menstrual extraction is no more a method of abortion than the intra-uterine (contraceptive device. Others stress that under the Offences Against the Person Act, it is illegal to use an instrument with the intention of performing an abortion whether the woman is pregnant or not. Because of this confusion and because this issue has not yet been tested in law, menstrual extraction is being carried out shrouded in secrecy. This means that only those women known and trusted are given menstrual extractions by women's groups, and that every one of these menstrual extractions carried a potential legal risk.[4]

The second problem which has been debated extensively is that in performing menstrual extractions secretly, women's groups can only communicate to limited numbers of women how abortion is 'demystified' by this procedure. Not only that, but women's groups are effectively giving an alternative but highly restricted service, rather than using their energy and time to put pressure on the NHS to provide a service generally. Some members of women and health groups argue that they should give priority to making the NHS ensure the ready availability of abortion in all regions, and to putting pressure on various Area Health Authorities to provide out-patient abortion facilities as part of widely available well-woman clinics.

Perhaps priority should also be given to pressing for proper sex education in schools about menstruation, for doctors to be more sympathetic and understanding of menstrual disorders, and to persuading general practitioners to perform menstrual extraction. However by doing menstrual extractions themselves, at least women and health groups can show that it is technically possible, and that it can be done by groups of lay women on each other gently and efficiently.

## National meetings

The first National Women and Health Conference was held in Sheffield in 1974. All the various strands mentioned above were represented, and enormous differences were apparent in the multiple approaches to women's health[5] (Women's Health Conference Collective 1974).

A very large number of women attending were basically opposed to virtually all medical intervention, and all drugs, and took a stand rather similar to that of Illich (1975). They were also very strongly hostile to anybody working in medicine or nursing, even feminists, as they believed they would be unable to throw off their male-dominated medical conditioning. Many of this group, though not all, were militant organic vegetarians, and saw solutions to ill-health mainly in terms of diet.

Other groups showed their interest in herbal healing, acupuncture, osteopathy, and homeopathy. Self-examination was demonstrated, followed by a discussion on the problems associated with menstrual extraction.

Women from the Women's Abortion and Contraception Campaign (WACC) reported their activities to the Conference, as did various other groups. One group in Leeds was involved with giving a Workers' Education Association Women's Health Course as part of an attempt to reach out more widely beyond the woman's movement. A Sheffield group talked of the campaign they had waged at one of the Sheffield hospitals, to persuade the doctors and nurses to accept natural childbirth as an option.

One analytical paper, very relevant to the kind of discussions mentioned above, concluded that the self-help movement was vitally important because it had begun to demystify health and sexuality – but that if it remained as an alternative, bypassing the majority of women, it would do nothing to force the State to provide adequate health care. The paper saw the way forward as incorporating the best ideas of the women and health self-help movement into the struggle for an adequate democratic health service.

To say a consensus emerged from the conference would be to distort the truth. However, there were areas of agreement. The importance of getting together nationally, and airing our many different views on the NHS, was recognized. The importance of women and health groups meeting and exploring, learning, and finding out what women want, was agreed. The need to see health as being more than the absence of disease, and to approach it in a preventive way (which would essentially include nutrition), emerged. The fundamental fact that the 'medicalization of everything' was causing illnesses as well as curing them, and was leading to many aspects of people's lives being 'taken over', was recognized and condemned. The importance of women taking action to improve their own health individually and collectively was agreed.

In many areas, though, differences remained, and perhaps the basic one was whether, on the one hand, individuals could provide solutions in 'drop-out' terms, with emphasis on alternative lifestyle, health food, alternative women's clinics and deprofessionalization, herbalism, etc.; or, on the other, whether the NHS should be supported, whether it could be changed, and how change could be effected. In one way, this was part of the long-standing debate between anarchists and the traditional left in the 1960s. In another sense, it could be seen as part of the debate started off by Illich (1975) and Szasz (1961). Finally it was part of the feminist debate on the male domination of health and of women's minds and bodies.

The second National Women and Health Conference took place in 1976 in Manchester. This time there was less emphasis on 'alternative medicine', although there were workshops on nutrition, astrological birth control, and herbalism, and there were massage, movement, and yoga sessions. The meeting concentrated rather more on such matters as women health workers, fighting the cuts in the NHS, radical midwifery, setting up a well-woman clinic and what it could encompass, pamphlet writing, menopause, home confinements, sex education, and industrial diseases and women. Most of the women at this conference were adopting a more practical approach, and considered the isolation of the women and health groups from the majority of women as a problem.

There was far less of the 'hippy' approach, far more of the need to work out how more women could be informed of the important discoveries, in order to make them more accessible. Most women felt that it was important to defend the health service, and to support hospital staff in their fight for decent conditions for themselves and for their patients. It was also generally considered important to give leaflets out at clinics and general practitioners' surgeries, on patient rights and about specific illnesses.

The continuation of women and health groups was felt to be essential. They provided women with a way of coming together to discuss experiences and to decide on needs and demands. They enabled women to share and increase their expertise and therefore inform their demands. Finally, they are the base from which women can stretch out their arms to sister health workers, without being afraid to challenge and criticize existing practices.

## The way forward

Women health workers are beginning to get organized into trade unions to demand their rights as nurses, doctors, cleaners, physiotherapists, radiologists, laboratory technicians, etc. They demand the right to decent pay and good, safe work conditions, to a career, equal opportunities, nursery facilities, and paid maternity leave.

Health service and other trade unions are slowly taking a stand on matters affecting the health of their women members and of women as a whole. As more women join trade unions, become more active in them, and insist on more priority being given to their needs, on positive discrimination in favour of women, on more women being employed as full-time union officials, on more women being elected to official posts, these gains will be consolidated and extended.

Over the last ten years women in voluntary bodies have been playing an increasingly vocal role in our society; moreover, the impact of the Women's Liberation Movement has been enormous. There is however a great gap between these two forces with respect to health. On the one hand, few voluntary bodies have any conception of the role of the trade unions and the very real problems faced by health workers, nor do they take these questions into account when deciding their policies or working out campaigns. On the other hand, few unions involved with health ever discuss such things as the doctor-nurse relationship, the position of women patients relative to health workers, the kind of treatment given to women in childbirth, or the way women are defined as neurotic by so many doctors (and even nurses).

If women health workers are to make the strides they wish to make they will need the sympathy and 'critical support' of many of the very powerful voluntary bodies. If women consumers of the NHS are to get the kind of health service they deserve, responsive to their needs, they will have to win the help and understanding, and supportive action, of women health workers. The development of well-women clinics opens possibilities in these directions. As we have shown, they are more likely to attract women users if the staff are women, and we are confident that involvement of local women in their operation will ensure an even wider response.

Further dialogue is necessary. One small beginning was made at an MPU conference in Manchester in May 1977, where representatives of patients' groups, health workers, and CHC members came together to discuss many health topics. It is possible that as a result further conferences will take place in the future. Also the local Trades Union Council has indicated its willingness to open its health sub-committee to CHC members and representatives of patients' groups from time to time.

Patients' Committees associated with health centres are another means of dialogue, and we welcome them and the 1977 initiative of the Manchester Central Community Health Council in calling together local residents and health workers to discuss the possibility of a new health centre having such a committee, probably the first in the north-west of England.

A better known example is the magnificent campaign, involving staff, patients, and the community, to resist the closure of the Elizabeth Garrett Anderson Hospital in London, one of the few women's hospitals staffed by women.

The seeds of a democratic NHS lie in such efforts to join together. Genuine democracy in the health service must involve health workers and patients' groups in a more meaningful way than the present appointed Area Health Authorities and relatively powerless Community Health Councils allow.

Discussions and campaigns involving patients and health workers will not be all sweetness and light. Inevitably there will be many conflicts, reflecting the very real differences of immediate interest, and the sectionalism of many health workers and many voluntary groups.

Another difficulty will be that of involving women to the extent necessary. The two or more jobs that most of us do leave little time for meetings, and most have been reluctant to speak up, even if they can attend. But without women, who form the majority of health service providers and users, democracy cannot be achieved, and the many important problems we have documented cannot be solved.

Women have been prominent in all the moves towards democracy mentioned above, and this encourages us to be optimistic. We believe that the time is ripe for imaginative developments in the provision of health care for women, and that women will respond to such developments.

This is the reason we have put together in one book a discussion of women as providers and as utilizers of health services; we hope that now you have read it, you will join us in going forward from this beginning.

# Notes

## Introduction

1 In 1965, a Government Social Survey (*Social Trends* 1974) found that one in ten women out at work, and one in eight of those at home, were also responsible for the care of at least one elderly or infirm person.

2 As we shall see, at present legislation plays a part on the other side of the scale. For example, it prevents the sharing of responsibilities at home by assuming that women are dependent on men.

## Chapter One

1 Not everyone agrees – Malkin (1961) suggests that 'husbands' were the first specialists, although he gives no evidence other than a passing mention of couvade (the practice of men taking to their beds after their wives give birth) to justify this proposition which is contrary to most historical and anthropological evidence.

2 The two main rivals for the title, prostitute and mercenary, surely arose only with the development of class society, representing as they do the ultimate in the commercialization of human relationships – sale of oneself.

3 Very soon after this the physicians attempted to correct the omission, and a subsequent act in 1525 confirmed the Charter of the Royal College of Physicians. Ignoring the 1512 Act, it also gave them and Oxbridge graduates the monopoly of the practice of medicine. This was still unrealistic from the logistic point of view if no other, and seems to have had little effect.

4 Did this mean contraception, we wonder?

5 Following which and because of which legislation was passed to exclude foreign graduates!

6 Whereupon the Society of Apothecaries changed their rules, to prevent a repeat of such a disastrous occurrence!

7 The scientific motive for educational reform thus happily coincided with the regular doctors' own restrictive policies.

## Chapter Two

1 These include Oxford (Robb-Smith 1962), Sheffield (Lunn 1964), Birmingham (Whitefield 1969), The Royal Free (Flynn and Gardner 1969), Glasgow (Timbury and Ratzer 1969, and Timbury and Timbury 1971), and the Middlesex Hospital (Aird and Silver 1971).

2 Incidentally, Eskin (1976) found that married medical women were very much more likely to be working or wanting to work than were other married women who had science degrees. Medical women are just one example, and not even an extreme one, of the under-use of trained female skills.

3 Most of these figures and many others in the book were kindly provided by Mr Bayne of the Statistics and Research Division of the Department of Health and Social Security.

4 About seventy or eighty supernumerary posts have been approved annually in recent years, with some regions having far more than others, although this may be partly due to variations in terminology used (Royal College of Physicians of London 1977).

5 On average 34 per cent of consulants have some sort of 'merit award' – a perk varying (in 1977) from £2,025 for a 'C' to £10,689 to an 'A+' on top of their income. Only in five specialties – anaesthetics, geriatrics, psychiatry, rheumatology, and community medicine did less that 26 per cent of consultants have awards.

6 'Honouraries', i.e. medical school appointed staff, comprise 9·6 per cent of all consultants. In VD only 1 per cent are honouraries, in geriatrics 3 per cent, in anaesthetics 2·8 per cent, and in mental handicap less than 1 per cent.

7  The arguments sometimes include a strand of racialism too –
   an unspoken 'it is better to have women doctors than overseas
   doctors in unpopular specialties'. In 1974, 14 per cent of all consultants were born outside the British Isles. Of those specializing
   in geriatrics, the proportion was 31 per cent, and in mental
   handicap and mental illness in children it was 22 per cent.

## Chapter Three

1.  The numbers are pathetically few. In 1972, the hospital services
    employed about 1,700 trained occupational therapists and 1,500
    assistants, 4,500 trained physiotherapists with 750 assistants,
    4,700 radiographers, 370 dieticians, 200 speech therapists, and
    170 chiropodists (DHSS 1973).
2   This man, a member of the family who introduced obstetric
    forceps into England (and kept them a trade secret for many
    years) attempted to take control of midwifery in 1633, by pro-
    posing a company of midwives with himself as its head. The
    Royal College of Physicians opposed this as keenly as they had
    opposed similar plans earlier including one from an older
    Chamberlen. Monopolies were not to be held by individuals –
    only by the Royal Colleges, representing the flower of the medi-
    cal profession.
3   This is an error, which, as McKeown and Brown show, 'fails to
    distinguish clearly between the interests of the *doctor*, and the
    interests of the *patients*'. The developments made medicine more
    interesting to its practitioners, but brought little relief to patients.
    The authors go on to argue convincingly that the major part of
    the fall in death rates in Europe up to the present day has been
    due to increased food production – and in truth rarely because
    of, but sometimes in spite of, medical activities.
4   A century later Florence Nightingale estimated institutional
    maternal mortality as 34 per 1,000 deliveries, more than seven
    times higher than in domiciliary deliveries.
5   The first to document the appalling ravages of puerperal sepsis
    in the maternity wards where medical students conducted de-
    liveries were ridiculed for it. Semmelweiss in Vienna learned
    from the women themselves that the death rates were higher
    on the professorial wards, confirmed it by analysing the figures,
    and deduced correctly that contagion was carried by the
    unwashed hands of the medical students. Few believed him,
    and he was unable to make lasting changes to the disastrous
    practices which killed so many women.
6   The Sex Discrimination Act allowed exceptions to the law that
    all jobs should be open to both sexes, in the case of jobs where
    the sex of the worker was crucial to the job – e.g. as a model.
    It has been ruled that this cannot be claimed for midwifery.
7   Oakley (1976) in a very important article argues that probably

the classification into sympathetic and unsympathetic atten-
dants in labour depends not on whether it is a doctor or a nurse,
or even a man or a woman, but whether the attendant is a
woman who has borne a child or not. She believes that the
issue of control by the users of the obstetric services should be
a crucial one for women's liberation.

8  In addition, from the vantage point of today, it can be seen
that class antagonisms have also figured prominently. Orthodox
nursing was about lady nurses, and the battle for professionalization was concerned to exclude all but ladies – that is, to exclude
working-class women, and men. The anti-men sentiments seem
excusable, given the very limited openings for women elsewhere
in the nineteenth century; but the class exclusiveness not only
seems deplorable, but led to a chronic shortage of nurses, who
were needed in increasing numbers as hospitals expanded.

9  Throughout this chapter we draw heavily on Abel-Smith's work.

10 Born Ethel Gordon Manson, she spent one year as a lady pupil
at a children's hospital, two years as a sister, and six years as
Matron of St Bartholomew's, before marrying a doctor and de-
voting the rest of her life, some sixty years, to nursing politics.

11 The RBNA did achieve a Royal Charter which empowered them
to compile a 'list' of nurses – a long way short of their proposals,
and ineffective in practice – but the campaign revived when
the Central Midwives Board came into being to register midwives and Fenwick regained her leadership.

12 The Incorporated Medical Practitioners Association, whose
members were relatively poor, opposed registration. They feared
undercutting by registered nurses, who might diminish their
already precarious livings – another facet of sex and class an-
tagonism in attitudes towards the professionalization of nursing.

13 It was expected that there would be between 70,000 and 80,000
eligible for registration, but the Minister had put Mrs Fenwick
and some of her associates on the new Council, who proceeded
to scrutinize every applicant in terms of their own elitist
aspirations for nursing. Only the several interventions by the
Minister of Health ensured progress, and even then only 40,000
nurses were registered by the closing date in July 1923.

14 The General Register had the highest status, and those on other
registers aspiring to it had to start from scratch – as did general
nurses, however, who wanted to specialize.

15 Today the shortage problem is accentuated by the fact that
most trained nurses are married women, who, as we have seen,
in our society generally have other, incompatible commitments
in the home.

16 By then Mrs Fenwick was eighty-two, but still very active and
fiery, it was said.

17 Although the nurses on the employees' side remained dominated by the 'professional organizations', trade unions began to

play a bigger part, even though they remained under-represented. An interesting example of 'professional' aims being used to promote sectional interests was the support given by the Royal College to the idea that probationers were actually students, rather than employees. In this way, although they were not eligible for full membership of the RCN, it could claim to speak for them, as future co-professionals; otherwise, as workers they might well join trade unions, as more and more nurses were doing, linking up with men who had long been excluded from the RCN. Abel-Smith suggests that the RCN was clever enough to use the improvements gained in nursing pay and conditions via the Whitley Council, where the experienced negotiators of NUPE, NALGO, and COSHE set the pace, to claim credit for the RCN as the big sister on the Council.

18  It should be remembered that until well into this century American medical schools, too, were largely private, profit-making institutions.

19  The roots too lie partly in reality which compounds the effect; a number of doctors actually do marry nurses: in the doctors' hospital residencies, there are frequent social events to which nurses are invited.

20  The conservative sex-stereotype is as resistant to change in hospitals as elsewhere, but is nevertheless being undermined in Britain as more and more women become doctors (now about 25 per cent) and more and more men become nurses (now about 17 per cent).

21  Increasingly shop stewards in general have refused to take part in joint consultative committees in which the RCN sought to play a dominant part. They insist on working only with bona fide elected trade unionists. Similarly junior hospital doctors, who face a need to negotiate contracts with their employers, are beginning in some areas, like the north west, to turn for help to the trade union expertise of ASTMS, and shop stewards.

22  The RCN's proposal that nurses should resign from the NHS and become agency nurses, on the other hand, does seek to undermine both the NHS and trade unionism. The growth, especially in London, of agencies who hire out nurses to the NHS and other employers is a serious matter. Agency nurses are paid more, while they work, but get no leave or sick pay, and are disposable by hospital and agency. They can work long hours, and can be moved from place to place at any time. In terms of patient care, they can hardly compete with regular nurses who know the ward and the patients, and in terms of expense they are a heavy burden on the NHS – but they enable staff to be cut without any disagreeable arguments with unions, and they are very profitable for the agencies.

23  In spite of the big expansion in intake of medical students, they are still drawn from a very restricted sector of the population.

Personal surveys in Manchester have found that each year more than 70 per cent of the students have fathers in Social Classes I or II – that is in managerial or professional occupations, and for women students the percentage is even higher. Only a handful of the 200 students entering each year have fathers who are manual workers.

24 Traditional medicine of various sorts persists of course, and provides what care is available to the peasants. Sometimes today it is a commercialized western-influenced descendant of traditional medicine (Frankenberg and Leeson 1976). However, sometimes this situation exists alongside medical unemployment in towns as in India, and often a great medical exodus or brain drain as from much of Asia.

25 Other commentators see it another way. Bicknell, Walsh, and Tanner (1974) considered that the Medex would be employed by the doctor and thus enable the doctor to make more money for doing less work.

26 We would also argue that women health workers, nurses, and receptionists in particular, who are sensitive to some of the issues raised in this book can use their traditional mediator roles to foster democracy in the health service at grass roots level. They can strive for an egalitarian health team, and can work towards bringing in the patient's voice too. We have in mind such developments as the 'Patients' Committee', at Aberdare (Wilson 1975).

27 There is an exact parallel in South African industry. White jobs, highly skilled and highly paid, are broken down into several components, and each part is done by a black man at a fraction of the pay. In the end, some black men may master them all, but they can never reach the level of pay for the skilled job.

28 Frances Cairncross (1977) testified to this after spending six weeks as an ante-natal patient.

29 Some are eclectic, others embrace psychonanalytic theories and many younger staff adopt a radical, community-action approach.

30 Administrative changes in the 1970s changed the headings under which some services were provided from 'health' to 'social services', which makes detailed financial comparisons difficult. However, although the number of social workers has increased, other essential features of community care, such as hostels, day centres, and home help services, have shown little expansion.

## Chapter Four

1 Studies in 106 general practices in 1956 recorded consultation rates of 3,385 consultations per 1,000 population per annum for males, and 4,076 consultations per 1,000 population per annum for females, a difference of 691 per 1,000 (Logan and Cushion

1958). Eliminating consultations associated with conditions and diseases of the breast and reproductive organs reduces them to 3,338 and 3,551 respectively, a difference of 213 per 1,000.

2 Some gynaecologists are associated with vasectomy clinics for men, and some see husbands in connection with proposals for female sterilization, investigation of involuntary sterility, and similar problems. Others seek the 'permission' of husbands before tampering with their property, e.g. inserting an intra-uterine contraceptive device in the wife. But in general, gynaecologists earn their living from women only.

3 In a work entitled 'Concerning the physiological and intellectual weakness of women', the German scientist P. Moebius wrote: 'If we wish woman to fulfil the task of motherhood she cannot possess a masculine brain. If the feminine abilities were developed to the same degree as those of the male, her maternal organs would suffer and we should have before us a repulsive and useless hybrid.'

4 Oakley (1974) discusses several other cultures. In one South-West Pacific society men are considered to need protection against sexual attack. In sexual intercourse both partners go through a long period of foreplay followed by a short period of coitus, resulting in orgasm for both. Malinowski in his study of Trobriand Islanders reported a similar equality in the sexual attitudes and behaviour of males and females. Crow Indians expect orgasm during every coitus and sit on top of men to achieve this, as do Caroline Island women.

5 There are, however, growing challenges to the prevalent ideologies, even within the medical profession itself. The existence of the group called 'Doctors for a Woman's Choice on Abortion', with more than 400 supporters is one example. As the Women's Liberation Movement grows in strength, and is able to score further victories in the field of legislation as well as ideology, then more and more doctors will begin to re-examine their previous assumptions about women. We have already witnessed one spectacular change in doctors' attitudes towards abortion, from almost total opposition to widespread support, following the British Abortion Act. This is a beginning, and it is up to all of us to ensure that the challenges continue and grow.

6 'Pre-menstrual syndromes' are not yet properly understood, and are most likely to be a mixed bag of various hormone imbalances. Individual women have very characteristic patterns, as far as timing in the cycle and type of problem are concerned, although severity may vary, but every woman has a different pattern. No doubt each different pattern would be best treated in a different way, for example, by one hormone or another or by Vitamin B6 (pyridoxine). But we are still very ignorant about the whole subject.

7 Although, mentally checking through a list of medical colleagues

and acquaintances, it seems to us that moody, unpredictable behaviour is in fact more common among the males. Maybe we are biased.

8   Many surveys of child behaviour testify to this – e.g. Shepherd, Oppenheim, and Mitchell (1971), Pringle, Butler, and Davie (1966), Rutter, Tizard, and Whitmore (1970), Miller *et al.* (1974), as do attendances at special schools and Child Guidance Clinics.

9   Clarke in America (Bullough and Voght 1973) and Maudsley (1874) were vociferous in their campaign. They had left it a little late; the enemy was within the gate, and another medical expert Dr Elizabeth Garrett Anderson (1874) was able to refute the prejudice disguised as science – see also Burstyn (1973).

10  Kessel and Coppen (1963) found in a community survey of 465 women that 45 per cent had some pain, 22 per cent headaches, 72 per cent swelling, 32 per cent irritability, and 23 per cent some other disturbance of feelings or mood.

11  The balance between two of these, the luteinizing hormone (LH) and the follicle-stimulating hormone (FSH) may change too.

12  The latest worry (Hoover, Gray, and Fraumeni 1977) is that a current increase in ovarian cancer in the US may be related to HRT, especially to one specific substance used, stilboestrol.

## Chapter Five

1   Various more picturesque names are in popular use, like the Liverpudlian 'getting off at Edge Hill instead of going through to Lime Street'.

2   It is said that the Arab trader put stones in the uterus of his camel to prevent conception during long desert journeys. Nearer home, early this century, silver and cat gut rings were inserted in the uterus by a German doctor called Grafenberg, but there were adverse reports of infection occurring, and the method was not widely used until the Americans developed polyethylene rings in the early 1960s.

3   It may be partly a matter of technique. Some centres report no increase in menstrual loss after sterilization (Kasonde and Bonner 1976).

4   In theory sterilization may be reversible, and some successful 'unsterilization' operations have been performed, but in practice it should be assumed that the operation is permanent.

5   Much of the material which follows is based on Greenwood and Young (1976).

6   Prominent among these are several hundred doctors associated with the 'Doctors for a Women's Choice on Abortion' group.

7   A step forward that may not be permanent. In 1977 anti-abortionists combined with economic cut-back lobbies to oppose abortion being financed by Medicaid.

8  Recent figures do suggest, however, that the escalation in 'active management' has been slowing down, and that some hospitals are now seriously reconsidering this issue.

9  Delay in seeking ante-natal care until pregnancy is well advanced is particularly likely if the conception was unwelcome. Women who become pregnant extra-maritally may desire to conceal the fact during the early stages. Attendance at an ante-natal clinic may be regarded as a public announcement of the matter, to be deferred until other crucial questions such as marriage are sorted out (McKinlay and McKinlay 1972).

10  It is extraordinary how rituals like this persist. The object is to prevent infection. Studies have shown that there is no difference in the infection rate in women who have been shaved compared with women who have not; but the procedure is still often carried out.

11  What happened to the wet nurse's own baby does not seem to have been taken into consideration at all.

12  Women made to breast-feed in hospital, even though they do not intend to continue at home, do not receive advice on artificial feeding and may feel reluctant to seek it. Arneil (1967) found more rickets in babies who had ceased breast-feeding soon after leaving hospital than in other groups.

## Chapter Six

1  As one child aptly remarked after being told the 'facts of life': 'Ingenious – but couldn't they have thought of something simpler?!'

2  Or the male model is not fully equipped, if you like to think of it that way.

3  As women doctors, we are not 'typical patients' of course. Doctors, male and female, are usually handled warily by colleagues, and seem to have an undue tendency to develop complications – or perhaps to have their complications noticed?

4  The logical treatment was a stick and carrot approach – foul smells to the head and sweet smells down below, to drive and lure it back.

5  They have also cast doubt on another common gynaecological diagnosis – cervical erosion. The appearance of the cervix may change during the month, sometimes seeming to have an erosion and sometimes not.

6  The cervix protrudes into the upper end of the vagina, and so can be seen with the help of a light and a speculum (and a mirror, if a woman wants to see her own cervix).

7  In some countries fluid is collected from the vagina using a pipette, and cells obtained for examination that way. The Americans call this a Pap. test.

8   One factor in this may be that there has been an increase in the women who have had their uteruses removed.

9   It is rare in nuns, and in wives of Orthodox Jews. But what causes it? Again there are many theories, particularly involving viruses, but no certainties. It seems to be related to sexual activity, particularly in the very young, and perhaps to male hygiene; partners of circumcised men seem less at risk. Some have called it a sexually transmitted disease with a very long incubation period (Beral 1974). Whilst this may be strictly true, we would oppose stressing it since such terminology is unlikely to encourage people to come forward readily for screening. If the popular image of young people being sexually active with multiple partners to a much greater extent today than in the past, is correct, we may be in for an epidemic in years ahead. In fact, it seems that cancer of the cervix is already rising in women under fifty years of age in England and Wales (Hill and Adelstein 1967), but not in women in the United States (Higgins 1971).

10  Thorne *et al.* (1975) calculate that it costs less to screen everyone and treat all those found to have pre-symptomatic, pre-clinical diseases, than to await the development of cancer and treat then.

11  Medical 'non-communication' can seriously disrupt a cervical screening programme. Often women do not respond to invitations to attend for repeat smears. Sansom, Wakefield, and Pinnock (1971) found that many women either did not even know they had had a smear taken (it was presumably done during an examination for another purpose), or had not understood that they should attend for another one later. In another study it was found that 'non-attenders' mostly had good reasons, such as they had been done elsewhere, or just could not make it for reasons of family or work.

    A recent campaign in Wigan, using a mobile caravan, and involving much grassroots work with women and women's organizations on the part of the woman doctor who conducted it, suggested that the right approach *can* reach many more high-risk women than the standard screening programmes attract (Parr 1977).

12  Fortunately an erstwhile favourite treatment for dysfunctional uterine bleeding is not used so often now. That is what is called induction of a radiation menopause. Radioactive material was placed in the vagina and left there for some time to 'knock out' the ovaries. It seemed to lead to a particularly unpleasant menopause, and the evidence is now strong that quite often the radiation was followed by, and probably caused cancer (Bamford and Wagman 1972). Hysterectomy, although a bigger operation at least cannot have this result.

13  The hysterectomy rates are higher in doctors' wives than in

wives of other professional men – but women doctors have low rates (Bunker and Brown 1974).

14 The pioneer birth controller, Marie Stopes (1934) introduced a slogan which caused an uproar, but which is still good advice for today: 'Don't put anything into the vagina which would be dangerous or unpleasant in the mouth.'

15 Recent studies suggest that stilboestrol medication, one of the early hormone replacement therapies, may be associated with later ovarian cancer (Hoover, Gray, and Fraumeni 1977).

## Chapter Seven

1 'Contact tracers' are yet another group of under-paid women with no adequate career structure, who are vital to the efficient functioning of the health service. Many but not all come to it from nursing or health visiting, and obviously the job requires large amounts of tact, persistence, and devotion to duty.

2 Although there is a lot of alarm and despondency about the English figures, most of which were rising from about the mid-1950s, but which seem to have levelled out now, we have some of the lowest rates in the western world. This difference is not because of under-recording; although this occurs, records are believed to be even less complete elsewhere, e.g. in the United States.

3 Many other patients may and almost certainly do receive treatment elsewhere.

4 As its name implies, it is something of an unsolved problem; current speculation is that it is caused by either a small germ half way between a virus and a bacteria, called chlamydia, or by another organism called mycoplasma (Dunlop 1975).

5 It seems thrush thrives on the Pill; oral contraceptives produce an environment in the vagina which is favourable for candida to grow in.

6 In one study, 13 per cent of apparently healthy first attenders at a family planning clinic had thrush.

7 Assuming there are no faults in the gut's ability to absorb it, such as lack of acid in the stomach. Absorption is influenced by other factors too, such as the presence of vitamin C (ascorbic acid) which helps.

8 Tablets are another problem. Swallowing iron tablets has many unwanted side effects, from nausea to constipation, which do not encourage one to take them for weeks and weeks. Unlike some medicines, you do not experience any quick improvements to encourage carrying on, either.

9 Robinson (1971) found that wives of manual workers regarded tiredness in their husbands as 'normal', whereas middle-class wives regarded tiredness in their husbands as a symptom that should take him to the doctor.

10 These include one of the authors of this book.

11 Incidentally, excessively high haemoglobin levels do not seem to be good for you either, in terms of life expectancy. An excess of deaths was found in a later follow-up study among those with very high haemoglobin levels, as well as those with very low levels. As in body weight, a happy medium seems desirable.

12 It seems that as far as the USA is concerned, the transition from male excess to female excess in admissions to mental hospitals is quite recent, occurring round about World War II (incidentally, many current US studies give an overestimate of the excess of women, because they do not include the Veterans' Administration Hospitals where virtually all patients are men) (Gove and Tudor 1973). A recent report from Finland notes that, in this relatively unindustrialized country, unlike its highly developed Swedish neighbour, there is little female excess in hospital cases of mental illness. In northern Finland, in fact, there are more males than females admitted (Haavio-Mannila 1976).

The female excess in mental hospital patients in Britain is actually largely an excess of *admissions*. Of those in hospital at any one time, men exceed women among patients aged under fifty-five years, and it is only among those aged over sixty-five, and particularly aged over seventy-five that there is a large excess of women – as there is in the general population, of course (DHSS 1975).

13 We are well aware that sex stereotyping constricts men, as well as women, and it may be that it is easier for you if you are a loser when you are a woman. This hardly seems to compensate for the fact that you are much more likely to *be* a loser *because* you are a woman.

14 Clinical reports that schizophrenic patients have abnormal mothers may derive from the lack of consensus about women's roles today. The mothers may behave 'abnormally' in the eyes of the doctors, or may be inconsistent in their attempts to combine motherhood with self-realization, thus increasing the confusion of the disturbed child. However, the work of Hirsch and Leff suggests that they do not differ significantly from other mothers, whose children are not schizophrenic.

**Chapter Eight**

1 Recently a national organization of CHCs was set up to act as a forum for opinion and to exchange experiences, but this has yet to produce any data. The information which follows about CHC campaigns on women's health issues is therefore largely gleaned from copies of *CHC News*, from personal contact with some CHC secretaries, and from the proceedings of the York

Conference of CHC members, organized by the British Sociological Association's Medical Sociology group in April 1976.
2  Some are part of a national network of Feminist Women's Health Centres offering gynaecological services, self-help, and paramedical training, and are beginning to get involved with childbirth. Others are grass roots community clinics formed by women who are tired and angry with the lack of services.
3  An instrument shaped like a duck's bill which is inserted into the vagina and then opened, to keep the walls apart so that the cervix can be seen.
4  Recently, the Director of Public Prosecutions was reported to have issued a warning to a gynaecologist in the north west of England, instructing him to stop performing abortions before a pregnancy test could be done (earlier than the sixth week of pregnancy).
5  Such diversity is not unique to women and health. There are at least as many strands present *within* orthodox medicine.

# Bibliography

ABEL-SMITH, B. (1960) *A History of the Nursing Profession*
London: Heinemann.

*Abortion Services in Liverpool* (1976) Liverpool: Liverpool Central
and South Community Health Council.

AIRD, L. A. and SILVER, P. H. S. (1971) Women Doctors from
the Middlesex Hospital Medical School (University of London)
1947–67. *British Journal of Medical Education* 5: 232–41.

ALDERSON, M. R. (1974) Self-poisoning – What is the Future?
*Lancet* 1: 1040.

ALMENT, E. A. J., BARR, A., REID, M., and REID, J. J. A. (1967)
Normal Confinement: a domiciliary and hospital study. *British
Medical Journal* 1: 530.

ANDERSON, E. G. (1874) Sex in Mind and Education: A Reply.
*Fortnightly Review* 15: 582–94.

ANTLER, J. and FOX, D. M. (1977) The Movement towards a Safe
Maternity; Physician Accountability in New York City. *Bulletin
of the History of Medicine* 50: 569–95.

ARIE, T. (1976) A New Deal for Half our Doctors. *Lancet* 2: 1073.

ARNEIL, G. C. (1967) Dietary Study of 4,365 Scottish Infants, 1965. Scottish Health Service Studies No. 6. Edinburgh: Scottish Home & Health Department.

ASHLEY, J. A. (1976) *Hospitals, Paternalism and the Role of the Nurse.* Columbia University, New York: Teachers' College Press.

AVELING, J. H. (1872) *English Midwives.* Reprinted 1967. London: Hugh Elliot.

BAIRD, D. (ed.) (1969) *Combined Textbook of Obstetrics & Gynaecology.* Edinburgh: Churchill Livingstone.

BAIRD, D. (1976) Induction of Labour (letter). *British Medical Journal* 1: 896.

BAIRD, D., WALKER, J., and THOMPSON, A, M. (1954) The causes and prevention of stillbirths and first-week death. *Journal of Obstetrics and Gynaecology of the British Empire* 61: 433.

BALLINGER, C. B. (1975) Psychiatric Morbidity and the Menopause; Screening of General Population Sample. *British Medical Journal* 2: 344.

BAMFORD, D. S. and WAGMAN, H. (1972) Radium Menopause: a long term follow-up. *Journal of Obstetrics & Gynaecology of the British Commonwealth* 79: 82.

BARRETT, M. and ROBERTS, H. (1976) Why do women go to the doctor? Paper given to the British Sociological Association, Manchester (April).

BATESON, G., JACKSON, D. D., HALEY, J., and WEAKLAND, J. H. (1963) A note on the double bind. *Family Process* 2: 154.

BEAUVOIR, S. de (1972) *The Second Sex.* Translated by H. M. Parshley. Harmondsworth: Penguin Books.

BELL, E. M. (1953) *Storming the Citadel: The Rise of the Woman Doctor.* London: Constable.

BERAL, V. (1974) Cancer of the Cervix, a sexually transmitted disease? *Lancet* 1: 1037.

—— (1976) Cardio-vascular disease mortality trends and oral-contraceptive use in young women. *Lancet* 2: 1047–52.

BEWLEY, B. R. and BEWLEY, T. H. (1975) Hospital doctors' career structure and misuse of medical womanpower. *Lancet* 2: 270–72.

BIBBY, C. (1945) *Sex Education.* London: Macmillan.

BICKNELL, W. J., WALSH, D. C., and TANNER, M. M. (1974) Substantial or Decorative? Physicians' Assistants and Nurse Practitioners in the United States. *Lancet* 2 : 1241.

BLACKSTONE, T. and FULTON, O. (1976) Discrimination is the Villain. *The Times Higher Educational Supplement* (September 9).

BOSTON WOMEN'S HEALTH BOOK COLLECTIVE (1971) *Our Bodies, Ourselves: A Book By and For Women.* New York: Simon & Schuster.

BOWLBY, J. (1946) *Forty-four juvenile thieves: their characters and home-life.* London: Baillière Tindall.

—— (1951) *Maternal Care and Mental Health.* Geneva: World Health Organization.

217

*British Medical Journal* (1976) Women in Medicine (leader) 1:56.

A'BROOK, M. F., HAILSTONE, J. D., and MCLAUGHLAN, I. E. J. (1967) Psychiatric Illness in the Medical Profession. *British Journal of Psychiatry 113*: 1013.

BROVERMAN, I. K., BROVERMAN, D. M., CLARKSON, F. E., ROSENKRANZ, P. S., and VOGEL, S. R. (1970) Sex Role Stereotypes and Clinical Judgements in Mental Health. *Journal of Consulting and Clinical Psychology 34*: 1970.

BROWN, C. (1975) New Role for Women in Health Care Delivery. Proceedings of the International Conference on Women in Health. Washington, D.C.: Department of Health Education and Welfare.

BROWN, C. A. (1975) Women Workers in the Health Service Industry. *International Journal of Health Services 5* (2): 173–84.

BROWN, G. W., BHROLCHAIN, M. M. I., and HARRIS, T. (1975) Social Class and Psychiatric Disturbance among Women in an Urban Population. *Sociology 9*: 225–54.

BROWN, G. W., BONE, M., DALISON, B., and WING, J. K. (1966) *Schizophrenia & Social Care. Maudsley Monograph No. 17.* London: Oxford University Press.

BULLOUGH, V. and VOGHT, M. (1973) Women, Menstruation & Nineteenth Century Medicine. *Bulletin of the History of Medicine 47*: 66.

BUNKER, J. and BROWN, B. W. (1974) The professional patient as an informed consumer of surgical services. *New England Journal of Medicine 290*: 1051.

BURSTYN, J. (1973) Education and Sex: The Medical Case against Higher Education for Women in England 1870–1900. *Proceedings of the American Philosophical Society 117* (2): 79–84.

BUTLER, N. and BONHAM, D. G. (1963) *Perinatal Mortality: The First Report of the 1958 British Perinatal Mortality Survey.* Edinburgh: E. and S. Livingstone.

BYWATERS, J. L. and KNOX, E. G. (1976) The organization of breast cancer services. *Lancet 1*: 849.

CAIRNCROSS, F. (1977) Special delivery. *Guardian* (August 17).

CAMPBELL, B. (1973) Sexuality and Submission. *Red Rag 5.*

CAMPBELL, M. A. (1973) *Why would a girl go into medicine?* New York: Freemont Press.

CANADIAN MINISTRY OF HEALTH (1976) Report of a Task Force on Cervical Cancer. *Canadian Medical Association Journal 114*: 1003.

CANNINGS, K. and LAZONICK, W. (1975) The Development of the Nursing Labour Force in the United States: a basic analysis. *International Journal of Health Services 5*: 185–216.

CANTILE, N. (1974) *A History of the Army Medical Department.* Edinburgh: Churchill Livingstone.

CARPENTER, M. (1977) The New Managerialism and Professionalisation in Nursing. In Stacey, M. *et al.*, *Health and the Division of Labour.* London: Croom Helm.

CARTWRIGHT, A. (1970) *Parents and Family Planning Services.* London: Institute for Social Studies in Medical Care, Routledge & Kegan Paul.

—— (1976) *How Many Children?* London: Routledge & Kegan Paul.

CARTWRIGHT, A. and LUCAS, S. (1974) *Survey of Abortion Patients for the Committee on the Working of the Abortion Act. Report of the Committee on the Working of the Abortion Act,* Volume III. London: HMSO.

CARTWRIGHT, A. and O'BRIEN, M. (1976) Social Class Variations in Health Care and in the Nature of General Practitioner Consultations. In Stacey, M. (ed.) *The Sociology of the NHS. Sociological Review Monograph* 22, University of Keele.

CAVENAGH, A. J. M. (1968) Place of Delivery: Dutch Solution. *British Medical Journal* 1: 688.

CHALMERS, I., LAWSON, J. G., and TURNBULL, A. C. (1976) Evaluation of different approaches to Obstetric Care. *British Journal of Obstetrics & Gynaecology* 83: 921–29 (Part I); 930–33 (Part 2).

CHALMERS, I., NEWCOMBE, R. G., and CAMPBELL, H. (1977) Induction of Labour and Perinatal Mortality (letter). *British Medical Journal* 1: 707.

CHESLER, P. (1972) *Women and Madness.* New York: Avon Books.

CHESSER, E. (1956) *The Sexual, Marital and Family Relationships of the English Woman.* (Chesser Report). London: Hutchinson.

CIS (1976) *Crisis: Women under Attack.* London: Counter Information Services.

CLAYDEN, J. R., BELL, J. W., and POLLARD, P. (1974) Menopausal Flushing: A Double Blind Trial of a Non-hormonal Medication. *British Medical Journal* 1: 409.

COLE, P. (1974) Elective Hysterectomy: Pros and Cons. *New England Journal of Medicine* 290: 264.

COMAROFF, J. (1977) Conflicting Paradigms of Pregnancy: managing ambiguity in ante-natal encounters. In Davis, A. and Horobin, G. (eds.) *Medical Encounters: The Experience of Illness and Treatment.* London: Croom Helm.

COMFORT, A. (1967) *The Anxiety Makers.* London: Nelson.

CONSUMER'S ASSOCIATION (1971) Maternity Services. *Which?* (June).

COOPE, J., THOMSON, J., and POLLER, L. (1975) Effects of 'Natural Oestrogen' Replacement Therapy on Menopausal Symptoms and Blood Clotting. *British Medical Journal* 4: 139.

COOPER, W. (1975) *No Change: A Biological Revolution for Women.* London: Hutchinson.

COPEMAN, W. S. C. (1967) *The Apothecaries of London, A History, 1617–1967.* Oxford: Pergamon.

COSER, R. L. (1963) Alienation and Social Structure: A Case

Analysis of a Hospital. In Freidson, E. (ed.) *The Hospital in Modern Society*. London: Collier Macmillan, Glencoe: Free Press.

Court Report (1976) *Fit for the Future: Report of the Committee on Child Health Services*. London: HMSO.

Cranbrook Report (1959) *Report of the Maternity Services Committee, Ministry of Health*. London: HMSO.

CURRAN, D., PARTRIDGE, M., and STOREY, P. (1972) *Psychological Medicine: An Introduction to Psychiatry* (7th Ed.). Edinburgh: Churchill Livingstone.

DALTON, K. (1969) *The Menstrual Cycle*. Pelican Original. Harmondsworth: Penguin Books.

DAVIS, A. and HOROBIN, G. (eds) (1977) *Medical Encounters: The Experience of Illness and Treatment*. London: Croom Helm.

DEPARTMENT OF EMPLOYMENT (1975) *Women and Work*. Manpower Papers Nos. 11 and 12. London: HSMO.

DEPARTMENT OF HEALTH AND SOCIAL SECURITY (1973) *Health and Personal Social Service Statistics for England*. London: HMSO.

—— (1975) *Health and Personal Social Services Statistics for England*. London: HMSO.

—— (1972) *National Health Service Reorganization: England*. Cmd. 5055. London: HMSO.

—— (1975a) *On the State of the Public Health, 1974*. London: HMSO.

—— (1975b) *Psychiatric Hospitals and Units in England & Wales. In-patient Statistics, 1970*. London: HMSO.

—— (1976a) *Report of Joint Working Group on Oral Contraceptives*. London: HMSO.

—— (1976b) *Sharing Resources for Health in England*. Resource Allocation Working Party. London: HMSO.

DICK-READ, G. (1963) *Childbirth Without Fear*. London: Pan.

DINGWALL, R., HEATH, C., REID, M., and STACEY, M. (eds) (1977) *Health Care and Health Knowledge*. London: Croom Helm.

DONNISON, J. (1977) *Midwives and Medical Men*. London: Heineman.

DUNLOP, E. M. C. (1975) In Morton, R. S. and Harris, J. R. W. (eds) *Recent Advances in Sexually Transmitted Diseases*. Edinburgh: Churchill Livingstone.

DUNN, P. M. (1976) Obstetric Delivery Today. For Better or for Worse? *Lancet 1*: 790.

ECKSTEIN, H. (1960) *Pressure Group Politics*. London: George Allen & Unwin.

EDWARDS, D. (1974) Gynaecological Abnormalities Found at a Cytology Clinic. *British Medical Journal 4*: 218.

EHRENREICH, B. and ENGLISH, D. (1974a) *Witches, Midwives & Nurses: A History of Women Healers*. Glass Mountain Pamphlet No. 1. London: Compendium.

—— (1974b) *Complaints and Disorders: The Sexual Politics of Sickness*. Glass Mountain Pamphlet No. 2. London: Compendium.

ELLIOT, P. M. and JEFFERYS, M. (1966) *Women in Medicine*. London: Office of Health Economics.

ELSTON, M. A. (1977) Women in the Medical Profession: Whose Problem? In Stacey, M. *et al.* (eds). *Health and the Division of Labour*. London: Croom Helm.

ELWOOD, P. C. and WOOD, M. M. (1966) Effects of Oral Iron Therapy on the Symptoms of Anaemia. *British Journal of Preventive & Social Medicine* 20: 172–75.

ELWOOD, P. C., REES, G., and THOMAS, J. D. R. (1968) Community Study of Menstrual Iron Loss and its Association with Iron Deficiency Anaemia. *British Journal of Preventive & Social Medicine* 22: 127–31.

ESKIN, F. (1976) Comparison of Employment Status of Women Medical Graduates and Women Science Graduates, University of Sheffield, 1960–65. *British Journal of Medical Education* 10: 456–62.

ESSEX, B. J. (1976) *Diagnostic Pathways in Clinical Medicine*. Edinburgh: Churchill Livingstone.

ETTEN, G. M. van (1976) *Rural Health Development in Tanzania*. Assan/Amsterdam: van Gorcum.

ETZIONI, A. (ed.) (1969) *The Semi-Professions and their Organizations*. New York: Free Press.

FAIRBAIRN, A. S. and ACHESON, E. D. (1969) The extent of organ removal in the Oxford area. *Journal of Chronic Disease* 22: 111–22.

FAULDER, C. (1973) In the search for self-knowledge, how much of yourself are you prepared to see? *Nova* (August).

FIELD, F. (1977) *A Budget for Children*. London: Child Poverty Action Group.

FIELD, M. (1975) A US Response to 'A look at the USSR'. In Approaches to Correct the Under-Representation of Women in Health Professions. Proceedings of the International Conference on Women in Health. Washington, D.C.: Department of Health, Education and Welfare.

FLEXNER, A. (1910) *Medical Education in the United States and Canada*. Boston: Updike.

FLYNN, A. C. and GARDNER, F. (1969) The Careers of Women Graduates from the Royal Free Hospital School of Medicine, London. *British Journal of Medical Education* 3: 28–42.

FLYNN, A. and KELLY, J. (1976) Continuous Fetal Monitoring in the Ambulant Patient in Labour. *British Medical Journal* 2: 842.

FOGARTY, M. F., RAPOPORT, R. R., and RAPOPORT, R. N. (1971) *Sex, Career & Family*. London: George Allen & Unwin.

FORBES, T. R. (1966) *The Midwife and the Witch*. New Haven and London: Yale University Press.

FORSYTH, G. (1966) *Doctors and State Medicine: a Study of the British National Health Service*. London: Pitman Medical.

FOUCAULT, M. (1973) *The Birth of the Clinic*. Translated by A. M. Sheridan Smith. London: Tavistock.

FRANKENBERG, R. and LEESON, J. (1976) Disease, Illness & Sickness: Social Aspects of the Choice of Healer in a Lusaka Suburb. In Loudon, J. (ed.) *Social Anthropology & Medicine. ASA Monograph 13*. London: Academic Press.

FREIDSON, E. (1970) *Profession of Medicine*. New York: Dodd Mead.

GAVRON, H. (1966) *The Captive Wife*. Harmondsworth: Penguin Books.

GAYMANS, R., VALKENBURG, H. A., HAVERKORN, M. J. and GOSLINGS, W. R. O. (1976) A Prospective Study of Urinary Tract Infections in a Dutch General Practice. *Lancet* 2: 674.

GEORGE, W. D., GLEAVE, E. N., ENGLAND, P. C., WILSON, M. C., SELLWOOD, R. A., ASBURY, D., HARTLEY, G., BARKER, P. G., HOBBS, P., and WAKEFIELD, J. (1976) Screening for Breast Cancer. *British Medical Journal* 2: 858.

GISH, O. (1973) Doctor Auxiliaries in Tanzania. *Lancet* 2: 1251.

GOLDTHORPE, W. O., (1977) Ten Minute Abortions. *British Medical Journal* 2: 562.

GOODE, W. J. (1969). The Theoretical Limits of Professionalization. In Etzoni, A. (ed.) *The Semi-Professions and their Organisations*. New York: Free Press.

GORDON, H. and ILIFFE, S. (1977) *Pickets in White; the Junior Doctors' Dispute of 1975 – a Study of the Medical Profession in Transition*. London: MPU Publications.

GOVE, W. (1972) The Relationship between Sex Roles, Mental Illness and Marital Status. *Social Forces 51* (September).

GOVE, W. and TUDOR, J. (1973) Sex Roles and Mental Illness. In Haber, J, (ed.) *Changing Women in a Changing Society*. Chicago and London: University of Chicago Press.

GREENWALD, H. (1958) *The Elegant Prostitute*. New York: Ballantine Books.

GREENWOOD, V. A. and YOUNG, J. (1976) *Abortion in Demand*. London: Pluto Press.

HAAVIO-MANNILA, E. (1976) Ecological & Sex Differences in the Hospitalization of Mental Illness in Finland and Sweden. *Social Science & Medicine 10*: 77–82.

HAIRE, D. (1973) The Cultural Warping of Childbirth. *Journal of Tropical Paediatrics*. (June special issue).

HAMPSON, M. (1976) The Operation was Successful, but the Patient Wants to Die ... *World Medicine* (November 3): 35–7.

HARRIS, A. (1971) *Handicapped and Impaired in Great Britain*. London: HMSO.

HART, J. T. (1974) Proposals for Assisted Entry to Medical Schools for Health Workers as Mature Students. *Lancet* 2: 1191.

HART, N. (1977) Parenthood and Patienthood: A Dialectical Autobiography. In Davis, A. and Horobin, G. (eds) *Medical Encounters: The Experience of Illness and Treatment*. London: Croom Helm.

HAWORTH, A. (1968) Personal communications concerned with Chainama Hills Hospital, Lusaka, Zambia, where he was Medical Superintendent.

HENRYK-GUTT, R. and SILVERSTONE, R. (1976) Career Problems of Women Doctors. *British Medical Journal* 2: 574.

HIGGINS, I. T. T. (1971) Recent Mortality from Cervical Cancer in the United States and the United Kingdom. *Lancet* 2: 1141.

HILL, A. B. and ADELSTEIN, A. M. (1967) Cohort Mortality from Cancer of the Cervix. *Lancet* 11: 605.

HIRSCH, S. R. and LEFF, J. P. (1975) *Abnormalities in Parents of Schizophrenics*. London: Oxford University Press.

HITE, S. (1976) *The Hite Report*. New York: Dell Books.

HOCKEY, L. (1976) *Women in Nursing*. London: Hodder & Stoughton.

HOOVER, R., GRAY, L. A., JR., and FRAUMENI, J. F. (1977) Stilboestrol (Diethylstilboestrol) and the risk of ovarian cancer. *Lancet* 2: 533.

*Hospital In-Patient Enquiry* (1974) London: HMSO for DHSS and OPCS.

HOWELL, M. C. (1974) What Medical Schools Teach about Women. *New England Journal of Medicine* 291: 304.

HUBER, J. (ed.) (1973) *Changing Women in a Changing Society*. Chicago and London: University of Chicago Press.

ILLICH, I. (1975) *Medical Nemesis: The Expropriation of Health*. London: Calder & Boyars.

JAMOUS, H. and PELOILLE, B. (1970) Professions or Self-Perpetuating Systems. Changes in the French University Hospital System. In Jackson, J. A. (ed.) *Professions & Professionalisation*. Cambridge: Cambridge University Press.

JEFFCOATE, T. N. A. (1967) *Principles of Gynaecology*. London: Butterworth.

JEFFERYS, M., GAUVAIN, S., and GULESON, D. (1965) Comparison of Men and Women in Medical Training. *Lancet* 1: 1381–83.

JOHNSON, M. (1971) Non-Academic Factors in Medical School Selection. *British Journal of Medical Education* 5: 2648.

JOHNSSON, I. (1975) How to improve the ultilization of nurses and allied health support personnel: the Swedish model. Proceedings of the International Conference on Women in Health. Washington, D.C.: Department of Health, Education and Welfare.

JONES, C. (1977) The Nursing Process: Individualized Nursing Care. *Nursing Mirror* (October 13): 13.

KANNER, L. (1954) *Nervous Child* 2: 217.

KASONDE, J. L. and BONNER, J. (1976) Effects of Sterilization on Menstrual Blood Loss. *British Journal of Obstetrics & Gynaecology* 83: 572–75.

KESSEL, W. I. N. and COPPEN, A. J. (1963) The Prevalence of Common Menstrual Symptoms. *Lancet* 2: 61.

223

KILMARTIN, A. (1973) *Understanding Cystitis*. London: Heinemann.

KING, M. (ed.) *Medical Care in Developing Countries*. London and Nairobi: Oxford University Press.

KINSEY, A. C. (1953) *Sexual Behaviour in the Human Female*. Eastbourne, East Sussex: W. B. Saunders.

KITZINGER, S. (1975) Some Mothers' Experience on Induced Labour. Submission to the DHSS from the National Childbirth Trust, London.

KLEIN, R. and LEWIS, J. (1976) *The Politics of Consumer Representation: A Study of Community Health Councils*. London: Centre for Studies in Social Policy.

KLOPPER, A. (1977) How necessary was your D & C? *World Medicine* (February 23): 26–7.

KNOX, E. G. (1969) Cervical Cytology: a scrutiny of the evidence. In McLachlan, G. (ed.) *Problems and Progress in Medical Care*, Vol. 2. London: Oxford University Press.

KOOS, E. (1954) *The Health of Regionville: what people thought and did about it*. New York: Columbia University Press.

LAING, R. D. and ESTERSON, A. (1970) *Sanity, Madness and the Family*. Harmondsworth: Penguin Books.

*Lancet* (1977a) The Doctor's Role in Fertility Regulation (leader) 1: 1041.

—— (1977b) What Every Women Needs to Know (leader) 1: 232.

*Lane Report* (1974) *Report of the Committee on the Working of the Abortion Act*. London: HMSO.

LAND, H. (1975) The Myth of the Male Bread Winner. *New Society* (October 9).

LAURIE, J., NEWHOUSE, M. L., and ELLIOT, P. M. (1966) Working Capacity of Women Doctors. *British Medical Journal* 1: 88–91.

LEACOCK, E. (ed.) (1972) *Fredrick Engels: The Origin of the Family, Private Property and the State*. London: Lawrence & Wishart.

LEESON, J. and SMITH, A. (1977a) Induction of Labour and Perinatal Mortality (letter). *British Medical Journal* 1: 707.

—— (1977b) Induction of Labour and Perinatal Mortality (letter). *British Medical Journal* 1: 1354.

LEIGHTON. D., LEIGHTON, A., HARDING, J., MACKLIN, D. and MACMILLAN, A. (1963) *The Character of Danger*. New York: Basic Books.

LENNANE, J. K. and LENNANE, R. J. (1973) Alleged Psychogenic Disorders in Women: a possible manifestation of sexual prejudice. *New England Journal of Medicine* 288: 288–92.

LEVY, J. (1923) Maternal Mortality and Mortality in the First Month of Life in Relation to Attendant at Birth. *American Journal of Public Health* 13: 89.

LINDSAY, R., AITKIN, J. M., ANDERSON, J. B., HART, D. M., MACDONALD, E. B., and CLARKE, A. C. (1976) Long-term

Prevention of Post-Menopausal Osteoporosis by Oestrogens. *Lancet* *1*: 1038.

*Liverpool Central and South Community Health Council Annual Report 1975–6.*

LOGAN, W. P. D. and CUSHION, A. (1958) *Morbidity Statistics from General Practice Part 1.* General Register Office Studies in Medical and Population Subjects, No. 14. London: HMSO.

LUNN, J. E. (1964) A Survey of Sheffield Medical Women Graduating over Years 1930–1952. *Medical Care 2*: 197–202.

MCCONAGHEY, R. S. M. (1961) The History of Rural Medical Practice. In Poynter, F. N. C. (ed.) *The Evolution of Medical Practice in Britain.* London: Pitman Medical.

MACGREGOR, J. E. and TEPER, S. (1974) Screening for Cervical Cancer (letter). *Lancet 1*: 1221.

MACKEITH, N. (1978) *The New Women's Health Handbook.* London: Virago.

MCKEOWN, T. (1976) *The Modern Rise of Population.* London: Edward Arnold.

MCKEOWN, T. and BROWN, R. G. (1955) Medical Evidence Related to English Population Changes in the Eighteenth Century. *Population Studies IX* (2): 119–41.

MCKINLAY, S. M. and JEFFERYS, M. (1974) The Menopausal Syndrome. *British Journal of Preventive & Social Medicine 28*: 108–15.

MCKINLAY, J. B. and MCKINLAY, S. M. (1972) Some Social Characteristics of Lower Working Class Utilizers of Maternity Care Services. *Journal of Health & Social Behaviour. 13* (December 4): 369–82.

MCNAY, M. B., MCILWAINE, G. M., HOWIE, P. W., and MACNAUGHTON, M. C. (1977) Perinatal Deaths: An Analysis by Clinical Cause to Assess Value of Induction of Labour. *British Medical Journal 1*: 343.

MALKIN, H. J. (1961) The Rise of Obstetrics in British Medical Practice and the Influence of the Royal College of Obstetricians and Gynaecologists. In Poynter, F. N. C. (ed.) *The Evolution of Medical Practice in Britain.* London: Pitman Medical.

MAMDANI, M. (1972) *The Myth of Population Control: Family, Caste and Class in an Indian Village.* New York: Monthly Review Press.

MANSON, T. (1977) Management, the Professions and the Unions: A Social Analysis of Change in the National Health Service. In Stacey, M. *et al.*, *Health and the Division of Labour.* London: Croom Helm.

MANT, A. and DARROCK, D. B. (1975) Media Images and Medical Images. *Social Science & Medicine 9*: 613–18.

MANTON, J. (1965) *Elizabeth Garrett Anderson.* London: Methuen.

MARCHANT, J. (1975) Breast Prostheses (letter) *Lancet 2*: 187–88.

—— (1976) Breast Prostheses (letter). *Lancet 1*: 360.

MARIESKIND, H. I. (1975) New Roles for Women in Health Care Delivery. Proceedings of International Conference on Women in Health. Washington, D.C.: Department of Health, Education and Welfare.

MARSH, G. N. (1976) Further Nursing Care in General Practice. *British Medical Journal* 3: 626.

MARTIN, D. V. (1968) *Adventure in Psychiatry* (2nd Ed.). Oxford: Cassirer.

MARTIN, M. (1969) *Colleagues or Competitors.* Occasional Papers in Social Administration No. 31. London: Bell.

MASTERS, W. H. and JOHNSON, V. E. (1966) *Human Sexual Response.* Boston: Little, Brown & Co.

MAUDSLEY, H. (1874) Sex in Mind and in Education. *Fortnightly Review* 15: 466–83.

MEAD, K. H. (1938) *A History of Women in Medicine from the Earliest Times to the Beginning of the Nineteenth Century.* Haddam, Conn.: Haddam Press.

MEAD, M. (1962) A Cultural Anthropologist's Approach to Maternal Deprivation. In *Deprivation of Maternal Care: A reassessment of its effects.* Geneva: WHO.

MILLER, F. J. W., COURT, S. D. M., KNOX, E. G., and BRANDON, S. (1974) *The School Years in Newcastle Upon Tyne.* London: Oxford University Press.

MITCHELL, J. and OAKLEY, A. (eds) (1976) *Rights and Wrongs of Women.* Harmondsworth: Penguin Books.

MODLIN, H. C. (1963) Psychodynamics in the Management of Paranoid States in Women. *General Psychiatry* 1963. (Quoted in Chesler. P. *Women and Madness.* New York: Avon Books.)

MULLER, M. (1975) *The Baby Killer.* London: War on Want.

MULLEY, G. and MITCHELL, J. R. A. (1976) Menopausal Flushing: Does oestrogen therapy make sense? *Lancet* 1: 1397.

MURRAY, R. M. (1976a) Alcoholism amongst Male Doctors in Scotland. *Lancet* 2: 729.

—— (1976b) Characteristics and Prognosis of Alcoholism in Doctors. *British Medical Journal* 2: 1537.

NATHANSON, C. A. (1975) Illness and the Feminine Role: A Theoretical Review. *Social Science & Medicine* 9: 57–62.

NATIONAL FEDERATION OF WOMEN'S INSTITUTES (1976) *Health Services in Rural Areas; a survey of the views of a selected sample of Women's Institute members,* (duplicated). London: NFWI.

NAVARRO, V. (1975) Women in Health Care. *New England Journal of Medicine* 292 (8): 398–402.

—— (1976) *Medicine under Capitalism.* London: Croom Helm.

NEIL, J. R., HAMMOND, G. T., NOBLE, A. D., RUSHTON, L., and LETCHWORTH, A. T. (1975) Late Complications of Sterilization by Laparoscopy and Tubal Ligation. *Lancet* 2: 699.

NEW YORK ACADEMY OF MEDICINE (1933) *Maternal Mortality in New York City: a study of all puerperal deaths in 1930–32.* New York: Commonwealth Fund.

OAKLEY, A. (1974) Cultural Influences on Female Sexuality. In Allen, S., Sanders, L., and Wallis, J. (eds) *Conditions of Illusion.* Leeds: Feminist Books.

—— (1975) The Trap of Medicalized Motherhood. *New Society* 34, (689, December).

—— (1976a) *Housewife.* Harmondsworth: Penguin Books.

—— (1976b) Wisewoman and Medicine Man: Changes in the Management of Childbirth. In Mitchell, J. and Oakley, A. (eds) *Rights and Wrongs of Women.* Harmondsworth: Penguin Books.

OCCASIONAL SURVEY (1961) The Maternity Services: Need for Changes in Attitude and Practice. *Lancet* 1: 873.

O'DRISCOLL, K., STRONGE, J. M., and MINOGUE, M. (1973) Active Management of Labour. *British Medical Journal* 2: 135–37.

OWEN, L. (1977) The Myth of the Hairy Lady. *Guardian* (July 28): Women's Page.

PARR, A. (1977) Personal communication.

PAULY, I. B. (1971) *Australian & New Zealand Journal of Psychiatry* 5: 206.

*Peel Report* (1970) *Domiciliary Midwifery and Maternity Bed Needs: Report of the Sub-Committee of the Standing Maternity and Midwifery Advisory Committee of the Central Health Services Council.* London: HMSO.

PENNELL, M. and SHOWELL, S. (1975) *Women in Health Careers: Chart Book for International Conference on Women in Health.* Washington D.C.: American Public Health Association.

PIRADOVA, M. D. (1975) A Look at the USSR. In Approaches to Correct the Under-representation of Women in the Health Professions. Proceedings of the International Conference on Women in Health. Washington, D.C.: Department of Health, Education and Welfare.

PORTER, A. M. W. (1970) Depressive Illness in a General Practice: a demographic study and a controlled trial of imipramine. *British Medical Journal* 1: 773–78.

POWERS, I., PARMELLE, R. D., and WIESENFELDER, H. (1969) Practice Patterns of Women and Men Physicians. *Journal of Medical Education* 44: 481–91.

POYNTER, F. N. C. (1961) The Influence of Government Legislation on Medical Practice in Britain. In Poynter, F. N. C. (ed.) (1961).

—— (ed.) (1961) *The Evolution of Medical Practice in Britain.* London: Pitman Medical.

POYNTER, N. (1971) *Medicine and Man.* London: C. A. Walls & Co.

PRATHER, J. and FIDELL, L. S. (1975) Sex Differences in the Content and Style of Medical Advertisements. *Social Science & Medicine* 9: 23–6.

227

PREECE, P. E., HUGHES, L. E., MANSEL, R. E., BAUM, M., BOLTON, P. M., and GRAVELLE, I. H. (1976) Clinical Syndromes of Mastalgia. *Lancet* 2: 670.

PRINGLE, M. L. K., BUTLER, N. R., and DAVIE, R. (1966) *11,000 Seven-year-olds*. London: Longman.

Proceedings of the International Conference on Women in Health (1975) Washington, D.C.: Department of Health, Education and Welfare.

REGISTRAR GENERAL (1974a) *Statistical Review of England & Wales for 1973: Medical*. London: HMSO.

—— (1974b) *Statistical Review of England and Wales for 1973: Supplement on Abortion*. London: HMSO.

RICHARDS, D. H. (1973) Depression and Hysterectomy. *Lancet* 2: 430.

—— (1974) A post-hysterectomy syndrome. *Lancet* 2: 983.

RICHARDS, M. P. M. (1975) Innovation in Medical Practice: obstetricians and the induction of labour in Britain. *Social Science & Medicine* 9: 595–602.

RICHMAN, J. and GOLDTHORP (1977) When was your last period? Temporal aspects of gynaecological diagnosis. In Dingwall *et al.* (eds) *Health Care and Health Knowledge*. London: Croom Helm.

ROBB-SMITH, A. H. T. (1962) The Fate of Oxford Medical Women. *Lancet* 2: 1158.

ROBINSON, D. (1971) *The Process of Becoming Ill*. London: Routledge & Kegan Paul.

ROBINSON, J. (1974) Mothers Object Mainly to Lack of Consultation. London. *The Times* (August 12).

—— (1977) Address to Conference of Health Workers and Patient Groups, Manchester (May).

ROEMER, R. (1975) Innovations in the utilization of nurses, allied health and support personnel. Proceedings of International Conference on Women in Health. Washington, D.C.: Department of Health, Education and Welfare.

RONAGHY, H. A. and SOLTER, S. (1974) Is the Chinese 'Barefoot Doctor' Exportable to Rural Iran? *Lancet* 1: 1331.

ROYAL COLLEGE OF GENERAL PRACTITIONERS (1974) *Oral Contraceptives and Health*. London: RCGP.

—— (1977) Mortality among oral-contraceptive users. *Lancet* 2: 726.

ROYAL COLLEGE OF PHYSICIANS OF LONDON (1977) *Part-time postgraduate training in medicine*. London: RCP.

RUE, R. (1975) Organization and Service Problems. Proceedings of a Conference on Women in Medicine. London: HMSO, for DHSS.

RUSH, F. (1971) The sexual abuse of children. A feminist point of view. Paper given at New York Radical Feminists Conference on Rape (April).

RUTTER, M. (1972) *Maternal Deprivation Reassessed*. Harmondsworth: Penguin Books.

RUTTER, M, TIZARD, J., and WHITMORE, K. (eds) (1970) *Education, Health & Behaviour*. London: Longman.

*Salmon Report* (1966) *Report of the Committee on Senior Nursing Staff Structure in the National Health Service*. London: HMSO.

SANSOM, C. D., WAKEFIELD, J., and PINNOCK, K. M. (1971) Choice or Chance? How women come to have a cytotest done by their family doctor. *International Journal of Health Education 14* (3): 127.

SCULLY, D. and BART, P. (1973) A funny thing happened on the way to the orifice: women in gynaecology textbooks. In Huber, J. (ed.) *Changing Women in a Changing Society*. Chicago and London: University of Chicago Press.

SELIGMAN, M. (1975) *Helplessness: on depression, development and death*. San Francisco: Freeman.

SEWARD, M. H. (1976) *The Provision of Dental Care by Women Dentists in England and Wales in 1975*. London: British Postgraduate Medical Federation.

SHAINESS, N. (1968) Sex. Sexuality & Sexual Love. *Jamwa:* 127–29.

SHAW, G. B. (1931) *The Doctor's Dilemma*. London: The Bodley Head.

SHEPHERD, M. OPPENHEIM, B., and MITCHELL, S. (1971) *Childhood Behaviour & Mental Health*. London: University of London Press.

SHYROCK, R. H. (1967) *Medical Licensing in America 1650–1965*. Baltimore: Johns Hopkins.

SIDEL, R. (1975) New Roles for Women in Health Care Delivery: Conditions in the People's Republic of China. Proceedings of the International Conference on Women in Health. Washington, D.C.: Department of Health, Education and Welfare.

SIDEL, V. W. and SIDEL, R. (1973) *Serve the People: Observations on Medicine in the People's Republic of China*. Boston: Beacon Press.

SIMPSON, L. and SIMPSON, I. H. (1969) Women and Bureaucracy. In Etzioni, A. (ed.) *The Semi-Professions and their Organizations*. New York: Free Press.

SMITH, A. and MACDONALD, I. S. (1965) Social circumstances related to child bearing in Glasgow, 1963. *Health Bulletin*, Scottish Home and Health Department XXIII (3) (July).

SMITH, R. A. (1973) Medex. *Lancet* 2: 85.

*Social Trends 1974*. London: HMSO.

SOKOŁOWSKA, M. (1975) A look at Poland. In, Analysis of the role of women in health care decision making. Proceedings of the International Conference on Women in Health. Washington, D.C.: Department of Health, Education and Welfare.

STACEY, M., REID, M., HEATH, C., and DINGWALL, R. (eds) (1977) *Health and the Division of Labour*. London: Croom Helm.

STANLEY, G. R. and LAST, J. M. (1968) Careers of Young Medical Women. *British Journal of Medical Education* 2: 204–9.

STIMSON, G. (1975) Women in a Doctored World. *New Society* (May 1): 265-67.

STOPES, M. (1934) *Birth Control Today.* London: Alex Moring.

SZASZ, T. S. (1961) *The Myth of Mental Illness.* New York: Hoeber/Harper.

TACCHI, D. (1971) Towards Easier Childbirth. *Lancet* 2: 1134.

TAULBEE, E. S. and WRIGHT, H. W. (1971) A Psychosocial Behavioural Model for Therapeutic Intervention. In Spielberger, C. D. (ed.) *Current Topics in Clinical and Community Psychology, III.* New York: Academic Press.

THORBURN, J. (1884) Female Education from a Physiological Point of View. In *Six Introductory Lectures in the Victorian University of Manchester. Manchester:* Cornish.

THORNE, J. B., MACGREGOR, J. E., RUSSELL, E. M., and SWANSON, K. (1975) Costs of Detecting and Treating Cancer of the Uterine Cervix in N.E. Scotland in 1971. *Lancet* 1: 674.

TIMBURY, M. C. and TIMBURY, C. C. (1971) Glasgow Women Medical Students: some facts and figures. *British Medical Journal* 1: 216.

TIMBURY, M. C. and RATZER, M. A. (1969) Glasgow Medical Women 1951-4: Their Contribution and Attitude to Medical Work. *British Medical Journal* 1: 372.

TRADES UNION CONGRESS (1950) Reports 1950, 1964, 1965, 1975. London: TUC.

ULYATT, K. and ULYATT, F. M. (1971) Some attitudes of a group of women doctors related to their field performance. *British Journal of Medical Education* 5: 242-45.

—— (1973) Attitudes of women medical students compared with those of women doctors. *British Journal of Medical Education* 7: 152-54.

VESSEY, M. P., DOLL, R., and SUTTON, P. M. (1972) Oral Contraceptives and Breast Neoplasia; a retrospective study. *British Medical Journal* 3: 719.

VEITCH, A. (1977) Pause for Serious Thought. *Guardian* (October 18).

VINCENT, C. E. (ed.) (1968) *Human Sexuality in Medical Education and Practice.* Springfield, Illinois: Charles C. Thomas.

WALTON, H. J. (1968) Sex differences in ability and outlook of senior medical students. *British Journal of Medical Education* 2: 156-62.

WEBB, S. and WEBB, B. (1929) *English Local Government & English Poor Law History. Part II.* London.

WHITE, R. (1975) The Development of the Poor Law Nursing Service; and the social, medical and political factors that influenced it: 1848-1948. M.Sc. Thesis: University of Manchester.

WHITEFIELD, A. G. W. (1969) Women Medical Graduates of the University of Birmingham. *British Medical Journal* 2: 44.

*Willink Report* (1957) *Report of the Committee of Enquiry to con-*

*sider the future number of medical practitioners and the appropriate intake of students.* London: HMSO.

WILSON, A. (1975) Initial experiences of patients' committees. *Medicine in Society* 2 (4).

WILSON, E. (1977) *Women and the Welfare State.* London: Tavistock.

WING, L. G. (ed.) (1976) *Early Childhood Autism* (2nd Ed.). Oxford: Pergamon.

WINNER, A. (1975) Women in Medicine: the Caroline Haslett Memorial Lecture. *Royal Society of Arts Journal XXIII*: 337–48.

WINSTON, R. M. I. (1977) Why 103 Women asked for Reversal of Sterilization. *British Medical Journal* 2: 305.

WOMEN'S HEALTH CONFERENCE COLLECTIVE (1974) *First Women & Health Conference.* Manchester: Moss Side Press.

*Women's Trades Union Congress Reports* (1972) (1975) (1976).

WOOD, M. M. and ELWOOD, P. C. (1966) Symptoms of Iron Deficiency Anaemia: A Community Survey. *British Journal of Preventive & Social Medicine* 20: 117–21.

WYNN, M. and WYNN, A. (1976) *Prevention of Handicap of Perinatal Origin.* London: Foundation for Education and Research on Child Bearing.

YUDKIN, S. and HOLME, A. (1963) *Working Mothers and their Children.* London: Michael Joseph.

# Name Index

233

235

# Subject Index